UP, UP, AND AWAY!

Cartoon producer Max Fleischer was the first to bring the Man of Steel to movie screens. Then it was Sam Katzman, who with action-director Spencer Gordon Bennet transformed Superman into a Saturday-matinee serial star. Through television, Superman became the most popular and enduring hero of all time, as played by George Reeves. Those 104 memorable episodes continue to enthrall millions around the world.

Now those golden years, those triumphant adventures, and the fascinating people who pooled their talents to make Superman super, are brought back in a book as exciting as its subject. On these pages Superman lives again at the peak of his power—with fascinating detail on every filmed adventure and many rare photos that trace his movie and television "career." This is also the story of two dedicated actors whose lives were never the same after playing the super-hero.

It's up, up, and away!—to the thrilling heights of nostalgia-filled pleasure.

Oversized Books in the Big Apple Film Series
Available from Popular Library:

HOLLYWOOD CORRAL
ROBERT REDFORD
ABBOTT AND COSTELLO
TEX AVERY: KING OF CARTOONS
STANLEY KUBRICK   A FILM ODYSSEY

And soon to appear in rack-size:

ABBOTT AND COSTELLO
STANLEY KUBRICK   A FILM ODYSSEY

SUPERMAN®
SERIAL TO CEREAL

by GARY H. GROSSMAN

Popular Library Film Series
Leonard Maltin, General Editor

POPULAR LIBRARY • NEW YORK

POPULAR LIBRARY EDITION
September, 1977
Copyright © 1976 by Leonard Maltin

ISBN: 0-445-04054-8

To Ruth Ann,
May she, as George Reeves,
live in the hearts
of those she touched

We welcome your thoughts and comments on the Popular Library Film Series. Address all correspondence to Leonard Maltin, 200 West 79 Street, 5-L, New York, New York 10024.

TABLE OF CONTENTS

———————————————

ABOUT THE AUTHOR—

Gary Grossman is a free-lance writer on the media and an instructor in Popular Culture at Boston University.

ACKNOWLEDGMENTS

To Irene, who let me watch "Superman" even when it was on opposite reruns of "Perry Mason." To all those associated with the Superman serials and television broadcasts, including Whitney Ellsworth, Natividad Vacio, Noel Neill, Kirk Alyn, Jack Larson, Robert Shayne, Phyllis Coates, Thomas Carr, Spencer Bennet, Thol Simonson, Sterling Holloway, Herburt Vigran, Harry Gerstad, Joseph Biroc, Robert Justman, Milton Frome and Ben Welden. I must also thank the following people for their patient help and understanding: Susan Barer; Arthur Hook, WLVI-TV; Brian Higgins, WSMW-TV; Gerald Haber, WTIC-TV; Gene Harris, WSBK-TV; Peter Affe, Warner Brothers Sales Representative, and Allan Asherman and Bernard Kashdan of National Periodical Publications. Additionally, Bob Porfirio, Betsy Goldman, Andi Jacobs, Mindy Roiter, Michael Berzak, Eric Hoffman, Gene Roddenberry, Paul Campanis, Mannie Levine, Edward Milkis, Madeleine Silber, and the staffs of the Lincoln Center Reference Library, the Galesburg, Illinois, Public Library, and the National Academy of Motion Picture Arts and Sciences Library. And in memory to Henry Cusano who helped originally broadcast "Superman" through my home TV station, WRGB.

Finally, my appreciation and special thanks (forever understated) to my parents, Evelyn and Stanley Grossman; Jeffrey Davis, David L. Miller, Michael Blowen, Bob Rubin (for his outstanding photographic efforts), and Leonard Maltin.

INTRODUCTION

For more than thirty years Superman has overshadowed Clark Kent. That may change now. The work of newspapermen Bob Woodward and Carl Bernstein tells Clark Kent that the reporter need not duck into an office storeroom and don a flashy uniform. He can keep his double-breasted suit and fight his battle for truth and justice with an earthbound typewriter instead of his intergalactic superstrength.

But Kent will find this new role difficult, for he is a child of the thirties, groomed in an era needing escapism and adventure, a time requiring a hero of extraordinary qualities; an ordinary reporter wouldn't do. Cartoonists Jerry Siegel and Joseph Shuster created a character to fit the bill. They premiered "Superman" for Harry Donenfeld's *Action Comics* in June 1938.

The Herculean character was appropriate to the needs of his generation.

Two years later Superman shifted to radio, making his debut on February 12, 1940, as a three-times-per-week program. Soon it became a top entry on the Mutual Network with Clayton (Bud) Collyer as the Man of Steel, Joan Alexander as the famous girl reporter Lois Lane and Julian Noa as the gruff Perry White. (The program was narrated by Jackson Beck, produced by Robert and Jessica Maxwell, and directed by Allen DuCovny and Mitchell Grayson.) Bob Maxwell, who later produced "Adventures of Superman" on television, utilized a recently introduced comic book character, the bumbling James Bartholomew Olsen, played by Jackie Kelk. The radio drama also discovered Superman's Achilles' heel—Kryptonite, the green rock that could kill the otherwise indestructible crusader.

The radio show brought together two longtime business partners, Superman and Kellogg's. It was a profitable relationship that lasted until 1957, when production on the television series ended. For years, Superman and the breakfast foods were inseparable. Characters from the cast peddled Corn Flakes moments after being saved from an almost certain demise.

On radio, Jimmy Olsen chimed:

> *Hep Hep Kellogg's Pep*
> *Keep in Tune*
> *Keep in Shape*
> *With Kellogg's Pep*

Superman also appeared in seventeen expensive, full-animation color cartoons produced by Fleischer Studios and Paramount Pictures. Again, Bud Collyer's voice shifted three octaves lower as Clark Kent shed his worldly costume, claiming "This is a job for Superman!" Unlike the limited-animated cartoon adventures later produced for television, these Fleischer mini-dramas are handsomely inked films originally designed to challenge the Disney market in style and brilliance.

Superman later became a live-action film hero in two fifteen-chapter motion picture serials produced by Columbia: *Superman* (1948), and *Atom Man vs. Superman* (1950). George Reeves took the role for a feature film, *Superman and the Mole Men,* in 1951, and starred in the television program from 1951–57. Today his adventures appear in eight different comic books, on sale in thirty countries, and written in fifteen different languages.

The actual character evolved throughout the Superman chronology. In an early edition of *Action Comics,* the Man of Steel risked his secret identity in order to secure an interview with an alleged murderer. In another issue, his parents, originally Jor-L and Lora, were renamed Jor-El and Lara. John and Mary Kent, his foster-parents on Earth, were renamed Eben and Sarah. Meanwhile in the comics, *Daily Planet* editor George Taylor woke up one morning as Perry White. And on radio, the audience discovered Superman had grown up in transit between Krypton and Earth.

The origin of Superman's powers differed from medium to medium. His flying was first attributed to gigantic leaps, possibly due to Earth's lesser gravity.

Yet Columbia's Superman, Kirk Alyn, actually flew, once boasting ". . . two thousand miles away. I can be there in thirty seconds!" The serial shared common ground with the radio scripts, agreeing that Krypton was a planet of supermen, and that Kal-El's feats on Earth were no mere accident. Meanwhile, an episode from the television years, "Divide and Conquer" (1957), attributes Superman's powers to the proximity of atoms within his body. According to Professor La-Serne:

Yours happen to have greater density, they're packed closer together, giving you your superstrength, making it impossible for you to be injured or hurt.

Clark Kent's career as a reporter on the *Daily Planet* also varied. On radio, Clark Kent edges out the competition with a scoop on wholesale destruction of our Western railroads. In the first serial, Superman saves Lois (Noel Neill) Lane and a coal miner, and on television, he rescues a man dangling from a dirigible.

Today the comics are contemporary. Superman has obtained rights from the United Nations to violate international air space, lest he be considered a red-caped missile from a hostile country. He's been humanized. Clark Kent joins the ranks of David Brinkley and Walter Cronkite, sporting styled hair, tinted glasses and Johnny Carson suits. Morgan Edge, president of the *Daily Planet* and heir apparent to the "Great Caesar's Ghost" role, puts Kent on the air.[1] He changes into Superman during commercials, flies to the other end of the globe, and returns in time to straighten his tie; all supposedly within sixty seconds. In addition, the format has changed. National Periodicals adopted the style of Stan Lee's *Marvel Comics*, linking individual issues together by narrative subplots and continuing peril, and the Man of Steel no longer fears the once deadly rock, Kryptonite.

[1] Television viewers see Clark Kent in this position as he broadcasts the news in the 1951 episode "The Monkey Mystery."

While Superman is still the character we identified with in our childhood, he has come of age in the 1970s. He's not as simplistic as his ancestor from bygone days. Today there is more conflict between Clark Kent/Superman than George Reeves was ever asked to portray on television. The character is complex. Still innocent and uncommitted, he is less chauvinistic, and remains conscious of being on the outside of normal life. As cartoonist Jules Feiffer suggests in *The Great Comic Book Heroes*, there exists a "schizoid chaste ménage à trois" surrounding Clark Kent, Lois Lane and Superman: Clark Kent loves Lois Lane. She in turn loves Superman, only tolerating Clark. But Superman wants Lois to respect him for his alter ego, "To love him when he acted the coward. She never did—so, of course he loved her. A typical American romance."

The paradox exists because Clark Kent is not real. He is not Superman's true identity as Don Diego is Zorro's or Bruce Wayne is Batman's. Clark Kent is the sham. The glasses, suit and manner constitute the Halloween costume. As Clark Kent, he can feign interest in Lois or any other woman. As Superman, fearing his identity revealed, he can't "keep up" what Kent started. He remains the perennial celibate. Reeves, summing up this priestly predicament, once told a reporter, "I'm so super, I've never kissed my leading lady. Superman is above that sort of thing."

Today, the comic book character wonders why he must feign weakness, then be ridiculed by those he loves. His heroic efforts are often foiled because legal restrictions prevent him from intervening. In other cases, he realizes that committing himself to action might rob others of the initiative to solve their problem. Clark Kent alludes to this in the 1955 television episode "The Big Freeze":

Sometimes, Lois, it's not wise for everyone to depend on Superman to keep their own house in order.

The "Adventures of Superman" developed its own

format. Batman never appears on television with Superman as he did on radio. Nor does Superman regularly crash through the time barrier, visit his Fortress of Solitude, fight Bizarro, or protect the miniaturized city of Kandor. The hero debuted on television, as he had in print, as a crusader for justice who operates outside the law, but toward similar goals. He is often anti-intellectual but still retains the ability to break up every marriage between corrupt politicians and organized crime ("The Big Freeze," "Crime Wave," and "Beware the Wrecker"). He is a pacifist in the tradition of Zorro and the Lone Ranger. He can tolerate only a "legitimate" use of force.

During World War II, Superman's emblem became synonymous with the American flag. There were never any greater symbols. In hundreds of colorful pages Superman handily downs drooling, slanty-eyed Japanese pilots and screaming Germans.[2] Germany's propaganda minister Joseph Goebbels, recognizing Superman's hold over the American foot soldier's morale, leveled a massive counterattack. "Superman is a Jewmonger," said Goebbels. But to the Nazi's extreme displeasure, Superman remained standard issue in GI duffel bags, outlasting Betty Grable, and outselling the Bible!

Today "Superman" reruns are challenged in longevity only by "I Love Lucy" and an occasional appearance by "The Today Show's" retired Frank Blair. From an embossed "K" on a Henry Kissinger book jacket to articles in *Playboy*, *New Times*, *New York Magazine* and *Newsweek*, there are daily takeoffs on the Superman motif. ABC telecast a remake of the Broadway play *It's a Bird . . . It's a Plane . . . It's Superman* and a recent Air Force recruiting campaign suited up "Mission Impossible" strong man Peter Lupus for the pitch. *Godspell* producers Edgar Lansbury, Stuart Duncan and Joseph Beruh clad their omnipotent Jesus Christ in a Superman shirt. There is even a book titled *The*

---

[2] 1942 Paramount cartoon *The Japoteurs*.

Gospel According to Superman, and now, of course, the Mario Puzo "Superman" motion picture.

The Superman formula is quite simple. He does not have the enlightened ratiocination of Sherlock Holmes. After all, Superman is a child of *Action Comics,* not *Detective Comics.* His saving grace is swift action and brute force. Luckily, most of his foes are slightly below Neanderthal man on the evolutionary scale. Meanwhile, the interior of Clark Kent's apartment reinforces *his* reliance on invincible strength rather than aesthetic judgment. Nothing is revealed except Santa Monica Avenue antiques, Goodwill furniture and Woolworth paintings. But we need not tire ourselves over nonverbal clues. The character has remained middle-class; a Walter Mitty who could command an evil power. However, thanks to those wholesome formative years in the corn belt he chooses the path of total righteousness.

It is surprising, however, that more comic book heroes haven't followed the experience of Superman's low budget–high return television years. There have been spinoffs; a Western caricature on "Wild, Wild West," and a mechanical marvel, "Six Million Dollar Man." "Batman" and "Green Hornet" had short runs and "Wonder Woman" was a forgettable television pilot from Warner Brothers. Perhaps comic book creators have realized that luck played out in the Superman success, and such a turn might not come up again.

The "Adventures of Superman" began on television amid Dr. Frederic Wertham's attacks against sex, sadism and violence in comics. At a time when other comic publishers were turning from a horror and science fiction genre to docile characters in fairylands, National Comics stayed with their old kingpin, Superman, who had survived World War II, a court suit against Captain Marvel and the assaults of Dr. Wertham. Countless youngsters must have grown up as I did, with Mom's kitchen stepladder firmly planted under the tummy, arms and legs outstretched, makeshift

Clark Kent and Lois Lane in their motion picture debut, the 1941 Paramount Pictures—Max Fleischer cartoon "Superman" (also known as "The Mad Scientist").

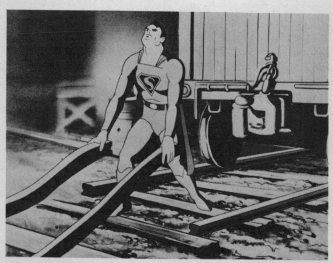

Superman in his first screen uniform, from the 1942 Paramount Pictures—Max Fleischer cartoon "Billion Dollar Limited."

Superman, as he appears in television cartoons today.

cape flowing in the breeze of a Vornado fan, watching, with sweaty palms, the weekly "Adventures of Superman." I triumphed every time he leaped out that inevitable window or did in heavies with his "old one-two." It never occurred to me why the same footage was used repeatedly, why Ben Welden, Richard Reeves, Tris Coffin, Herb Vigran and Billy Nelson kept coming back as different nasties, or why Inspector Henderson never solved a crime by himself. Anyway, who cared?

The ubiquitous eye of television has raised the Siegel-Shuster character to the pinnacle of popular culture heroes, standing taller than John Henry, Paul Bunyan, Casey Jones, Charlie Chaplin and Buster Keaton. "For some weird reason," says Jimmy Olsen actor Jack Larson, "Superman will continue to draw fans of every age to the tube, just as the Superman comic book covers still catch our eyes when we pass the newsstand. I can't explain it. I don't know how it became a classic, but we must have done something right."

The Superman families from the serials and television.

Superman television producer Whitney Ellsworth would like to believe it, yet modesty prevents him. Instead, Ellsworth insists, "It still might be too early to tell whether the Man of Steel is made of tempered metal or is merely chrome-plated." But you know, Mr. Ellsworth, after more than two decades of exposure to the tube, there are no signs that Superman is rusting away!

CHAPTER I

FROM TWO THOUSAND TWO HUNDRED EIGHTY-EIGHT SATURDAYS . . .

There used to be a time when serials were what you went to the theater for, and if they threw in a two- or three-reeler, that was extra. Serials were very important for Saturday matinees. For fifteen weeks you never knew how the story would turn out. They were originally called cliff-hangers, because each week either the heroine or hero was left in a very precarious position. You didn't know how they were going to get out of it, so you'd come back next week. Those were serials.

Kirk Alyn

"You couldn't wait to see Pearl White again next week," remembers actor-director Thomas Carr. "There was more spontaneity in serials than in many feature films. We'd work hard." "Some days," according to Kirk (Superman) Alyn, "we did seventy-six setups and thought nothing of it."

Serial's roots extend well into the silent era. The Edison Company experimented first. The idea was pure genius; the early producers simply cashed in on the audiences' support for their daily print favorites and constructed complicated film adventures around them. Serials pioneered women's liberation with sensational, death-defying women, long before comparable feminine roles were the vogue in features. From the 1912 Edison Company *What Happened to Mary* through Phyllis Coates's 1955 *Panther Girl of the Kongo*, the serial queen ruled; forever naïve, innocent and always beautiful.

Perhaps the most famous and most often imitated serial remains *The Perils of Pauline*. First produced in 1914, the cliff-hanger catapulted Pearl White to heights no other serial star has since attained.

During the thirties, Mascot, Universal and Republic were king; they had the capital, facilities and stars. RKO entered the field for only one film, a Lon Chaney western (*The Last Frontier*, 1932). Mascot had a youthful and trim John Wayne in *Shadow of the Eagle* (1932), *Hurricane Express* (1932) and *The Three Musketeers* (1933), while Universal countered with Buster Crabbe in four *Buck Rogers* and *Flash Gordon* serials from 1936—40. Republic Pictures joined the action in 1936, using a small lot in the San Fernando Valley previously dedicated to the filming of low-budget Westerns.

Film historian Alan G. Barbour feels that Republic's staff, the underdog in the industry, refused to be moved by the criticism of the day. Republic had been dubbed "Repulsive Pictures" and was considered the rock bottom of the industry. It was said that working there "was the first step down the ladder to obscurity and unemployment." Yet the crew would not be moved; they produced films at a rate no other studio could match. Republic even succeeded where Mascot and Universal had failed: pacing and music. Chapter plays had

Kirk Alyn and James Dale explain the law to veteran heavy Roy Barcroft in a scene from "Federal Agents vs. Underworld, Inc." (Republic, 1949)

Kirk Alyn holds the gun as James Dale checks Tristram Coffin for a concealed weapon in "Federal Agents vs. Underworld, Inc." (Republic, 1949). Coffin also appears regularly in television's "Adventures of Superman."

previously dragged so much that the chases seemed to last forever. Not Republic's; their musicians composed a library of mood vignettes that their directors used lavishly throughout the fifteen minutes of action.

Republic also had directors with moxie. William Witney, John English, *Superman*'s Tommy Carr and Spencer Gordon Bennet kept audiences on the edge of their seats with even the most mundane of scripts. The special effects of Howard Lydecker's winged batmen, exploding cars and daredevil planes rounded out Republic's expertise. It seemed fitting that Republic should bring America's most famous comic book hero to the screen. Studio executives talked of filming Superman as early as 1940, but negotiations with National Comics were postponed. Republic held the edge over the competition for many years, twice announcing they would bring the man from Krypton to local theaters. But Republic was not willing to give up control to the omnipresent comic book owners, who insisted on absolute control of script and production. It wasn't Republic's style to submit, despite the optimism of a two-page spread on Superman in the studio's 1941 promotion book. Seven years passed before the next major development occurred. In 1947, Columbia acquired the serial rights to Superman. The production was awarded to Sam Katzman, a benevolent despot, noted for never having lost money on a film.

Columbia serials were often as flat as the characters upon which they were based, very often comic book heroes: *Mandrake the Magician* (1939), *Terry and the Pirates* (1940), *Batman* in 1943 and again in 1949, *The Phantom, Brenda Starr, Reporter, The Vigilante* in 1943, and Kirk Alyn's 1951 *Blackhawk*. The studio also sent their crime fighters to other worlds: *Brick Bradford* (1947), *Captain Video* (1951) and *The Lost Planet* (1953). Unfortunately, they lacked the enthusiasm of the Flash Gordon serials they copied. The productions looked every bit the shoddy, low-budget quickies they were. Nonetheless, the surviving triumvirate of a dying industry gathered in 1948 on the Columbia lot for an all-out effort. *Superman* was finally on the call-board. Bennet, Katzman and Alyn were doing it!

Spencer Gordon Bennet is a living Hollywood legend. He began calling the shots on early Pearl White serials, continuing to direct Saturday fare through 1956. The last theatrical serial produced in the United States, *Blazing the Overland Trail*, bore the Bennet signature. He was considered the most prolific of action directors, and could move from studio to studio, serials to features and features to television. Bennet could claim the honors whenever serials improved. "I didn't think that much of any one I completed," says Bennet. "I just figured how much better the next one could be." His years at Republic brought lavish fights, trick photography and thrilling musical scores. Bennet controlled the show.

Republic was a factory, the best in serial production. "In order to make pictures fast in those days, as soon as I said 'cut' in one scene I'd begin another. We had to keep moving, we were working sixty or seventy set-ups per day! While one crew was rehearsing, another was shooting." Bennet says it was normal to shoot a ten- or fifteen-episode serial each month. The large studios, Fox, RKO and M-G-M, never scheduled work at Republic's pace. "There was a waste of time in big features, compared to what I did. But then the major studios never had Pearl White teetering in a basket above a vat of boiling oil!"

Bennet was a master of trick work. "In one film I had to have an ocean liner leave a dock in Jacksonville, Florida. Well, the dock was there, but no ocean liner. To get an ocean liner to steam up and move away would have cost at least $25,000. I couldn't afford that. Luckily there was a big vessel anchored about a half mile from shore in the St. James River. I hired a tugboat and a big scow, the type used on the Hudson to carry freight trains. They look like docks. I towed one out against the ship; behind it was the tugboat. The shot before had Charlie Hutchinson running through the streets to catch the ship before it left. He ran past the camera, and I cut to him running on the barge. I moved the dock, that is the barge, instead of the ship. The illusion was the ship going away!"

For years Bennet was Hollywood's most accomplished illusionist. "I could total a $35,000 Rolls-Royce without giving it a scratch." The former Coney Island polar bear edited most of his early serials in the camera as well. "When a producer told me he had a low budget, I had to visualize what every scene would cost in terms of film, otherwise I'd be shooting over. I shot three-to-one." The ratio has to do with the amount of film shot to the amount used. For every foot edited into the final print, Bennet would throw away only three. The lower the ratio, the more money a director would save, and Bennet's ratio was very low.

Bennet had a good reputation in town for frugality, consequently he could demand top dollar for himself. "Katzman was used to directors who would show him a great deal of repetition in the dailies. When he first hired me I demanded a certain salary. He claimed he couldn't pay, so I turned around and said, 'You don't want me then. I would have saved you money in a big lab bill, and overtime for actors. Would you rather pay them or me?' " Katzman saw the light.

Film editors liked Bennet's style. "All they had to do was cut it the way I shot the picture. They didn't have to plow through hundreds and hundreds of feet and wonder which angle to use. I shot it the way it was to be edited."

Bennet was a perfectionist, demanding of all just what their jobs called for. Nothing more, nothing less. "He knew his business," recalls Kirk Alyn. "I learned a great deal from him."

Noel Neill adds, "Spencer was a real love, a wonderful person . . . just a gentleman, a word used sparingly in the business years ago. But he was a dear person, very kind and easy. He could do all the stunts if he wanted to. He was a real believer, and every day after work he would go to the 'Y' on Sunset Boulevard to play handball."

Spencer Gordon Bennet can still be seen beating all comers at the game of handball. The veteran director has lived eight full decades with unceasing vigor. No doubt he'll be teaching the freshmen in town for a long while.

Kirk Alyn reminisces about the late Sam Katzman. "He was a nice guy, maybe one of the sweetest in the world, once we got past the money stage." Alyn's view is widely held by those who worked with the producer. Noel Neill feels that Katzman helped keep Columbia alive. "The studio didn't have the class of M-G-M, Twentieth Century–Fox and Paramount. But Katzman kept grinding out the serials and B movies in those last years."

"He was cheap only to a certain degree," adds Kirk Alyn. "He knew how to cut production costs and overwork people, but we'd always be able to dicker with him on salary. Sam would say, 'You know I always take good care of you, kid.' " Katzman liked to show off his talent. He'd say to Alyn, "Hurry up and get rid of that uniform, we'll go to lunch." Inside the Brown Derby Sam would ask the unknowing maître d', "Do you know who this is?" After a short pause and a smile, "This fellow is Superman!"

Jim Harmon and Donald Glut, authors of *The Great Movie Serials*, damned all Katzman motion pictures: "The low budget showed everywhere in money-saving short cuts and inadequacies." But Spencer Bennet defends Katzman's tightness. "Sam wasn't getting up-front money. His serials were supporting Columbia's big flops, and not getting the return themselves." His last features were no exception: *Rock Around the Clock, Get Yourself a College Girl, Harem Scarem* and *Girl Crazy.*

Another serial director, Tommy Carr, was a bit miffed by it all, but now, actively retired, he is able to be philosophical. "On *Superman* and his other more important serials we cracked down, paid more attention to details, made better scenes and took more time with the first three episodes than the others. Sam would run the first three for a prospective distributor on hopes of selling the entire package. If they liked them, they'd take whatever else we'd deliver. The first three weeks usually ran three reels instead of two. From then on it was downhill. While this was normal for other studios as well, Sam didn't hesitate telling us to make the first three good, especially on *Superman*."

Katzman was King of the Serials at Columbia during the 1940s and 1950s. He was famous for getting the most out of his people for the least amount of money. "Sam hired me because I knew serials," says Spencer Bennet. "And in the eight years I was with him he never bothered me once."

"We all did a lot of cheapies that Spencer directed for Katzman," says actress Phyllis Coates, "but I feel he forgot about us, we were Katzman one-dimensional stick figures."

Tommy Carr wanted out after Katzman's 1948 *Superman*. "As far as my work was concerned, I felt I had more control over television than over Katzman serials. He didn't care what the pictures looked like. His idea was just to get it on film as cheaply as possible. That never set well with me."

Robert Shayne speaks of the stranglehold Katzman kept on some of his people. "Many actors, like other people, gambled their money away. When that happened Katzman would be there with a fast deal. He'd lend them money and the only way they could pay him back was to work on his terms." But the Katzman legend also tells of a compassionate man who kept hundreds of people working and millions of viewers entertained. His features and serials, including the long-running East Side Kids–Bowery Boys productions, filled movie screens for three decades, and it's unfortunate that Katzman's last two serials were probably the worst made anywhere——*Perils of the Wilderness* (1956) and *Blazing the Overland Trail* (1956). The industry's last two gasps relied on incredible amounts of stock footage. Some chapters contained an assortment of ten-year-old action wide shots, fights and tumbles. It was an old technique cultivated at Republic, but Columbia was guilty, too. The studio kept in the black by choosing leading men on the basis of their resemblance to others already on film.

Meanwhile, television began to lure away crews and actors with production values slipping at Columbia and Republic. However, the new medium offered only a dream of steady employment and a myth of better production. Actually it was no better. The fulfillment of television's early promise for actors, directors, and producers was probably nonexistent, or at best, still years ahead.

Serial production that began with Pearl White ended with Sam Katzman. His two Superman releases, though the top-grossing cliff-hangers of all time, marked the beginning of the end of Columbia.

RADAR PATROL
VS. SPY KING
A
REPUBLIC
SERIAL IN
12 CHAPTERS
KIRK ALYN
JEAN DEAN
GEORGE J. LEWIS
EVE WHITNEY
FRED BRANNON

Kirk Alyn was one of the last great serial heroes. He arrived at the Columbia B lot not knowing what to expect from *Superman*. As Alyn tells it in his book, *A Job for Superman*, Katzman telephoned asking whether the character interested him. "We've been auditioning all the fighters, wrestlers and stunt men in town, more than a hundred of them, I don't know why we didn't think of you before."

Alyn went to the familiar office at Columbia. He had previously made a few "parlor-bedroom-sink" pictures for Katzman. As Alyn walked in, the producer bellowed, "What the hell have you got on your face!" The actor had a beard from two Westerns he'd shot. National Comics, of course, was not looking for a Samson; they had their idea of Superman, and Kirk Alyn with a beard was not it. But the next day he walked the studio halls sans beard, ready to be measured for tights, boots, cape and S. Kirk Alyn's tenure as Superman had begun.

He did not spring forth fully formed in a Superman outfit. Alyn began his stage career by accident. He auditioned for a Broadway show as a gag and won the role. From Columbia University to a New York musical was an impressive accomplishment for a shy youngster from New Jersey. Over the next few months he moved into a Ginger Rogers musical, *Girl Crazy*, and a summer stock production with Joseph Cotten, *Band Concert*. Yet Alyn still experienced the traditional ups and downs of an acting career in the Depression. He worked for a time in a modeling agency, until he was selected for the George S. Kaufman–Morrie Ryskind musical *Of Thee I Sing*.

But the most unforgettable days, remembers Alyn, ". . . were those fifty-three weeks spent on tour with Olsen and Johnson, two of the zaniest guys in the business. I did everything in *Hellzapoppin*. We never had a completely rehearsed program. It would change every night. Sure, we'd have a short meeting while the stage was being set to tell us which acts were likely to go up that day, but anything could happen . . . everything did. Ole must have fired me a dozen times before the show opened, but Chic would always say, 'Kirkie, come back, we need you!' ''

Throughout the early thirties, Alyn appeared in Warner Brothers one- and two-reelers in New York, working with Shemp Howard and Dizzy Dean. He subwayed to the Bronx for some shorts with Hal LeRoy in the old Bronx Biograph studios and later emceed musical acts for Ben Blake's Long Island pictures.

Kirk also pioneered New York television in 1939: "We got fifty bucks for doing a show. They were detective plots, unsponsored. It was illegal to take commercials because it was just for industry research. Only a few bars around town had receivers, and the thing was a complete monstrosity, costing about $1,000. No home could afford it, in fact who would have wanted one? The cabinet was huge, and the screen was only about six inches wide. You watched the picture in a mirror. . . . So we never thought much of it. After the war it was different. Television started to boom. It hurt the Saturday matinee, the afternoon shows when all our serials ran. After mine, studios made a few more with edited stock footage and a leading man just to tie the story together. It was television that caused the serials to fade out, the same way vaudeville disappeared when talking pictures emerged."

Alyn continued to work up dance routines with new partners Imogene Coca and Bob Burton. He also moved into comic sketches with Billy De Wolfe. During July and August, he often returned to his old stamping grounds, summer stock, opening a new play every week; rehearsing next week's play in the daytime hours and playing the current show at night.

A chance at a Hollywood contract offered a way off this treadmill. Alyn was a quick study, and this stab at Hollywood was a godsend. His first Columbia screen test turned into a role as a Portuguese sailor in *My Sister Eileen* (1942). He was later cast with Fred Astaire and Rita Hayworth in *You Were Never Lovelier* (1942).

After the war there were parts in *Little Miss Broad-*

This is one fight Kirk Alyn loses—temporarily. There's no doubt why. Utility double and stuntman Tom (Captain Marvel) Steele throws the punch while character actor Anthony Warde holds. ("Radar Patrol vs. Spy King"—Republic, 1950.)

way, *The Life of St. John the Baptist, Lucky Jordan* and a Charlie Chan feature, *The Trap*.

Amid these roles, the former New Jersey ballet dancer endured himself uncomfortably on a horse. "It's perfectly safe," the director of *Overland Mail Robbery* told Alyn. "All you have to do is give the horse a kick when the camera truck pulls up next to you. The horse is perfectly trained and he knows exactly what to do. All you have to remember is hang on and look back once in a while because those fellows behind are shooting at you." If only things had gone that well. When they picked up a sore-bottomed, bruised Kirk Alyn he made no bones about his riding. "I don't like horses! I want no further contact with them!" said the New Jersey native. However, he remained at the Republic lot in the forties for *Man from Rio* and *Call of the Rockies*.

Kirk Alyn on location in the San Fernando Valley with the production of "Blackhawk" (1952).

Republic continued to churn out a Western every two weeks. They did so, however, without the fast guns and champion equestrian abilities of Kirk Alyn. "With or without my horse I think I did eight pictures at Republic, out of one into another . . . out of one into another. I seemed to be working all the time. I did nine features for Katzman, seven at Columbia. And there were six serials from 1946–52, split between Republic and Columbia. So you see I didn't really come out of the woods to do Superman, then go back into the woods when I finished. There was more to my career."

"But with all the nostalgia," adds Alyn with a little pride, "if you ask what did I have the most fun in pictures doing, I'd say *Superman*."

Although Kirk Alyn will be remembered most for his Superman role, Alan Barbour believes he was superior as a straight actor in his other serials: *Daughter of*

Don Q (Republic, 1946), *Federal Agents vs. Underworld, Inc.* (Republic, 1949), *Radar Patrol vs. Spy King* (Republic, 1950) and *Blackhawk* (Columbia, 1952).

Kirk Alyn's days of fighting crime as a secret agent, crusader and ace do-gooder were over with the completion of *Blackhawk*. Reviewing his career, Alyn says, "I'm proud I never did anything in my life that made me unhappy. If I didn't like it I would quit. But *Superman*, unlike *Blackhawk* and all the rest, was something else. I was hard pressed to find a decent role. Everyplace I'd go they'd say 'Hi ya, Superman!' I didn't think of that at all when I went into it. Not that I regret it; I just didn't expect it." But Alyn did work again. He traded his tights for tapping shoes, and returned East for plays with Veronica Lake, Ilona Massey and June Havoc. He also appeared in *When Worlds Collide* (1952), *Highway Patrol*, *PJ* and *Annie Oakley*.

Today he looks back on his career. "I don't know whether *Superman* was a good thing for me to do, but I'm glad I did it. It was good, clean fun; you could distinguish the hero from the bad guys. No matter how formidable the perils I faced I always won in the last chapter!"

Kirk Alyn, the original screen Superman, as he looks in the 1970s.

CHAPTER II

. . . Came Thirty Saturdays with Superman

There was no doubt about it; by the time Kirk Alyn suited up for *Superman*, serial production was on the wane and box office receipts were dropping. Soon Hollywood would know the sounds of facades crashing on cement, leaving only rubble for a quick auction or an obscure collector's garage. However, before the bulldozers leveled the sets to make room for shopping centers and parking lots, two Superman serials were sealed in the can. Kirk Alyn starred in both.

When you play a human being everybody expects certain things. But something like Superman has to be just a little different, so the audience will always think that it *is* plausible; that it can be.

With Superman properly cast, producer Sam Katzman searched for the lead's romantic counterpart, Lois Lane. Her parameters had been explicitly defined in the comics; she remained the no-nonsense reporter with an obsession for a scoop. Katzman called in all the busty sweater girls before deciding upon Noel Neill, a contract player in Paramount's Henry Aldrich films and Monogram's "Teenagers" series.

"I was doing good movies at Paramount before *Superman*," says the pert actress. "It was just work. We didn't care what we did, the main idea was to work. Work the major lots, then pick up anything extra along the way. In 1948, I thought *Superman* was one of those extra things."

Pierre Watkin signed on as Perry White. The busy character actor, already a veteran of over one hundred films, brought practical experience to his new role. Watkin had been editor of the *Sioux City Tribune* and *Sioux Falls Argus*. Filmgoers may remember him for his serial appearances in *Brick Bradford* and *Jack Armstrong, the All-American Boy*, and features including *Country Gentlemen* (1936), *Young Dr. Kildare*

Noel Neill as Lois Lane in the 1948 serial "Superman."

(1938), *Mr. Smith Goes to Washington* (1939), *The Road to Singapore* (1940), *Meet John Doe* (1941) and the controversial *Mission to Moscow* (1943). Coincidentally, Pierre Watkin concluded his career with guest shots on the "Adventures of Superman": "The Case of the Talkative Dummy" (1951), "The Jolly Roger" (1955) and "The Last Knight" (1957).

Finally, "Our Gang" graduate Tommy Bond rounded out the cast, portraying Jimmy Olsen. Bond had appeared in dozens of the Hal Roach comedies as Butch,

DAILY PLANET

Former "Our Gang" regular—Tommy Bond—as Jimmy Olsen in the 1948 serial, "Superman."

the little tough guy with angled baseball cap. Today he keeps up with the industry as prop department supervisor at Los Angeles television station KTTV.

Columbia opted for complete secrecy, adding infinite drama to the eight years of anticipation. Few beyond the studio paymaster knew who would portray Superman. No visitors were permitted on the set, and Alyn was billed solely as the newspaperman. At Katzman's first official press briefing he announced that it had proved quite impossible to find any actor to play Superman. No human possessed the unique capabilities the role demanded; the solution was obvious. The authentic Superman had been persuaded to accept the assignment himself.

Alyn describes the strategy: "All production secrets were supposed to remain privileged information for the duration of the series and hopefully beyond. Personal appearances were to be screened and supervised to protect the Superman image, and it went without saying that the conduct of Clark Kent, not to mention me, was under the evil eye of the legal department."

The first test of the "image clause" was not good. National prefers not to remember the incident, "But I enjoy telling it," jokes Alyn. Leading comedians and actors formed two baseball teams to junket the country for the purpose of raising funds for the City of Hope Hospital. The first game was scheduled for a warm September evening in Chicago. Hopalong Cassidy gave up prairie justice for the moment, assuming a position of far greater power. He became umpire. Bob Hope, Anthony Quinn, Buddy Rogers, Wayne Morris, Roddy McDowall and Sonny Tufts provided the action. Ava Gardner and a crew of healthy Hollywood lovelies cheered from the sidelines.

The serious actors were collecting more runs. The comedians and novelty players were behind, but not out of the game; their secret weapon hadn't stepped forward yet. The scenario was perfect: bases loaded, two outs, two strikes. The call went out for a pinch hitter. Dave Garroway, public address announcer, tested the strength of the crowd.

> **A pinch hitter—who will it be?**
> **Is it a bird?**
> **Is it a plane?**
> **Oh no! It's Superman!**

The crowd erupted with cheers as the costumed serial hero bounded out of the dugout with a forceful stride. Superman was at bat! Babe Ruth, Lou Gehrig,

NOW THE ONE AND ONLY

Copyright 1948
National Comics Publications, Inc.

SUPERMAN

AT HIS MIGHTIEST AS A REAL LIVE HERO ON THE *SERIAL SCREEN!*

Adaptation by George H. Plympton and Joseph F. Poland
Screenplay by Arthur Hoerl, Lewis Clay
and Royal Cole
Directed by SPENCER BENNET
and THOMAS CARR
Produced by SAM KATZMAN

A
COLUMBIA
SERIAL

Based on the SUPERMAN adventure feature
appearing in SUPERMAN and ACTION COMICS
magazines, in daily and Sunday newspapers
coast-to-coast and on the SUPERMAN radio program
broadcast over the Mutual Network.

Ty Cobb . . . nobody was ever a more awesome figure at the plate. The pitcher looked at the sign, wound up and served up the "special ball." It was constructed to shatter when hit, suggesting the awesome power of the batter. There was only one hitch.

Superman struck out: "I missed the ball entirely," remembers Alyn, "and Superman, like the mighty Casey, had struck out! Waves of laughter echoed throughout the stadium; there wasn't a dry eye in the crowd." In the meantime, a second "special ball" was ordered up on a fabricated technicality. Superman would have another swing.

Alyn carefully pointed out toward the last row of bleachers with the aplomb of a ninth-inning slugger.

Summoning all the dramatic effect of the Superman "uniform," I followed the Babe's famous gesture, and as the fans quieted to see what was going to happen next, the pitch came. I whacked the ball, and it shattered with a most satisfying splat. Up went the roar again, but this time there was a difference.

A JOB FOR SUPERMAN

The hero saved the day for everyone and the wire service ate it up. Alyn pleaded that he was not deliberately lampooning Superman, "I just missed the ball because of the photographers. I didn't want to hit one of the cameras. They were standing all around me. As soon as I missed it they [reporters] disappeared so fast to run to their stations with the story: 'Superman Strikes Out, the Mighty Superman Strikes Out!' "

Alyn believes his interpretation of Clark Kent/Superman was true to the character. "When I was Clark Kent, I played him for light comedy. When I got to be Superman I puffed out my chest, pushed my voice down and became authoritative."

"Kirk looked like Clark Kent in real life. That's what impressed me," says Spencer Bennet. Unlike Reeves's Superman, Alyn didn't use padding. He simply wore a cutaway sweat shirt beneath his costume to keep the perspiration from showing. His uniform, however, was not the colorful red and blue. In order for the differences to be distinguishable in the black and white serials, Spencer Bennet used gray and brown. Alyn stepped into his newly fitted boots, standing slightly taller than any of his formidable opponents. Tailored from head to toe, a dashing Kirk Alyn began the grind of over a month of fourteen-hour days.

Alyn sat out the earliest tumbles and falls in favor of a double named Paul Stader. The ace stunt man used his own wardrobe, a duplicate uniform. But the truth of the darkened projection room revealed to Spencer Bennet that no one could successfully double for Kirk Alyn.

"They realized he didn't look like me from either the back or the sides," says Alyn. "He just didn't move like me."

Shooting and reshooting stunts absorbed Katzman's budget. The production went beyond the usual twenty-one days, and expenses rose proportionately. The budget of $10,000 per episode was fast doubling and Katzman began to worry about the entire project. However, his nervous concern was soon dissipated by the release of the serial to a resounding public and a busy box office. Kids everywhere were marching their empty soda bottles to the market, anxiously collecting pennies so they could see *Superman*.

The serial opens as the doomed planet Krypton comes into focus and the narration begins:

There once was a tiny blue star . . . billions of miles separated the star from the Earth. We discovered it was, in reality, a planet like our own. This was the ill-fated planet Krypton which revolved about the brilliant sun of its own. . . . Krypton was a rugged planet laden with jagged mountain chains, rich in strange minerals, unknown to Earth. And on a wide plateau by the capital of Krypton, the nerve center of a civilization that was far advanced . . . for it boasted a race of super men and women. Among the leaders was Jor-El, the fore-

most man of science. Jor-El had concluded that Krypton was being inexorably drawn toward its sun and would one day explode like a giant bubble and disintegrate. Jor-El's wife, Lara, inspired him in his feverish race to construct a trial spaceship. If successful, he planned to build a mammoth fleet to carry the inhabitants of the doomed planet to safety on Earth. (Sound of rumbling.) New giant subterranean pockets of gas exploded, touching off long-sealed volcanoes; columns of fire lit the sky, molten lava scarred Krypton's surface. The fears of Jor-El and Lara were intensified by their concern for the safety of their infant son. To Jor-El, the tremors and shocks, which were now more frequent and violent, were an indication that the cataclysmic day was not far off. . . .

Bennet composed his opening montage from materials at hand: leftover sketches of a Brick Bradford city, an alien San Fernando Valley landscape and dusty costumes from a silent biblical epic. The council of elders is dominated by a most courageous Jor-El (Nelson Leigh) and sinister Robert Barron. For all their superpowers, the wise men of Krypton simply refuse to give credence to Jor-El's prediction. As time runs out, Jor-El and Lara (Luana Walters) realize they must rocket their infant son toward his destiny—planet Earth.

The first chapter continues as Kal-El's animated trip targets him for Middle America. Eben (Edward Cassidy) and Martha Kent (Virginia Carroll) discover the star child. Following adoption proceedings, the Kents raise the odd lad,[1] who eventually learns of his origin during a facts-of-life discussion with his parents.

Eben Kent:

Clark, we've had you with us as long as you can remember. You know we're only your foster-parents. You came to us out of the sky, from what distant place we can't even imagine. You're different from other people.

[1] Played by progressively older actors—Alan Dinehart III, Ralph Hodges and Kirk Alyn.

Your unique abilities make you a kind of superman. Because of these great powers, your speed and strength, your X-ray vision and supersensitive hearing, you have a great responsibility. The world needs a man of such extraordinary capability. That's why you must leave the farm.

Taking it like a real trouper, Clark proclaims, "I'll get a job that will keep me close to world events." Next, his mother produces a uniform she has made from his baby blankets.

Clark Kent:

I'll only wear it when I'm . . . when I'm Superman. I think it's better that no one know that he and Clark Kent are the same person.

Clark begins his quest for truth and justice. En route to Metropolis he spots a break in a stretch of railroad tracks. The music builds to a crescendo, the station agent (Jack George) yells to Kent, "The express has already passed the last station. I couldn't stop it!" And a seemingly passive observer emerges—for the first time—as the mighty Superman! As the death train roars toward certain destruction, Spencer Bennet and Tommy Carr end "Superman Comes to Earth."

Chapter II, "Depths of the Earth," begins where the first twenty-six minutes leave off. Superman easily twists the rails back into place just as the train carrying Lois Lane and Jimmy Olsen thunders by. However, the real-life practicality of accomplishing this stunt worried Alyn on his first day at work. Columbia won permission to shoot along the right-of-way, but the railroad ruled the train would roll by at full throttle. "I think you'll be okay," the technical advisor for the railroad told Alyn. "Just be sure you stay back fifteen inches from where I told you." The expert, meanwhile, pulled back a good twenty-five feet. Kirk describes the scene in his book, *A Job for Superman*:

I began to feel funny in my stomach. Even the cameraman on the opposite side of the tracks put the camera on automatic and retired to a more pleasant vantage point. .... I was absolutely deserted, with my cape thrown casually over my shoulder, down on my knees, holding the railroad tie. .... It's amazing how many things can pass through your mind at a time like that. I could even feel a vibration in the rails.

Kirk held his ground to everyone's astonishment. The dancer from New Jersey electrified the crew with his willpower.

Metropolis rises amid a combination of backlot magic and stock footage. Here Kent looks for work as a newspaperman. But before he reaches the *Daily Planet*, he heeds a call from a damsel in distress. Kent vaults over some bordering bushes, ducks behind a parked car and proclaims, "This looks like a job for Superman!" A swish pan to the sky, the sound of a rocket taking off, and Columbia's famed animation unit takes over.

"We hadn't planned it that way," reminisces Spencer Bennet. "We had Kirk on wires but they showed in the rushes. So when he was ready to take off, Kirk ran, assumed a ballet plié and fifth position and leaped into the air. As he did that, I took an imaginary flight with the camera: a dry pan. Then the animators picked up the action right when Kirk was in the middle of his takeoff. At that point they drew him over my travel shots."

Bennet feels that if Katzman had forked up $64 instead of the going $32 per foot, the animator would have drawn his figure "in relief," creating a third-dimension effect. But Katzman had originally intended to have Alyn fly "live." Columbia's special effects wizards guaranteed they could opaque wires, rendering them invisible to the camera. Alyn was to be fitted with a steel breastplate, then suspended from wires and filmed from various angles. It looked plausible on paper.

"I went through torture getting fitted for that breast-

Professor Leeds (Forrest Taylor) shows Clark Kent a sample of the meteor from Krypton. The next moment, the reporter is on the floor, apparently dead. ("Superman"—Columbia, 1948.)

plate," says Kirk Alyn. "Special effects made a plaster cast of my torso. They fitted me with a mold, poured warm plaster onto me, but as the thing began to harden I couldn't expand my chest. I couldn't breathe! The plaster contracted as it hardened. When they finally got ready to take it off they started from the bottom. It pulled off the hairs on my chest even though they had put vaseline on earlier. It hurt like hell! After about half an hour they called in a doctor who reached in with a long cutting edge. I went through sheer torture."

The crack special effects team also failed to consider the limits of human endurance. Kirk Alyn was Superman on film, not on his own time: "Once they hoisted me up, we all realized the plate didn't hold my legs. I was up there over eight hours trying to hold my legs out as if I were flying. I pulled my stomach muscles out of whack trying to act nonchalant."

While Alyn strained, the camera dipped, panned, dollied and zoomed, creating the illusion of Kirk's speed and maneuverability. However, the screening room again presented the truth for all to see—Columbia's special effects predictions had turned sour. The rushes revealed with little subtlety the visibility of the so-called "invisible wires." Katzman immediately requisitioned the animation.

Superman's rescue of the woman from a blazing inferno wins a *Daily Planet* headline: "Man from Sky Saves Girl."

The stern editor has his own words about the story: "Of all the stupid stories that have come across my desk," screams Perry White, "this is the worst. Flying man in the burning building rescues woman. It's a case of mass hysteria and that's how I want it played. Now get out of here, all of you." Everyone leaves but Kent, who has been observing from an inconspicuous corner.

Perry White:

Well, what do you want?

Clark Kent:

A job.

Perry White:

Any special kind or would mine do?

Clark Kent:

I'd like to be a reporter. I haven't any experience in writing, but . . . well, I have other special qualifications that might be [with a smile] valuable.

Before Kent finishes his pitch, Lois telephones from the scene of a mine disaster. Ten men are trapped in the lower shaft. White orders her to obtain a firsthand interview; however, Kent's powerful ears overhear the conversation from across the room. White is flabbergasted, he demands to know how. "My hearing is better than average," answers Clark modestly.

Clark Kent's retort is the first in an endless supply of one-liners. Television producer Whitney Ellsworth calls it "titillating the kiddies," letting us in on something a major character doesn't know. (George Reeves perfected the repartee with a touch of his glasses and a wink to the camera.)

Meanwhile, White offers Kent a position on the staff under one condition. "If you can get inside that mine and bring me the story, the job is yours!"

Pop Andrews (Tom London) is looking for help when Clark arrives. The novice reporter learns that Lois has stumbled into the gas-filled mine. For the second time in as many weeks, Lois needs help. Clark cocks his eyes toward the mine wall and sees the young miss unconscious on the other side of the rock. It is the screen's first encounter with Superman's famous X-ray vision, which is capable of penetrating earth, rock, steel and concrete. "There are only two things the X-ray vision cannot see through," says Whitney Ellsworth. "One is that real-life baffler of X rays—lead, which is also Superman's only defense against the element Kryptonite; the other is apparently clothing.

Thus, though Superman might locate Lois through tons of solid granite, it never violates her maidenly modesty."

Chapter III, "The Reducer Ray," moves accordingly as Superman's feats are recorded in *Daily Planet* headlines: "Superman Saves 70 in Plane," "Superman Breaks Smuggling Ring," "Superman Traps Killer" and "Man of Tomorrow Foils Robbers." It becomes increasingly clear to the underworld that this is a force

Superman (Alyn) unties Jimmy Olsen (Tommy Bond) in a chapter from "Superman" (1948).

Lois Lane (Noel Neill) trapped in the Spider Lady's web ("Superman"—1948).

to be reckoned with. Enter the formidable Spider Lady, the sinister Queen of Crime (Carol Forman), who has plans for the Man of Steel.

Uncle Sam is understandably nervous about a lethal "Reducer Ray" falling into her hands. Superman proudly answers the call for assistance. After his first official Washington briefing, he turns to leave. "That's the window," he's told, "the door is here."

"Yes, I know," answers Superman. He continues, undaunted, proclaiming his famous "Up, up and away."

"I only said that once," remembers Kirk Alyn. "I suggested to Spencer that the line was ridiculous as hell. The same thing goes for 'This is a job for Superman.' On radio it might be okay, you don't see him, you want to know he's changing, so he has to say something. The same goes for flying. You don't know he's doing it unless he tells you. But when you see Superman on the screen you know what he's doing. He just changes and takes off. So I told Spencer I'm just not going to say it anymore. He agreed."

Jim Harmon and Donald Glut report an additional

45

Superman (Alyn) rescues the forever helpless Lois Lane in "Blast in the Depths" (Chapter 12 of "Superman"—1948).

unconfirmed anecdote in their book *The Great Movie Serials.* Scriptwriter George H. Plympton wanted to have Superman exclaim "Hi-yo Silver!" instead of "Up, up and away!" For better or worse, the joke never made it to the release print.

Still in Chapter III, local scientists announce that a meteorite is streaking toward Metropolis. Coincidentally, both the meteor and the city's number one citizen have the same origin—Krypton. Lois and Clark, by now fierce competitors, are assigned the story. However, Lois ditches her companion and stalks the story on her own. Kent, stranded when Lane speeds off, is luckily picked up by Professor Leeds (Forrest Taylor), the scientist who has already pirated the fallen meteorite.

The scientist shows the reporter his find, and explains his theory: "The exploded parts of the planet Krypton circled the sun for years in the form of asteroids. This one eventually came within Earth's gravitational pull."

When Leeds shows the inquiring Mr. Kent the meteorite, a mysterious glare emanates from the box and the reporter falls to the floor. The professor fumbles with the telephone. "Operator," he shouts. "Call the coroner; Clark Kent just died in my office!"

Spencer Bennet expectedly ends Chapter III with the apparent death of his lead. But Clark Kent is far from the obituary page. When Leeds closes the box, the stricken reporter regains consciousness. Leeds's theory is correct, the meteorite is indeed from Krypton, but he asks himself why Clark Kent should collapse. Kent dramatically turns off the lights, sheds his disguise and faces Leeds as Superman. The knowledge of Superman's secret identity inevitably leads to the anticipated demise of the unsuspecting professor.

"There were nine or ten rehearsals for that scene," recalls Alyn. "I was to enter, advance on the glowing meteor and pass out cold. They had to synchronize the dollying of the camera, the lights dimming as the glow from the box grew brighter, and my slow trembling advance." Alyn was by this time so much into the part that he began feeling its effects. "I had no trouble at all feigning the scene, my knees crumpled all by themselves."

Jack Ingram won't try to push Pierre Watkin out the window as long as Kirk (Superman) Alyn is handy. ("Superman"—Columbia, 1948.)

Superman (Alyn) hurtles thug Al Wyatt atop Rube Schaeffer in "Superman" (1948).

Outside the office one of Spider Lady's henchmen listens attentively. He reports the news of Superman's weakness; it's music to the ears of Spider Lady. She begins spinning a web to snare the previously invulnerable superhero, and baits her trap with the innocent, trusting Lois Lane.

Superman saves the susceptible reporter in and out of the next two chapters until Spider Lady realizes she can destroy the Man of Steel with the stolen Kryptonite from Dr. Leeds's laboratory. Although she fails in Chapter VII, "Into the Electric Furnace," she holds onto the green rock until she can fire it into Superman with a guided missile. In the meantime, Superman averts a second train disaster and rescues Lois from another bizarre peril. Shortly thereafter, the girl reporter is assigned an interview with Dr. Graham (Herbert Rawlinson), inventor of the Reducer Ray. However, Lois faces danger when Spider Lady substitutes her henchman for Graham. Since Lois knows too much she's prepared for electrocution, but naturally Superman intervenes in time to channel the high voltage through his own body.

Actually the stunt was not quite as simple as it

appears. As the charge shot between the two terminals, Alyn caught the sparks directly on the metal buckle of his belt. "I was damned fortunate I had rubber-soled boots on, otherwise I would have been fried to a crisp. It was a close call!"

In "Superman's Dilemma," Spider Lady orders Dr. Graham to jury-rig a duplicate Reducer Ray. In addition, Lois gets caught snooping, and Jimmy Olsen is nearly killed. In the closing weeks, Perry White rejoins the action and requires Superman's special abilities to keep him alive ("Superman at Bay"). After White's brush with death, Spider Lady becomes desperate.

In the final chapter, "The Payoff," she boldly announces that unless her terms are met she will turn the Reducer Ray on Metropolis.[2] A pack of investigators headed by Kent, Lane and Olsen shoot for her latest headquarters. In doing so, they manage to get captured for one more time.

Anticipating the showdown, Superman wears a lead lining under his uniform to shield his body from the deadly emanations of Kryptonite. Furious at the setback, Spider Lady orders the Reducer Ray to full power. It explodes, taking Spider Lady and her henchman to their just reward. As they go up in smoke, Superman boasts, "What you thought was my weakness turned out to be your undoing!"

The *Daily Planet* heroes gather around Kent's desk for the closing lines. Lois enters to find Clark yawning. "I was just having a wonderful dream," he says.

Sarcastic, as always, in speaking to mild-mannered Clark Kent, Lois asks, "You weren't dreaming by any chance that you were Superman?" "That's exactly what I was doing, Lois, and I was flying through the air!"

Lois harrumphs, "That wasn't a dream, Mr. Kent. As far as I'm concerned, it was a nightmare!"

The first Superman serial ends after fifteen weeks

[2] Reminiscent of 1941 Paramount cartoon, *Superman* (sometimes known as *The Mad Scientist*).

of adventurous stunts and disappointing animation. It was an enormous financial success despite its short-comings. Kirk Alyn has reason to be proud. His two Superman serials were giant money-makers, topping cash receipts above any other chapter ever released. However, Jerry Siegel, Joe Shuster and the entire Superman industry must be credited along with the star. Certainly Alyn was the guinea pig, but putting Superman in the uniform was no great risk. Superman was big business long before Kirk Alyn pumped life into him, and the actor realizes this. "I had an awful lot of fun despite the hard knocks. Yet it's crazy to think the Superman serials—so popular years ago—aren't around for new audiences to see. I think they'd be enjoyed by just about everyone."

He is probably correct, but Columbia's 1948 *Superman* press book provides a philosophical clue why they may never be available again.

Atomic-age kids, of course, would no more be satisfied with that old piecemeal thriller, "The Perils of Pauline," than their parents would want to return to the Stanley Steamer. Life these days is quick tempoed, if not earnest, and new scientific gadgets—not all of them harmless toys—are here to stay, apparently.

The actual reason the Superman serials will never be rereleased is quite a different story. Columbia would love to sell them to television or elsewhere, but the contract with National set a limit on the period of years during which they might be shown theatrically. The deal specifically excludes television, and in light of the 104 George Reeves TV episodes, National is not about to rescind its own order.

If audiences could see the serials they might think Superman was overplayed, but that was the style of the medium. "They would always look overplayed to the adult viewer even though we played it straight," says Alyn. "At the time, none of it looked funny, only looking back now does it seem humorous."

A fire prevents Superman (Kirk Alyn) from foiling a bank robbery ("Superman"—Columbia, 1948).

Noel Neill's serial Lois is different than her television portrayal. Alyn remembers when he was Clark Kent he was told to underplay her in order to appear timid and mild-mannered. "But when I was Superman, I was told to overpower her with my action."

"Personally, I liked her better on TV, and so do most kids!" says Whit Ellsworth. The producer believes that Noel managed to invest the role with a quality very much in keeping with the comic book Lois. "The young viewers felt an immediate and instinctive rapport with her, and even the crew occasionally rewarded her performance with a round of applause."

Tommy Bond's Jimmy Olsen differs little from the television interpretation. Bond brought nerve to the serial role. He was more the angry young man. On the other hand, the television Jimmy, as played by Jack Larson, is no sniveling coward. He has fight too, and regularly stands up to heavies in defense of his beloved Miss Lane.

To this day, Kirk Alyn hasn't seen all the chapters

of *Superman.* "I saw one segment back in 1948, just to measure the audience's reaction. Boy, did they love it! Other than that I haven't seen more than a ninety-minute feature re-edit job. Sam Katzman tried to drag me along to see the stuff, but I rarely checked into the rushes. I said, 'You look at them. I'll watch your face when you come out. If you're smiling, I'll stick around. If not, I'll hide!' "

There is no doubt that Superman is the star of the serial. "If anyone ever gets to see the serial again, and that's doubtful, they'll see Superman on the screen most of the time. But for ninety per cent of the television program, George Reeves is Clark Kent, because they relied so much on dialogue—and even that was too flippant. Clark Kent is supposed to be more mild-mannered; I think they forgot about that." Alyn consequently believes that the television version doesn't measure up to his Superman serials. "After all, he never stops trains, holds bridges up or lifts many cars as I did. They just didn't give George any of the sensational stuff."

Perhaps it was a case of television not repeating the inherent risks of the serial production. Alyn's frightful experience in the harness reinforced this concern to TV producers Bob Maxwell and Whitney Ellsworth. As Alyn recalls:

I was flying alongside an airplane. The idea of the episode was somebody had planted a bomb in the wing. It contained a homing device, so they could set it off at a certain time. I was in the plane, changed into Superman, and flew out, hauled the thing off, and tossed it into a lake. Sam cut to a stock shot of an atomic bomb explosion, so it made a hell of an effect. But while I was flying, the smoke from the bomb was going in my face. It gave me the illusion of speed in the air. The special effects people had a couple of smoke pots added to heighten the illusion. But they got overzealous and put too much air in the smoke pots. Instead of it smoking slowly, sparks flew out.

The Spider Lady (Carol Forman) and Brock (Terry Frost) are convinced that they've finally defeated Superman (Alyn). They couldn't be more wrong ("Superman"—1948).

Since I was flying, my shirt top opened up a little bit and the sparks went underneath. I had to hit the metal breastplate trying to put the fire out. I yelled, "Let me down from this damn thing! I'm burning up!" So they lowered me down on the pulleys and took a pitcher of water and poured it down my suit!

Columbia Pictures and National Comics made hay from the success of the serials. They inaugurated a gigantic licensing campaign that promoted Superman jackets, sweaters, watches, acrobatic toys and hand movie viewers. The market was flooded with Superman dolls, records, shirts, bubble gum, balloons, school-bags, pens and billfolds. Theaters offered "Superman Club Cards," which entitled the filmgoer to free admittance to the last chapter if he could prove perfect attendance at the previous fourteen.

Kirk Alyn remains convinced that playing Superman made it extremely difficult for him to find new work. "Pictures are funny," observes Alyn. "An actor can easily get typecast as a policeman or judge and keep busy with work. But once you've played the man that came from outer space, where the hell do you go from there? It's hard to play anyone else. I was indestructible one week, so who would believe me getting hurt in *Federal Agents vs. Underworld, Inc.* or *Radar Patrol vs. Spy King* another week?"

Typecasting was a bullet that Alyn and thousands of other actors have had to bite. Yet what is considered by many as a sinister Hollywood ploy often works to the advantage of those who are typecast. B actors can earn a solid living in their niche, and there's little humiliation in constant exposure. Carol Forman, for example, took advantage of the "type," weaving her web of evil in *Superman, The Black Widow* (Republic, 1947) and *Brick Bradford.* She tangled with Kirk Alyn again in *Federal Agents vs. Underworld, Inc.*, and *Blackhawk.* Realistically, however, Alyn's options were somewhat limited, so no one was surprised when he accepted Sam Katzman's second telephone call. "Kirkie, would you like to do another one?"

" 'Yes, but I want twice the money,' I said, and poor old Sam almost blew a blood vessel. He told me, "You know, Kirk, we can make this serial with someone else and call it *The Son of Superman!* '

"I said, 'Go ahead, Sam, make it. And make sure you tell the kids where the son came from, right?' "

Katzman stopped his huffing and puffing long enough to recall the money made on the first venture. The public wouldn't accept too many Supermen; he'd have to go with the veteran.

"I had a lot of fun on the second one," says Alyn. "We got the flying scenes down a little better, and we got the takeoffs to appear more realistic."

Spencer Gordon Bennet concentrated on the things that had worked before. He undercranked more when Kirk ran fast. As Alyn recollects, "It was pretty damn hard running along a train track or on the rocks because I couldn't look where I was stepping. I always had to look up in the distance while I was doing the running, so I essentially used ballet leaps. Fortunately, I never tripped or fell, but Spencer made it look good when he speeded up the action for the print." The director also undercranked the fight scenes to make them look more furious when projected at normal speed. Most importantly, however, the audience wasn't able to catch all the missed punches.

"The second serial was better," says Spencer Bennet. *Atom Man vs. Superman* utilized more close-up flying scenes. There was less animation because we devised a modified flying technique: Alyn stood on the floor, his arms raised above his head. The camera was placed in front of him on a special mount. Instead of suspending Alyn from wires, the camera tilted parallel to him, creating the illusion of flight with none of the strain and anguish." For additional effect, flat scenery was placed behind him, and a fan above. The scene was shot from a ninety-degree angle, so when the film was righted, Superman appeared horizontal and moving. "I did dialogue from up there, too. I yelled to the people down below!" (Television unsuccessfully returned to the wires, but soon discarded them for another variation of the breastplate for George Reeves.)

The daily grind of serial production, as in any B picture, afforded Alyn little time to catch his breath. "They came to me the night before and said, 'This is tomorrow's work.' I looked through it, went home, and usually slipped into bed without having dinner. Then up again at five for morning shooting. I read the script over once, but luckily there was never a lot of memorization. *Atom Man vs. Superman* was action, and that's exactly what the kids wanted!"

The sequel recalled all the regulars from the first chapter play and marked the screen debut of Superman's archenemy from the comics, Luther (Lyle Talbot), in his only film experience. For fifteen weeks the two chased one another around Metropolis like cat and mouse. Talbot wore a flesh-colored headpiece that emphasized the comic book villain's fanatical nature.

Luther disguises himself as the diabolical Atom Man, complete with long black robe and lead helmet. He "transports" his jailed henchman, Lawson (Paul Stader), to freedom. Earlier, Superman had captured the gang and thought the mad scientist was safely be-

Clark Kent (Kirk Alyn) and Lois Lane (Noel Neill) interview Superman's arch enemy, Luthor (Lyle Talbot), while a henchman (Jack George) observes ("Atom Man vs. Superman"—Columbia Pictures, 1950).

hind bars, but the Man of Steel never expected Luther to double in the outside world as Atom Man.

Luther introduces a devilish array of inventions, including synthetic Kryptonite which stops Superman "At the Mercy of Atom Man." He later turns on another creation leaving Superman a ghost-like figure, impotent and unable to prevent Atom Man from thoroughly terrorizing the city. Finally, the criminal aims a deadly torpedo and a fleet of flying saucers at Metropolis. However, Luther's magnum opus is also his Waterloo. In "Superman Saves the Universe," Chapter XV, the fully recovered crusader diverts the torpedo, destroys the flying saucers, disrupts a sonic vibrator, saves the indefensible Lois and overtakes Luther's fleeing spaceship—all in a day's work.

The Great Movie Serials says the second serial was "far more gimmicky and gadget-prone than the first . . . but was flawed by the same Katzman cheapness in production values, despite the cast and crew." Yet Spencer Bennet, Sam Katzman and Kirk Alyn gave audiences fifteen more weeks of their favorite hero. "And after all," says Kirk Alyn, "isn't that what they paid for!"

CHAPTER III

Serial to Cereal

By 1948, Columbia could see the handwriting on the box-office wall. The serials were dying, and television was to blame. "Television killed the serials," says Tommy Carr. "And don't forget, when you talk about television it killed everything in the theater business. It was free, and you can't beat that price."

Early in that first year of commercial broadcasting, only eight cities had television outlets. By the end of the year the number had risen to twenty-three. The East Coast enjoyed armchair comfort for a young Uncle Miltie, the 1948 political conventions and the inevitably stonefaced Ed Sullivan. Recognizing the rising popularity of the medium, the Federal Communications Commission ordered a four-year "freeze" on additional frequency authorizations. They outlined a comprehensive policy for equitable telecasting service throughout the country. In the interim, 108 stations operated; some failed, while others busied themselves profitably with the new technology. The transcontinental microwave relay was completed in 1951, and on September 4, the inaugural coast-to-coast hookup offered viewers the Japanese peace treaty conference *live* from San Francisco. The National Broadcasting Company (NBC) followed with the World Series and the first nationally sponsored program, the "NBC Comedy Hour."

The FCC terminated the freeze in June 1952, to the tune of 2,000 new channel assignments available for 1,300 communities. To accomplish this almost unbelievable task, the Commission extended telecasting from VHF (Very High Frequency) channels, 2 through 13, to seventy more UHF (Ultra High Frequency) channels, 14 through 83.

The "gold rush" came in 1952. The year marked the end of radio's great era, for the combined annual revenues of national television finally exceeded those of the four long-established radio networks. NBC and CBS were solidly in the market. ABC merged with Paramount in 1953 to rank a poor third. Mutual remained out of the picture; the Dumont Network should have done the same.

The Federal Communications Commission reviewed 521 new television applications within one month after the freeze was terminated. Many groups had filed for the same channel, so the process took longer than had been anticipated. By the end of the first year, seventeen new stations were broadcasting. In January 1954, 356 commercial stations were on the air, and nearly 300 others were under construction. Expansion declined thereafter, with many cities boasting two or more outlets.

Not all stations were prosperous. The choice VHF stations reported consistently high earnings. They, of course, were in the largest markets. Dumont, at the bottom of the heap in cities already three and four stations deep, acknowledged their mistake too late. The network left the air in 1955, after a four-year battle that saw no clear path out of the cellar. Other stations were doomed in markets too small, or unlucky enough to draw rarely viewed UHF frequencies.[1]

During the early and middle fifties, only six cities had more than three stations; NBC and CBS owned the most desirable outlets; ABC grabbed up the best of whatever was left. Ratings became the name of the game. Instead of box-office success, Hollywood lives depended upon the feedback from a telephone questionnaire. "I knew television was going to be a big thing," says Tommy Carr. He recalls a Directors Guild meeting in 1948 at the Hollywood Athletic Club. The old-timers were certain of television's inconsequential effect on the movies. " 'Come on, that's a Mickey

[1] Few television sets had UHF tuning before the FCC so ruled in 1964; consequently, of the approximately 190 UHF commercial stations that had signed on from 1952 through 1964, half went dark.

Mouse thing anyhow. It's never going to mean anything for years,' they told me. But I insisted, 'Don't kid yourselves. I'm going to get into this with both feet, and just as soon as I can. This is the biggest thing that's ever hit the entertainment world so far as those of us who make pictures are concerned.' "

Actor Ben Welden was also enthusiastic about the new medium; especially since the once great serial and feature market had begun to recede. "We couldn't afford to work in serials anymore. The leading man may have gotten a fair amount, but no one got off easy. It meant long hours, more of a grind than TV. We had to learn how to work in television, it was all new. Features were different as well. Just as you coudn't play a drawing room comedy like a Western, you couldn't do straight acting in a serial. We don't have them anymore, so there's no problem, but some of the television programs are as bad as the serials!"

The work schedules weren't anything to write home about either. Whit Ellsworth says, "When we started out, the television industry was on a six-day week, just like the movies. Under pressure from the unions we later went to a five-day week, but it was still rugged. From seven or seven-thirty in the morning to six, seven or later at night. It was hard work."

The conditions were hectic; those connected with "Superman" had little life outside the studio. Robert Justman, now a producer, was then a second assistant director. From his account of the twenty-six "Superman" shows in 1953, it sounds as though the personnel should have been attired in sweat shirts and Keds. He says, "Today we still work hard, but the schedule enables us to do things on weekends like other people do. 'Superman' was another era. In my own case, I would be at the studio at six in the morning. I'd probably leave at eight, five days a week, but on Saturdays we very often worked up to ten, eleven, or midnight. That left Sunday just to recuperate."

Jack Larson says he didn't even have Sundays. "After a week like that I slept! I was in a state of collapse. And then, at some point on Sunday, I had to begin lines for Monday. The weekend lasted, tops, eight hours if I woke up early. When shooting the program we knew no other life. Six days' work, between fifteen and twenty pages each day."

If the pace was difficult on the talent and crew, it fell heaviest on the producer. Whitney Ellsworth recalls the weeks of seven days and seven nights spent in pre-production, getting scripts in shape and ironing out details. "I can remember signing overtime checks for as much as $300 a week for the laborer who swept up the sets. Those checks were the cushion they all relied upon to take care of the inevitable periods 'between shows.' And though the pace of an A picture might have been slower than those of B pictures, serials and television, the hours were just as long and grueling."

The pace was phenomenal, and cameraman Joe Biroc says jokingly, "The only thing I can remember is that the paint on half the sets was still wet when we left them; we worked that fast!"

Thol (Si) Simonson, the longtime special effects expert who went directly from high-budget features to the Superman series, found the transition somewhat startling, but professionally challenging. "In television, you have just so much to put into it. You make the effect as cheaply as you can." This had never been the case with big motion pictures, says Simonson. "By taking a little longer, and doing it a little better, you might really help the picture and maybe even bring in some added box office—it was usually worth it. That was the kind of pace we were used to," continues Simonson, "but when television rolled in some producers said they wanted the gag finished and ready within twenty-four hours. At that rate we were lucky to get anything done right on the first take. But we tried, and somehow we did it!"

An actor couldn't expect to get rich quick in those days. Scale for bit players in 1951 was just under $70 per day. It had climbed to $80 per day by 1957 and to

$172.50 in the mid-1970s. The concept of residual payments for reruns did not take effect until July 21, 1952, long after the first twenty-six episodes of "Superman" were completed. Contract players weren't jumping for joy over their bank accounts either. The salaries were penurious. For example, Noel Neill's contract after five seasons on "Superman" was $225 per episode or $2,925 for the thirteen, plus the usual residuals. Jack Larson had it little better, $250 each episode.

Minimum payment for a low-budget half-hour television script was $650 in 1953, and $2,144.00 by the seventies. There are also residual payments for reruns, but with over three thousand members enrolled in the Writers Guild-West, one need not consult a pocket computer to figure out how many would be starving if everyone relied on full-time work. Still, Whitney Ellsworth, producer of 78 of the 104 Superman films for television, feels writers on his show got a better break than most.

Every year the New York Office would lend me Mort Weisinger for a few weeks to act as Story Editor. Mort had been my editor when I wrote for the pulp magazines in the late thirties, and I hired him when I became Editorial Director on the comics at National in 1940. Together we knew about as much about Superman as it was possible to know. So in advance of production we'd lock ourselves in a room and work on stories. Once we did it on the train trip from New York to Los Angeles. By the time we were ready to hand out writing assignments we were able to give the writers outlines of what we wanted—not just so-called premises but complete step-by-step story-lines in almost every case. Needless to say this made the writer's job much easier and less time-consuming. He could write three screenplays in the time he'd normally spend on two. Under the terms of the Writers Guild contract the producer is entitled to a "rewrite" and a "polish," but I chose to do the rewriting myself—not necessarily

because I thought I was a better writer but mostly because I found it easier than explaining to the writer exactly what I wanted. In any case, it was another break for the writer, who could be off and running on a new assignment for new money instead of doing a tiresome rewrite. I never encountered a script that didn't require rewriting—some less than others, of course—and I worked on every script I ever shot. I recall feeling a bit wistful about it when I signed residual checks for the writers—like $12,000 at one crack to a writer named Jackson Gillis.

Early television rarely touched on any relevant social issues. "Superman" was no exception, but the program need not have concerned itself with turbulent politics and philosophies of the times; it was the McCarthy era, an age of resurrected witch-hunts. For a time, government committees looked behind closed doors for alleged conspirators, known Communists and left-wingers. The guilty were those hiding, afraid to let the inquisitors in, ashamed to confess their crime. It was a time of guilt by association. Those who didn't cooperate in the heresy proceedings endangered themselves. Senator Joseph McCarthy was the chief inquisitor, a man of dark hallways, whose weapon was the innuendo.

The trouble was born from legitimate discontent within the industry. Any actor, director, writer or producer who was concerned over pay and working conditions became the prey of a handful of committee members. Reformers were equated with left-wing groups, and even studio bosses saw this as a prelude to Communism. Certainly some people in Hollywood did look toward Marxist doctrine, but most quickly turned away, completely disillusioned with the foreign ideology. While McCarthy and members of the House Committee on Un-American Activities were lopping off heads in the movie industry, a similar assault was launched upon the comic book market. Comics were held as culpable as motion pictures since both were considered the dupes of the Communist world. However, comic books were especially suspect because they were easily available to the young, whose precious minds might run astray from the sacred white Anglo-Saxon model.

Dr. Frederic Wertham, senior psychiatrist for the New York City Department of Hospitals and author of *Seduction of the Innocent*, sought to clean up the comic trade. Congress began investigating Wertham's thesis regarding the alleged relationship between comic books and juvenile delinquency, and although a special subcommittee ruled that the medium was entitled to the same latitude as other printed matter, Wertham had fuel for his crusade. For nearly every incident of abnormal behavior, Wertham considered comic books responsible, for he felt they led children to revolution, violence, lust. The psychiatrist favored a rating system which would have left little on newsstands except for happy-ending talking animals and safe Classic Comics.

Seduction of the Innocent extended its loose argument to the area of juvenile delinquency. The correlation was obvious, at least to Wertham. Crime was rising and comic books were the cause; youngsters saw Superman take the law into his own hands, so they did the same. His treatise was the culmination of fourteen years of research and by the time the book was published, Wertham was a household word—especially in households with children. Yet his arguments were ludicrous, full of the same reasoning used to attack vaudeville, motion pictures, popular music and television. What was at issue, but rarely discussed, was whether parents' social values could accept comics at face value—entertainment. However, after months of unsympathetic press, and a high-gear campaign directed by Wertham, the industry succumbed to the pressure. Comic book executives banded together to establish a line of defense: the Comics Code Authority. Not since the days of Will Hays in motion pictures had one regulatory body been given such sweeping power over a medium. The board affixed its seal to only those comics that met its strict canons of taste. All other comics were rated unacceptable, and vendors were discouraged from displaying them on their racks. A publication without the code could be threatened, boycotted or ruined.

Dr. Wertham was not a lone wolf in his campaign. Gershon Legman wrote that comic violence is a transformation for sexuality, repressed and restricted by society (*Love and Death*, 1949). Although his thesis is known for some creative thought, Legman also slipped into the name-calling syndrome: "That the publishers, editors, artists and writers of comic books are degenerates and belong in jail." In fairness to context, Legman implied the need to review, perhaps limit, those elements in comics that sexually and violently excited children.

On Superman, he wrote that hooded justice was a reprehensible model to display before children:

He [Superman] takes crime for granted, and then spends thirty pages violently avenging it. He can see through walls, he can stop the sun in its orbit like a second Joshua; and all this godlike power he focuses on some two-bit criminal or crackpot, who hasn't even pulled a trigger yet, but is only threatening to.

"Giant the Jack Killer" he calls Superman. And with the sanction of the law, the Man of Steel's might is right:

If Superman is punished at all, his punishment is something like Blondie's, implicit in his status, in the fact that he is really only an unvirile clerk who wears glasses and can't get the girl—like the reader. And this obvious flim flam suffices to blind parents and teachers to the glaring fact that not only Superman and his even more violent imitators invest violence with righteousness and prestige . . . but that the Superman formula is essentially lynching.

Contiguity was Legman's weapon. He enjoyed using "violence," "sex" and "anarchy" in the same sentence with "children's comic books." These associations were designed to alarm the House Un-American Activities Committee and shake up the comic book industry. Apparently they worked, for National Comics chose compromise; the corporation joined the Comics Code Authority.

Comics reacted with much more alarm than did its sister medium, film. Perhaps it was more vulnerable, easier to criticize. However, the comic industry's stars were drawn from inkwells; so no matter how harshly anyone demanded, neither Superman nor the other ten-cent heroes could testify in Washington. The guilty—if anyone was really guilty—had to be the writers and publishers, and Wertham went after them with vigor.

Although *Superman* magazine contended with verbal assassination, the television program remained free of organized criticism. Whitney Ellsworth adds thankfully, "Nobody ever told us what to say or who to use. This was never raised. No one even gave me a list of who were the red, white and blue Americans. Not only didn't Kellogg's or their agency, Leo Burnett, pressure me, they never mentioned it!"

CHAPTER IV

George Reeves . . . and Who Disguised as Clark Kent . . .

George loved life so much. With me he'd say, "Let's go off to South America," or "Let's buy a horse and go prospecting into Mexico." This would be in two minutes. Five minutes later he'd buy the damn horse and off we'd go. He didn't stop at anything. Every day was a ball with this man.

Natividad Vacio

I met Reeves for the first time on "Superman" and I liked him so very much. He had such a great sense of humor—he was so full of life, it was quite a shock when there was none left.

Sterling Holloway

If Kirk Alyn was concerned by his identification as Superman in 1948 and 1950, he didn't have much to worry about after 1951. For better or worse, the role belonged to George Reeves. One actor told Reeves he could have done it for the rest of his life. In truth he did. George Reeves died June 16, 1959.

Oddly, Reeves's background bears a striking similarity to that of the character he portrayed. Clark Kent was raised somewhere in Middle America. George Reeves was born in Ashland, Kentucky. Both faced conflict throughout their public and private lives. Both were the antithesis of what their roles portended. Reeves and Clark Kent desired to be known for their real identities. Neither was successful. Says director Harry Gerstad, "This was George's cross to bear. He was Superman. Nobody ever said, 'Hey, George!' if they saw him on the street. George went to bed with it every night and he had to get up with it in the morning." But George Reeves was a vital, dedicated actor who paid his dues long before he stole into the storeroom to become Superman.

Jack Larson knew him as well as anyone on the "Superman" set. "George was a wonderful person. He called himself 'Honest George the People's Friend.' " Larson remembers that George helped scores who were

CLOSE MATCHES RESULT IN JAYSEE TOURNAMENT

Emberson Loses Out In Boxing Event; Hatcher Wins Over Bessolo; Castro Wins

In one of the closest matches of the day in which the judges had to have an extra round before giving a decision, Leland MacGowan, lightweight, defeated Keith Emberson after four rounds of furious milling in one of the feature bouts of the semi-finals of Coach Leland C. Mac-Auley's Pasadena Junior College annual boxing tourney staged before a packed house yesterday afternoon.

Another fast bout was the light heavyweight scrap in which Max Hatcher and George Bessolo slugged for three rounds, Hatcher finally taking the decision

1933.

unemployed. "My suspicion would be that he loaned out nearly as much money as he earned."

Reeves's longtime Mexican-American friend Natividad Vacio has the same recollection. "George was an easy touch for a hundred anytime, day or night. He lost a lot of money in Hollywood by handing out thousands of dollars for which he was never repaid. This was one of the things he did which people do not remember."

George Reeves, born George Bessolo, was the son of a druggist. He moved from the Bible Belt to Southern California while still in elementary school. By the time he was a teen-ager, he was singing in church affairs and acting in local theater groups. In 1932, he enrolled in Pasadena Junior College, where he became fast friends with Natividad Vacio. It was the beginning of a lifelong relationship. The two played guitar together for a few hours each day, before Bessolo moved into the ring for a round of wrestling and boxing.

Mannie Pineta, a Pasadena sportswriter, once sparred with Reeves. "He was the greatest ring prospect in 1932, and he entered the Golden Gloves." At the last minute the 6'2", 195-pound light heavyweight collegiate champ canceled his bout. "His mother wouldn't let him fight. She was afraid he'd get bandaged up and ruin his acting career." She might have been right. Reeves suffered the pain and embarrassment of a broken nose—seven times. Surprisingly, however, the worst physical beating he took was totally unrelated to boxing. Reeves slipped and broke a bone in his foot during a fencing match. "But, you know, that didn't stop him," says Natividad Vacio. "Nothing did."

Reeves enrolled in the Pasadena Playhouse in the early thirties and worked with Robert Preston and Victor Mature. Mature made it to the screen in two years, Preston in three. Reeves, meanwhile, lingered under the nighttime lights for six years, while working by day in the shadows of a broker's office.

During a 1936 Shakespeare Festival at the Playhouse, he worked with actors Jan Arvan and Frank Ferguson, who would eventually guest with Reeves in

"King for a Day" and "Lady in Black." But Superman was still years off.

Top billing at the Pasadena Playhouse was almost like getting a part on Broadway. Director Gilmor Brown had to be selective about whom he would accept for enrollment and Reeves was lucky. Soon he was not only acting, but traveling as Brown's secretary on junkets through the United States and England. However, the Playhouse was also an important school for Reeves. He knew that Hollywood people watched for exciting performances, and hoped his opportunity wouldn't be too far off.[1]

Rumblings about a screen adaptation of Margaret Mitchell's *Gone with the Wind* had leaked from the Selznick studios. Max Arnow, casting director for the film, heard of the handsome twenty-three-year-old actor George Bessolo. George rehearsed his Southern accent and laid claim to his Kentucky birthright. Within days of his first screen test, Selznick signed him for the role of Brent Tarleton.

"You couldn't find a happier guy," says Natividad Vacio. "I remember his first film clearly. He played one of the Tarleton twins. George was so excited. He dyed his hair and went all the way out!" The studio certainly played it up in their public relations splashes. One landed in Louella Parsons' syndicated newspaper column:

Bloodcurdling screams rent the "refeened" air at Westmore's Beauty Emporium yesterday and I thought one of the glamour girls was being scalped—until two husky male voices started singing old Southern ditties. When the bedlam subsided, it turned out to be just the "twins" in "Gone with the Wind" (Fred Crane and George Bessolo) having their hair bleached for the roles. . . .

Early press releases from the Selznick camp announced that George Bessolo had been given the role

[1] Reeves appeared in Pasadena Playhouse productions through the 1950s.

of the talkative head-over-heels admirer of Scarlett O'Hara. However, between the signing ceremony and the Atlanta premiere, his name had been changed. Jack Warner, who held a portion of the actor's contract, decided that the name Bessolo lacked the necessary ring of a forthcoming star and consequently requested the alteration: Thus, as the opening credits of the film rolled by, George Bessolo disappeared, to be replaced by a Hollywood creation—George Reeves.

Although *Gone with the Wind* was Reeves's first im-

'SHOW MUST GO ON, SO ACTOR USES CRUTCHES

7/17/37

That even a young actor already knows well the traditions of his profession was shown yesterday by George Bessolo at the Community Playhouse.

Mr. Bessolo, who is playing the lead in "Heartbreak House," went home yesterday following a matinee and took part in a fencing match, during which he slipped and broke a bone in his foot.

A temporary splint was devised. At last evening's performance, Mr. Bessolo "trod the boards" on crutches.

portant picture, Warner Brothers had already sunk a few dollars into his career. In the late thirties, Reeves was put through the gristmill by the Warner "historical featurette" division. He portrayed Henry Clay's secretary in *The Monroe Doctrine*, a dastardly Mexican bandit in *Ride Cowboy Ride*, and Buffalo Bill Cody in *Pony Express*.

In short order, the handsome Reeves was moved up, proving his durability in a series of pre-war programmers. The first was *Smashing the Money Ring* (1939), a hapless Ronald Reagan melodrama about a counterfeit operation.

Reeves appeared in twelve other pictures over the next year, including a prophetic cops 'n' robbers film where he gets the drop on heavy Ben Welden. And the police chief, John Hamilton, was no doubt grateful for Reeves's help in *Tear Gas Squad* (1940).

For any insomniac who cares to wait up, there's a rare treat—George Reeves and James Cagney in three splendid films. In *The Fighting 69th* (1940), Reeves bites the bullet thanks to Cagney's cowardice on the World War I battlefield. They fight again in *Torrid Zone* (1940), and in *Strawberry Blonde* (1941) where Cagney beats Reeves at his own game, boxing.

There were other roles: *Till We Meet Again* (1941) with Merle Oberon, and *Gambling on the High Seas* (1940) with Wayne Morris and Jane Wyman. There were four B pictures directed in quick succession by Noel Smith, *Ladies Must Live* (1940), *Father Is a Prince* (1940), *Always a Bride* (1940) and *Calling All Husbands* (1940).

Before Reeves's contract expired, Jack Warner loaned him to Alexander Korda for what turned out to be an extravagant flop. *Lydia* (1941) was a strong picture for Reeves and star Merle Oberon, but the Alexander Korda costume drama never drew long lines outside the theaters. Universal then cast Reeves as their romantic lead in the Ritz Brothers musical *Argentine Nights* (1940). His rich baritone voice led the gaucho chorus along a mountain trail in the film's best production number, "Amigo We Go Riding Tonight!"

When Reeves satisfied his obligations to Warner Brothers, he moved to Twentieth Century–Fox. For his screen test, Reeves talked the director into accepting a rather unorthodox request: He brought his wife, actress Elenora Needles, onto the set to play opposite him in a love scene. "I couldn't do the scene with someone I'd never seen before," said Reeves to a newspaper reporter. "So the director let me do it my way and it all went well." Reeves cinched the contract.[2] Fox quickly cast him in their supersleuth series, Charlie Chan. In *Dead Men Tell*, he plays an escaped criminal posing as a newspaper reporter. Reeves strolls through the film with sinister intent until he ends up dead inside a bathysphere.

Fox's starring vehicle for Reeves was *Man at Large*, an aimless spy flick about a Nazi flier's escape from a Canadian internment camp and the FBI's infiltration of the German espionage gang. A December 10, 1941, *RKO Newsette* in New York promoted Reeves as ". . . a good-looking stranger who seems to be both an enemy agent and G-Man . . . in the spine-tingling enter-

[2] His marriage was not as successful. In 1949, he divorced his wife of nine years.

1937—a telegram from George's mother, Helen Bessolo.

tainment." *Variety* called the picture ". . . a wildly incredible tale . . ." But the most interesting item came from a Cleveland newspaper which described Reeves's performance as everything short of ". . . being a Superman."

Reeves was also assigned to a supporting role in the Fox remake of the 1922 Rudolph Valentino smash, *Blood and Sand.* The new version of the romance between a naïve bullfighter and a love temptress starred Tyrone Power, Linda Darnell, Rita Hayworth, Anthony Quinn, J. Carroll Naish and John Carradine. Reeves plays Captain Vincente Martinez.

When Reeves's one-year contract with Fox expired he free-lanced. *The Mad Martindales* was his only feature of note for 1942. During the next year, he dodged Hopalong Cassidy bullets in *Hoppy Serves a Writ, The Leather Burners, The Last Will and Testament, Colt Comrades* and *Bar 20.* However, Paramount had greater designs for Reeves than rustling cattle in B pictures. They threw away his spurs and chaps and outfitted him in army khaki for his most visible role, in *So Proudly We Hail* (1943) opposite Claudette Colbert. Hedda Hopper congratulated Reeves with a paragraph in her November 17 column:

When George Reeves got word that he'd won the lead . . . he and his wife bought up a stack of newspapers carrying the story, spread them on the living room floor and celebrated with a bottle of beer. . . .

Hopper and a few other reporters acknowledged that luck had a hand in Reeves's contract. The studio wanted a test of Teddi Sherman, "Pop" (Harry) Sherman's daughter.[3] But when director Mark Sandrich saw her seven-page test with Reeves, he thought only of his

[3] Reeves worked for Harry Sherman in a series of Hopalong Cassidy pictures: *Border Patrol, Hoppy Serves a Writ, The Leather Burners, The Last Will and Testament, Colt Comrades,* and *Bar 20.* He also appeared in *Tombstone* and *Buckskin Empire* for Sherman.

male lead. The scene had so won over Sandrich that the part immediately belonged to Reeves. With great promise for the future he went to Paramount on loan-out from Harry Sherman.

"No matter how good his career looked then," says Jack Larson, "George just missed being a big box-office leading man; it was one of the misfortunes of the war. Everything was going really well, then boom! He went into the army."

Columnist Fred Orthman wrote with noticeable concern about it when it was still only a possibility: "Like many other actors in a similar spot, Reeves is sorry it took the war to give him his big chance (*So Proudly We Hail*), yet he can't help be happy he finally got it. [The] Only trouble with Reeves, from Paramount's standpoint, is the fact that he and his wife have no children, and he's liable to be going to the war soon after this picture is finished. That's too bad for the movies because Reeves . . . knows his acting business. . . ."

By the time he returned to Hollywood, long after the war had ended, the heavyweights—Ronald Reagan, Jimmy Stewart, Clark Gable and the rest—were all re-established. "George never could get work in the same way," concluded Jack Larson. "He was disappointed, but the one and only time George ever talked to me about his career was when we began shooting 'Superman' in July 1951. I had just seen a film directed by Mark Sandrich, and unknowingly remarked to George, 'What a fine director. Did you ever know Sandrich?' George answered, 'Know him! He co-starred me in *So Proudly We Hail*. And if Mark Sandrich hadn't died, I wouldn't be here today!' Sandrich was obviously one director who believed in George, and it was the only time I ever heard him say anything like that."

Actually Reeves didn't have it that bad during the war. He was assigned to the Army–Air Force Special Forces division, and for a time, stationed in Manhattan with the stage version of *Winged Victory*. Moss Hart's

HE'LL PLAY TWIN

GEORGE BESSELO

Pasadena Community Playhouse actor, who has been signed for an important role in Selznick's production of "Gone With the Wind."

He will portray one of the Tarleton twins.

The actor, born in Ashland, Ky., was considered so fit for the role that his hair was dyed a fiery red instead of dark as pictured.

At the Playhouse he appeared in "The Boy David" and "Heartbreak House," among others.

The other twin will be played by Fred Cane of Tulane University. Mr. Besselo is a former amateur boxer.

The original make-up still of the Tarleton Twins, George Reeves and Fred Crane ("Gone with the Wind"—MGM, 1939).

drama premiered in November 1943 to rave notices and standing ovations, and on opening night the playwright delivered one of the shortest Broadway speeches on record: "I have just heard on the radio that we have bombed Berlin again. That's what this play is about." [4]

Some members of the cast simultaneously rehearsed a production of *Yellow Jack,* the ten-year-old Sidney Howard-Paul de Kruif play about Dr. Walter Reed's gallant fight against yellow fever. It starred Private John Forsythe, Private Whit Bissell, Corporal Gary Merrill, Sergeant George Reeves, and played in army camps far from the lights of Broadway.

A few months later, Reeves received a transfer back to Fox for the film version of *Winged Victory,* in which he re-created his New York role of Lieutenant Thomp-

[4] The audience's good cheer eventually subsided, for less than ten years later, on May 22, 1951, Hart's patriotism was falsely scrutinized before the House Un-American Activities Committee.

The Tarleton Twins—Stuart (Fred Crane) and Brent (George Reeves) woo Scarlett O'Hara (Vivien Leigh) in this famous scene from "Gone with the Wind" (MGM, 1939).

son. Other army actors who joined him included corporals Red Buttons, Lee J. Cobb, Barry Nelson, Karl Malden and sergeants Edmond O'Brien and Peter Lind Hayes.

When Reeves received his honorable discharge, he went to work rebuilding his civilian career. Following a stint in New York radio dramas and soap operas, he returned to Hollywood for a walk-on in *Variety Girl* (1947). It began his new paydays at Paramount, where Reeves met Joe Biroc, who eventually filmed the final Superman shows for television. "We made many, many tests with George," Biroc remembers. "He'd be the man who would come in and test with the girls. He was offstage, his back to the camera all the time. He knew they were testing the girls, not him. And he was always cheerful and helpful about it. He was a hell of a guy."

The next year Reeves was again the co-star, this time opposite Veronica Lake in *The Sainted Sisters*. A short while later, he was handed an interesting role in *Special Agent,* the concocted story of government railroad investigators pitted against evil Paul (George Reeves) Devereaux and his brother Edmond (Paul Valentine). In an unflattering review the *New York Times* wrote: ". . . Paul Valentine and George Reeves, as the bandit brothers, try hard enough, but the script and the direction provide too big a handicap." It was the story of his life, as it had been for others before him. Reeves's acting ability was sabotaged by poor vehicles. Hollywood had begun winding down after the war; choice parts were harder to come by, and Reeves, like Kirk Alyn, had to settle for whatever was left.

A Jungle Jim expedition with Johnny Weissmuller and a plane ride with Ralph (Dick Tracy) Byrd in *Jungle Goddess* (1948) garnered nothing for Reeves but a few more hours waist-deep in low-budget motion picture quicksand. However, it loosened him up for the 1949 Spencer Bennet–Sam Katzman bastardization of the tales of King Arthur in the fifteen-chapter serial *Sir Galahad.* Any similarity to Camelot was purely coincidental. For effect, Katzman selected an aging William Fawcett (resident studio professor and old-timer) for the cantankerous Merlin. Galahad's sidekick, Bors, was the familiar Charles King.

The serial served up a potpourri of the traditional Mack Sennett chase/Doug Fairbanks fight formula. Reeves squared off against the magic of Merlin, clinging vines, fire monsters, catapults, arrows and a nasty encounter or two with the Black Knight.

Except for the uniform, it all sounds like an audition for Superman. But Reeves was actually put through paces in *Galahad* that were in many ways more difficult than any he faced as the Man of Steel.

Once the challenges of a twelfth-century hero were finished, the actor returned to a contemporary pursuit of his film career. He appeared in the 1950 farce *The Good Humor Man,* and in 1952 and 1953, a pair of Fritz Lang features, *Rancho Notorious* and *The Blue Gardenia,* shot after "Superman" had already been in production one year.

Reeves's last films were *From Here to Eternity*

(1953), *Forever Female* (1954), and Walt Disney's 1956 *Westward Ho the Wagons!* His experience in *From Here to Eternity* was a pathetic sign to any interested casting director that the George Reeves name carried other implications to the box office. Fred Zinnemann cast Reeves as Sergeant Maylon Stark, but the press who gathered for the initial screening saw only Superman in army getup. The film went back to the editor, and George Reeves was severely cut from the final print. Some think his upward mobility in acting was written off that day.

Reeves's final film holds a particular irony. The well-known—perhaps *too* well-known—Man of Steel visage of George Reeves shows scarcely at all. Walt Disney director William Beaudine ordered the make-up department to outfit the television star with a beard before Reeves hopped aboard a wagon train full of Mouseketeers—Doreen, Tommy, Cubby and Karen. The studio poop sheet says it all:

George Reeves of Superman fame plays a pioneer in "Westward Ho the Wagons!" George Reeves, the indestructible Superman of television fame, has doffed his cape and tights for the first time in nearly four years to play a frontier expedition leader in "Westward Ho the Wagons!" Walt Disney's actionful story of pioneer adventure on the Oregon trail.

Reeves donned a broad-brimmed hat and the typical accouterments of wilderness-breaker James Stephens. He explained in one studio biography, "When I assume a screen role, I try to make it a real characterization. I never want to look like Superman in disguise."

When production on "Superman" closed down on November 27, 1957, the superhero turned mortal man, and flew cross-country (in an airplane) to appear on the Ed Sullivan show. Reeves was an accomplished guitarist, fluent in Spanish and a mellow baritone tenor. His television singing bid was well received the Sullivan appearance might have given a spinoff career had Reeves's life not s ended.

By the time Reeves flew East for the Sullivan show, he had been Superman for more than six years. He probably never intended to stay with the role for so long, and like many other serious actors, he may have told himself, "I'll do this bit just long enough to reestablish myself, then back to films." Accordingly, he worked in the bumptious new medium before he wore the Superman tricolors. In the early fifties he appeared in a variety of roles in such "live" shows as "Philco Television Playhouse," "Kraft Television Theatre," "Suspense," and "Danger." And on March 25, 1952, after he filmed his first twenty-six Superman shows, Reeves took the lead on the NBC "Fireside Theatre" production "Hurry, Hurry." During the next few years there were guest shots with Ray Bolger and a host of other programs, but none of these were any great shakes.

Then there was "Superman."

One popular story says Reeves was "discovered at Muscle Beach," a California strip replete with the weight-lifting set. There he was supposedly catapulted miraculously to stardom by "Superman" producer Robert Maxwell. Untrue. Tommy Carr and Maxwell screened nearly two hundred applicants, most of them professional actors rather than mere musclemen. Just to be sure, however, the two surveyed the studs at the 1951 Mr. America contest in Los Angeles. "But most of them," says Tommy Carr, "appeared to have a serious deficiency in their chromosome count." They pushed on. Maxwell seems never to have given serious consideration to Kirk Alyn, the Superman of the serials, and indeed Alyn may not have wished at that time to be a candidate for the job. In any event, the search ended when George Reeves dropped in one day with his agent. Tommy Carr remembers, "From that moment on he was my first choice. He looked like Superman with that jaw of his. Kirk had the long neck and fine features, but although I like Kirk very much, he never ~~ked~~ the Superman Reeves did." It was the semi-

Reeves as the bandit in "Ride Cowboy, Ride."

George Reeves serenades James Cagney and Andy Devine during a break in the shooting of "Torrid Zone" (Warner Brothers, 1940).

Roman profile and the determined Dudley Doright jaw that won the role for George Reeves.

"Superman? What's that?" said Reeves when he recalled his introduction to the character for a 1954 newspaper interviewer. He told the reporter, "Of course I'd heard of the comic strip, but that's about all I knew." He talked over Maxwell's offer with his close friend Natividad Vacio, but in the end the decision to take the role was his own. "I've played about every type of part you can think of. Why not Superman?" said Reeves.

By 1957 George Reeves had honorary press cards from every major newspaper in the country.

Reeves had a special feeling for the young. Robert Shayne remembers one incident that others say was rather typical of Reeves's good nature:

We were out on location shooting "Superman" in the Hollywood hills. My wife brought my little boy and girl out there. My son, just five, went wild watching George in his uniform. If was a trick shot where Superman kept an automobile from going over a precipice ("The Man Who Could Read Minds"), which of course was all tricked up. My son thought that was fantastic. It was the first time Bob Junior had ever seen pictures made. The trick shot really impressed him, he thought it was real. George was so nice that he later presented him with a little Superman outfit, the "S" and everything. He got the wardrobe man to make up the uniform. My boy had it for years around the home, it was one of the happiest days of his life.

Jack Larson thoroughly agrees, adding that adults often gave George the most grief. Once on a personal appearance in Memphis a rotor-mouthed mother faced the actor and declared, "Why, Mr. Reeves, I overheard somebody say you don't *like* children." George beamed at her in his best W. C. Fields manner and answered, "*Like* them, ma'am, I have one for lunch every day!"

Reeves felt that as Superman he had a particular re-

George Reeves holds Ben Welden (center) at bay in "Tear Gas Squad" (Warner Brothers, 1940).

Another future Superman villain, John Eldredge, with George Reeves in 1940 ("Always a Bride"—Warner Brothers).

sponsibility to his young audience. He pitched for their safety and well-being both in and out of the Superman uniform. Kellogg's booked him on a ten-city promotional-safety tour in 1955, visiting children's hospitals, speaking on jaywalking, bicycling and flying. In 1956, the Myasthenia Gravis Foundation honored him with an award for his dedicated efforts for victims of this serious neuromuscular disease. And Reeves eventually succeeded Roy Rogers as the national sponsor of another worthy cause—Little Helpers, the children's organization that works on behalf of leukemia victims in the City of Hope Medical Center, Duarte, California.

Reeves was always upset when he heard about young fans pretending to be Superman, trying to fly out of their second-story bedroom windows. Invariably, these stories proved to be just that—stories. Nonetheless, Reeves thought that Superman himself ought to make the point perfectly clear. He discussed it with his producer, and in the 1954 television episode "The Unlucky Number" he repeated the warning he had so often voiced in public appearances:

No one, but no one, can do the things Superman does. And that goes especially for flying!

Some observers are of the opinion that Reeves was compulsive over his sense of responsibility, that perhaps he carried a burden of guilt on his shoulders, but his friend Natividad Vacio says this was not true. "George was calm and at peace with himself, like any man who does his work honorably and well. His house was a Grand Central Station. You could eat or drink at any hour of the day or night. This was the type of man he was. Whenever anyone needed a buck, George Reeves was there. He was completely openhearted, and everyone in Hollywood knew it."

Reeves particularly enjoyed his association with some 160 underprivileged youngsters from the barrios of East Los Angeles whom he had been sponsoring for over ten years. He was their "Super Hombre," and many of the children considered him their best friend.

George Reeves struggles with Lloyd Nolan in "Blue, White and Perfect" (Twentieth Century-Fox, 1941).

Frank Sennes, who operated the famous Moulin Rouge nightclub, told George he'd give his boys a free dinner show if Superman would entertain. All was set for a very special public appearance, until Reeves discovered that some of his kids didn't have clothing suitable for dining out. He hustled on his own, canvassing friends for outgrown attire and bedeviling friendly shopkeepers for slow-moving merchandise. By the time the dinner rolled around every youngster was properly dressed. It was a highly successful party, and it was all Reeves's.

Still there were days when Reeves seemed to rebel against this "good guy" image. Perhaps, like most adults who are genuinely fond of children, it was entirely possible for him to become occasionally "fed up" with them. Or maybe he most resented grown-ups pushing their kids forward to fawn over him. Harry Gerstad, a two-time Academy Award winner, who worked as both film editor and director on the Superman series, has an appropriate story to make the point.

"Some neighbors of ours dropped in on my wife and me one evening," Gerstad recalls. "They were slightly embarrassed but determined. They said their little daughter was going to be nine years old the next day and wanted only one thing for her birthday—a visit with the real live Superman. They'd offered her every damn thing under the sun, but it was Superman or nothing. So, knowing that I was directing the show, they asked, 'Would it be at all possible?' "

Gerstad had a deep feeling he was on the verge of making a big mistake, but he said, "Sure." "I asked George the next day between takes. He blew sky-high. He said I knew how he felt about having kids on the set in the first place, that he was sick of beating his brains out for moppets in the second place, and that in the third place he just wasn't going to entertain this kid or any other kid while at work. I told him he was right, that I had no right to put him on the spot." But the couple and their daughter couldn't be stopped; they were already on their way. Just before the noon break Gerstad saw them standing in the shadows. "We

George Reeves wins Claudette
Colbert lead

★ Harry
Mines

Pasadena Playhouse's George Reeves found himself a western thespian not many weeks ago when Harry Sherman placed him under term contract, and told him to sneer and leer at Richard Dix in "Tombstone" and "Buckskin Empire."

The dirty doings paid off profitably yesterday and here's how it happened. Mark Sandrich ran the two Sherman productions in the projection room, spotted Reeves immediately and asked for him as Claudette Colbert's leading man in "So Proudly We Hail," the story of the Bataan nurses.

If Reeves starts climbing high, 20th-Fox is going to be in a state as that studio once had permitted the option to lapse. You saw the actor as Merle Oberon's first beau, the football player, in "Lydia."

George Reeves and Veronica Lake study lines for "Sainted Sisters" (Paramount, 1948).

Lita Baron, Virginia Grey, George Reeves, and Johnny Weissmuller march through the Columbia Pictures swamp in "Jungle Jim" (1948).

were about to do a scene," he remembers, "and we got it on the first take. Then as a surprise to all of us George strode directly toward the little girl, beaming from ear to ear, and knelt in front of her. He said, 'Your name is Merriam, and I love you!' He leaned forward and kissed her on the cheek. She wet her pants."

Reeves had his own cure-all whenever he became sharp with his associates. "Sometimes George would get very irritated with the way something would happen, or it would get too hot and they'd keep him in the uniform too long." When that happened, says Jack Larson, "It was inevitable you'd have to go to dinner with him, because he'd always regret the altercation. If you did something to upset him, he'd tell you off. But along about seven o'clock he'd demand, 'Let's go to Trader Vic's.' It was his way of apologizing."

Larson used to shy away because he wanted to go home. "I loved being with George, but when he wanted to go out it meant belting a few before sitting down to eat, and that meant getting home after eleven o'clock.

I wanted to go home and memorize my lines for the next day. George had it easier than most in this regard. He was a 'fast study,' the possessor of an almost photographic memory which literally made it possible for him to learn a script in a single reading. This, of course, left him more time for dinner and good cheer, and for me less sleep."

Phyllis Coates remained a close personal friend up until the end. "George was a very giving guy, he was very good to me. On many Saturdays or Sundays he would come by with a gift for my daughter. He'd check in and talk awhile, but there was a very lonely quality about George."

Jack Larson recalls, "My most vivid memory of George—the one I treasure and that's making me smile at this moment—is that George was one of the few people at that time who smoked with a cigarette holder. He held it very elegantly, and it used to be so funny: George with his Superman outfit, cape, tights, and the inimitable cigarette holder. It looked so funny, charming and mad. It was just completely incongruous." Jack pauses, still smiling in recollection, and it becomes touchingly evident that a deep feeling of comradeship can, after a decade and a half, still bring George Reeves to life in the memories of those with whom he shared the experience.

Bob Justman can also smile as he remembers the famous Reeves Superman pose: "George would stand there for the opening credits, his hands on his hips, looking slightly three-quarters to one side. Jaw out. In the meantime his knees would come together knock-kneed. This just tickled me. Here's this guy fierce and determined with his damn knees touching each other."

Reeves enjoyed being a character. He liked clowning around and playing philanthropist and beneficiary. He was by every measure "Honest George, the People's Friend." When adult admirers asked him how he flew, his answer was straightforward enough: "They just know how to touch me in the right place!" In a July 1958 press release for ABC, he added to the absurdity of the question.

I enjoy flying. It's really jolly up there zooming around in my blue longies and red cape. Sometimes I take my guitar along and sing appropriate songs like "Blue Moon," "Stars in My Crown," "I Got the Sun in the Morning" and "One Eyed, One Horned, Flying Purple People Eater." By the way, we've met!

Actually it wasn't easy for a grown man to run around all day in false muscles and a cape. "George wore stuffing to cover for his sloped shoulders," muses Whitney Ellsworth. "He was a great athlete and did all his own jumps—and he did them well. But in uniform he needed the extra help at the shoulders to look like Superman."

"It was hot under all that rubber and sponge padding," adds Jack Larson. "On hot days it was sweltering, and he was supposed to be in it only a couple of consecutive hours a day, then rest, otherwise his skin would break out." It was different in the uniform, but as everyone remembers, George bested the ordeal every day. The shoulder pads were sewn to a cut-down T-shirt in order to keep them from shifting around. The upper costume, in turn, was sewn at the crotch to prevent it from riding up. Under the heat and humidity of Los Angeles and the studio lights, Reeves went through at least four of the $500 uniforms each year and it was not unusual for him to lose a few pounds of water weight through the seams every time he suited up.

Still, Reeves often forgot himself in the uniform. Whitney Ellsworth tells one story that involves his daughter. "Pat was working in Audience Relations at ABC in New York, and George went there to make some publicity stills. When he got through he didn't even wait to change; he charged downstairs to Pat's department, and the looks she tells me he got were enough to make you cry. But that's how old George was."

The initial good fortune of the Superman role had its drawbacks. Wherever Reeves toured, he was apprehensive of arrogant youngsters who wanted to challenge his powers onstage. "Just as the program became very popular," says Jack Larson, "George learned not to wear his Superman outfit too long on public appearances. That's why newspaper pictures with George in his uniform are rare."

It was no less safe when other people stepped into makeshift Superman garb. When the show peaked in the mid-fifties, National merchandised uniforms for the younger set. A report tells of a Chicago department store where the Superman display was promoted by a muscleman parading around the stage in a home-sewn outfit. One ambitious child set his sights on the derriere of the male model, and his drawing compass left the department store Superman standing for weeks.

Reeves was not without his own brushes with danger. According to an early *L.A. Times* column by Walter Ames, "He has been kicked in the shins, slugged in the back and subjected to other such tricks by his admirers to test his endurance." Reeves's greatest challenge was in 1953. He told newspaper interviewers on many occasions that a Detroit child decided to impress his friends by shooting Superman with his father's .45 army Colt. He aimed the loaded gun point blank at Reeves's chest. Nervous moments later, Reeves had miraculously talked the weapon out of the young assassin's hand. He assured the little soldier that Superman could indeed stand the force of the shot, but, "When the bullets bounce off my chest, they might hurt you and others around here." From that day forward, he decided the same thing would not happen again.

Walter Ames's Sepember 27, 1954, column tried to suggest that Reeves asked National to ". . . halt the sale of Superman capes and other goods he thought might prove harmful to youngsters." Reeves expressed his own concern to Jack Larson. "Some kids think Superman is indestructible, a few even think the uniform will do the same for them." Happily, most youngsters who sat with cape flapping in the breeze of their own Vornado fan realized Reeves was not really Super-

HONEST GEORGE
also known as
"COL. REEVES"

man. "Kids, frankly, are not quite as stupid as they are often credited with being," says Whitney Ellsworth. "And George knew this."

One interesting exception was a visit to Hess's, an Allentown, Pennsylvania, department store. Mannie Levine, the director of public relations, vividly remembers the two visits. The first was as George Reeves, March 31, 1955. "Then in 1956, tied in with a promotion for U. S. Savings Bonds and Stamps for youngsters, 'Superman' accepted Max Hess's challenge to take over the duties of Hess's 1,600 co-workers in the store. The Man of Steel darted around in costume delivering goods, running elevators, driving store trucks and filling in as advertising director, show salesman, fashion director and gift wrapper." The promotion was climaxed by Superman taking over the toy department, ". . . giving youngsters his own version of a merry-go-round ride . . ." until he skinned a knee in a collision with a tricycle.

Levine considers Reeves's second appearance as one of the most successful promotions the store ever engaged in. When Superman knocked on Allentown's doors with department store deliveries, the women went wild. "They just glowed as if they were tapped by Lady Fortune. They wanted George to come in and join them for coffee." One can only imagine the explanation the wives offered their spouses later in the day.

Reeves took his act on the road with more regularity after the Hess's experiment. In 1958, manager Arthur Weissman worked out details with National Periodicals (né National Comics) for a cross-country hop for George, Noel Neill and Natividad Vacio. Reeves hired a wrestler called "Mr. Kryptonite," and Vacio threw together a trio of musicians. The kids were delighted with the format: Neill crossed the stage first, and the wrestler, a stunt man in traditional bad-guy black, attacked "yon fair lady." Her screams for help were heard by— Superman. Reeves bounded on the stage and tossed his partner about the mat. After the triumph, he changed into his civies for a song and dance fest with Noel Neill and Natividad Vacio. With the accordion, guitar and bass backup, they sang a Mexican song, then one country and western number.

"One little thing I learned from George Reeves," says actor Herb Vigran, "I remember George was signing autographs, pictures of Superman for a group of kids. He signed them George Reeves, and I said, 'Gee, George, why don't you sign Superman?' He answered, laughing, 'I don't want Superman to get the publicity, I want George Reeves to get it!' "

Vigran had known Reeves for years, but still wasn't quite prepared for an incident during the filming of "Blackmail" in 1955. The script called for Vigran to aim an anti-Superman weapon at the Man of Steel. He did so, and the stunt backfired. When the smoke cleared, Vigran was so saturated with dirt and soot that he was certain he'd be washing for days. "I was just another actor on the set, a day player being paid peanuts like everyone else, and after all George was the star, but he said to me, 'Come on over to my dressing room, get cleaned up and take a shower.' " It was an ordinary courtesy at best, but Vigran was still impressed. "You can take my word, it doesn't happen like that very often. It's just the kind of guy Reeves was."

Tommy Carr speaks on a more professional level: "I wish all the shows I ever did could have been as free of actor trouble as the ones I made with George. He was just wonderful, you couldn't ask for anyone better. He never held us up, he knew all his lines, he was a fast study and he didn't gripe about working hard." At least he didn't complain much on the set. Perhaps it was different at home. Phyllis Coates says he aired his grievances to her even after she left the program. But in spite of the hard knocks, she adds, he seemed to take some perverse satisfaction in playing the role, probably because he knew he could do it well.

George Reeves as Superman (1953).

94

"The Major Sportsmens' Show of Connecticut"

Connecticut Sportsmen & Boat Show Inc.

BOX 30
WHITE RIVER JCT., VT.

119 ANN STREET
HARTFORD, CONN.

. . . . *Held in the Heart of the Capitol City* . . . .
State Armory
Hartford   Connecticut

Only one full-length Superman motion picture was ever produced, *Superman and the Mole Men* (1951). Two more feature scripts—*Superman and the Ghost of Mystery Mountain* (1954) and *Superman and the Secret Planet* (1957)—have since been written but not produced. No one seems to know why, but the best guess is that National was more than satisfied with the success of the television series and did not care to risk a flop at the box office. In any evident, all that remains on film of George Reeves's Superman are the 104 television episodes, including an edited version of the *Mole Men*.

A valid perspective of George's post-series life is totally dependent on whom you talk to and what is asked. One source is certain that "George's career not only faltered and stumbled, but came to a crashing halt." There were those who thought George would never work again.

"Rubbish!" say his friends Natividad Vacio and Phyllis Coates. They both knew of impending work, related and unrelated to "Superman." There were offers for summer stock, road shows and state fairs. Vacio says Reeves had a proposal from a New York firm that wanted a new Dick Tracy face, but Reeves replied, "Oh no, not another series, I want to direct." Reeves had tried his hand at directing "Superman" ("The Brainy Burro," "The Perils of Superman" and "All That Glitters") and was looking forward to working with the new scripts he had written. 'Money was no problem, 'Superman' checks were coming in every week," says Vacio. "It's not that George had no work, he could pick and choose."

Reeves had formed his own production company in 1954, and George Reeves Enterprises planned a television series on Hawaii and Mexico. In 1955, Reeves announced he had acquired the Lowell Barrington novel *The Deserter* and intended to star himself in a feature production of the property. The new career offered the actor a perfectly reasonable opportunity to be known as George Reeves rather than Superman. There is, therefore, a special poignancy in the fact that the identity he sought in life was unattainable, even in death. The headlines screamed: "Superman Kills Self," "Superman Mystery Grows," "Probe Death of Superman." The press couldn't, or wouldn't, separate George Reeves from the role. The more dramatic headlines were simply too good to pass up. These stories are still in libraries across the country, where the yellowing they show is from age, not a mellowing perspective. Consequently, misinformation concerning the death of George Reeves still circulates. One bizarre rumor in particular has survived the years. Some people still believe that he had lost himself so completely in the Superman role that in the end he jumped out a window thinking he could really fly.

The unadorned fact is that George Reeves died of a gunshot wound to the head, and after a complete police investigation and autopsy, the county coroner officially ruled that George Reeves committed suicide.

Certain newspaper reporters sought the reasons behind the act, and came up predictably with the picture of the dejected star unable to find work.

Reeves had complained for years about the typecasting that resulted from the TV series. He said last year that whenever he went looking for another role it was like Hopalong Cassidy trying to get an acting job in white tie and tails.

Washington Post, June 16, 1959

Newspaper reports indicate Reeves put aside his dignity and was prepared to return to the ring. "He was a strong man, and he found that after twenty-eight years the only job he could get was a job as wrestler." According to this story, George had scheduled a whirlwind tour for a fair bankroll. "He went into training and after two weeks got into pretty good shape," the story continued, "but his mental attitude was bad; he didn't want wrestling."

A newspaper photograph caught Superman (Reeves) delivering merchandise from Hess' department store in Allentown, Pennsylvania (1956).

. . . Reeves was set for the dates in Pennsylvania at stated figures, but he received notice the fees had been cut. Then, Monday morning . . . he got a letter notifying him the wrestling engagements were off. On top of that a narration he was supposed to make for a children's record was canceled. It was devastating. His attitude was "Here I am doing something I shouldn't be doing in the first place, and now they don't want me."

New York Journal-American, June 24, 1959

The thought of having to become a wrestler to make a living—"this man who had been an actor for 28 years, a star—was too much . . . not that he feared boxing with Archie Moore or wrestling with Gene Labelle in Pittsburgh, July 3, it was just that his heart was broken because he couldn't get a job. . . ." For two years George walked around this town trying to get a job in some production. But they told him, "We know you're a good actor, but everyone thinks you're Superman. You're typed for him."

New York Post, June 17, 1959

The accounts are clouded in typical Hollywood fog because Reeves had a children's record and motion pictures in the works. In fact, Whitney Ellsworth tends to dismiss the entire wrestling story as bunk because he believes that Reeves was in no physical shape to step inside the ring at that late date. "George had work," says Natividad Vacio. "He had work and he had money." One source reports that twelve hours before his death, Reeves even talked of a proposed $20,000 whirlwind tour of Australia. "I'm in love with the project, and we'll have ourselves a ball," said Reeves.

Less than two weeks earlier, Reeves had telephoned Phyllis Coates. The former actress says he offered her a part in a film he was planning to direct. Ironically, another job offer had been called in the afternoon prior to his death, but he didn't check with his answering service and never received the message. This film, an occult feature, would have given Reeves another directing assignment.

Obviously, we can never know the answer, for Reeves left no note, no indication why. His longtime business manager and friend, Arthur Weissman, told Whitney Ellsworth that George once or twice said something about killing himself, but in such a kidding way that neither Weissman nor Ellsworth considered it significant. Some have suggested a losing spin at "Russian roulette," which can be ruled out since the weapon was a Lüger automatic with no revolving chamber.

My Favorite Recipe:

Well, here is Superman's favorite recipe: Corn Flake Cookies.

The famous birdman of comic book fame is in town this week to open the Arizona State Fair. Too, he appears on KOOL-TV at 7 p.m. Tuesdays.

Clark Kent or Superman gives this recipe:

SUPERMAN COOKIES
¼ pound butter, softened
½ cup white sugar
½ cup light brown sugar
1 large egg, beaten
¼ teaspoon baking soda
1½ cups flour
½ cup coarsely grated chocolate
1 cup corn flakes

Cream butter and sugar together. Blend in beaten egg. Blend in flour ½ cup at a time. Add soda dissolved in a tablespoon hot water.

Add nuts, grated chocolate and corn flakes.

Drop by teaspoonful on greased

Superman is disguised as Clark Kent, newspaper reporter.

cookie sheet. Bake in 375 degree oven for 10 to 12 minutes. Remove from sheet and cool on cake rack.

George Reeves with Sam, his pet Schnauzer (1956).

Others hint at despondency over an unrequited love affair. A few believe the death may have been accidental, but this is unlikely, if only for technical reasons. Whitney Ellsworth has a theory which he says is shared by many of those who were closest to the situation—including lawyer Jerry Geisler and ultimately Reeves's mother, both of whom are now deceased.

"Two weeks before his death," Ellsworth says, "George had a bad automobile accident and suffered a serious brain concussion. He was having violent headaches, and his doctors prescribed pain-killers. George added a little pain-killer of his own—booze—and everybody knows that alcohol and sedatives make a very dangerous combination."

As a result, Ellsworth believes, Reeves may well have been in a state of temporary insanity, or at least in a condition where he was not aware of what he was doing. "Knowing George as well as I did," he says, "I just can't credit any other conclusion."

Reeves died two days before he was to be married.

If everything was looking so rosy, why did George Reeves kill himself? In spite of the coroner's verdict of suicide, Reeves's mother at first suspected an even more sinister cause. She engaged Jerry Geisler, the famed criminal lawyer, to conduct an investigation. Geisler pressed the inquiry with his usual vigor but was unable to produce any evidence of foul play. He eventually reported that there was no reason to question the official version of Reeves's tragic death.

His death came as a tremendous shock to everyone. But actor Milton Frome says he felt the impact in the most unusual way. The day Reeves died, a rerun of one of Frome's guest appearances had been televised. In "Whatever Goes Up" Frome fires a gun point blank at Superman. "That night," recalls Milton Frome, "some neighborhood kids came by our house and told my son Michael, 'Hey, your father killed Superman!' It was too frightening to believe. Michael said, 'No, my daddy's an actor, and don't forget, after my daddy shot

Thanks for Watching
Your friend
George Reeves
"Superman"

him Superman got up.' " It was impossible to explain to anyone what had happened. "You have to remember, George was a very good actor, and somehow or other he wanted to get out of the series to do other big things. Still I told him, 'George, you're tremendous in this thing. Nobody could be Superman but you. Absolutely nobody could be as dedicated.' "

"Maybe," answered Reeves in despair, "but I only wish I knew whether or not I even have one fan who's an adult."

He would have been pleased to know he did, for Milton Frome says with a quiet sense of pride, "I'm happy I knew him, because in my mind, and to millions of others, George Reeves was a great man. A truly great man."

CHAPTER V

1951

On July 30, 1951, a stretch of the dusty old RKO set in Culver City posted a new sign: "Silsby, home of the world's deepest oil well." The Superman Company had moved in. *Superman and the Mole Men* was released theatrically less than six months later. The sixty-seven-minute feature introduced principals Reeves and Coates to one another and bought a few day's work for a long list of character actors. "Every midget in town who belonged to the Screen Actors Guild was canvassed for a job as a Mole Man," remembers Coates. Producer Bob Maxwell finally settled on Billy Curtis,[1] Jack Banbury, Jerry Marvin and Tony Baris. The four played the curious little creatures who surfaced from the bowels of the earth shortly after Clark Kent and Lois Lane pulled into Silsby. The feature, a serious attempt at marketable science fiction, joined the ranks of sci-fi entries preoccupied with the notion of a civilization inhabiting the center of the earth.[2] In the Superman adventure, the luminous Lilliputians poke their heads out of an oil shaft that has been driven deep into their community. With the same stupidity and callousness that marks Robert Wise's humans in *The Day the Earth Stood Still,* the townspeople of Silsby try to destroy the Mole Men as they do Klaatu (Michael Rennie) the same year. In *Superman,* we sink the oil well six miles deep into the creatures' home— we step uninvited into their domain. Blinded by our own fear we don't recognize their mission of peace.

[1] Curtis later reappeared as a Martian in the 1956 Superman episode "Mr. Zero," and the lead in National Periodicals Publications' 1960 pilot, "Superpup."

[2] John Agar and Hugh Beaumont returned underground to discover *The Mole People* in 1956.

The Richard Fielding (pen name of Bob Maxwell) script raises *Superman and the Mole Men* above many other early Superman efforts. The message implicitly encourages mankind to move slower—peacefully. Yet Luke Benson (Jeff Corey) and his mob think differently.

Game show host Jack Narz sets the somber tone with his voice-over narration as cameraman Clark Ramsey zooms past a new Clark Kent and Lois Lane. The audience is immediately treated to a tug-of-war rivalry between the two. Phyllis Coates's Lois never lets up on the poor soul. Kent is badgered, insulted and abused, often backed into compromising positions, forced to wield a tirade in his own defense. The two act like newspaper muckrakers involved in a real mystery, "Well, I hope you realize what a fool you made of yourself!" snips Lois. With that he walks off in a huff barely hearing Lois' next put-down, "He always does that, gets himself in a jam, and then runs away." The strings begin to vibrate, the horns trill, the timpani roll and the familiar Superman theme reaches its peak. A handsome George Reeves, airborne over the camera, flies above the angry mob.

Luke Benson and his cronies naïvely challenge Superman with their rifles and fists. This mysterious man, be he angel or devil, is as alien to the mob as the Mole Men. They're dangerous because they are different, and the crowd acts out of ignorance and fear to protect their homes and family from the unknown peril. Some popular-culture observers say that *Superman and the Mole Men* parallels the Pentagon's warning of Communism in "The Red Menace." To those who make the comparison, the Mole Men seemingly move like infiltrating Communists—under the cloak of darkness. The analogy almost comes full circle when the aliens are cornered in a wooden shack by the frightened townspeople. There, Luke Benson, like Senator Joseph McCarthy, decides to destroy the enemy with an old-fashioned witch burning. Benson strikes the first match.

(left to right) Robert Maxwell, National Comics President Harry Donenfeld, Mrs. Donenfeld, and Whitney Ellsworth (Selznick Studios, Culver City, July, 1951).

Superman and the Mole Men was not intended as a social commentary on McCarthy or the "Red scare." However, with the perspective of twenty-five years, some of the underlying themes of *Mole Men*, like those of Donald Siegel's *Invasion of the Body Snatchers*, unmistakably fit the argument.

The Mole Men turn out to be less than advertised. Their radioactive glow, originally feared deadly, is simply a harmless phosphorescence. Yet, in spite of their innocence, reason does not prevail. Benson ignores Superman's last-ditch plea:

They look strange to us, it's true. But we must look just as strange to them. Be reasonable, let me handle this.

Détente was not even an occasional word in a 1950s *Reader's Digest* vocabulary quiz. It has no meaning to the farmers, shopkeepers, bankers and deliverymen of Silsby driven by fear and ignorance. Despite the hatred rampant against the Mole Men, the creatures are depicted as sympathetic beings who marvel at life they have never seen before. They exhibit more humanity and compassion than the surface dwellers do, comforting one another when a snake—the real symbol of evil—crosses their path. The script leaves even the youngest viewer with a sense of awe over which is more dangerous—the unknown, or the systematic destruction of it. Words become Superman's greatest weapon. He demands that they "Stop acting like Nazi storm troopers!"

Ironically, the people of Silsby never admit they are at fault. Mine supervisor Bill Corrigan (Walter Reed) describes the original mining operation to Clark Kent before the horror unfolds: "It [the drill bit] was hanging in midair as if we had broken through to the center of the earth." The apparatus returned with microscopic organisms, prompting Corrigan to speculate on the existence of another civilization below: "Whatever is down there could come up!" His words end up as the most dubious understatement of the film. Later he amends his initial stand: "Human? Monsters? Whatever, they're here, and they've come up from the center of the earth!"

By the end of the night, Luke Benson scores a villainous victory over his prey. Superman returns a wounded ambassador to his Mole Men comrades. Moments later, a high-pitched whine breaks the calm of the night. The little creatures fix a blast from their souped-up vacuum cleaner ray gun into the oil shaft. The well explodes, sending flames high into the air; forever sealing the corridor between two worlds. Superman, his cape now blowing freely in the wind, stands next to Lois as she delivers the last line:

It's almost as if they're saying, you've got your home and we've got ours.

Director Lee Sholem filmed George Reeves's lift and flight with wires. His crew wasn't plagued with the problems that beset Spencer Bennet, but they didn't escape without some difficulty. The rushes showed Reeves's cape entangled in the master guidelines. Spe-

Luke Benson (Jeff Corey) threatens the invincible Superman, as Lois Lane and the people of Silsby watch in awe ("Superman and the Mole Men").

cial effects artist Ray Mercer suggested a different system. He fitted Reeves for a harness under his uniform, avoiding the ordeal of Kirk Alyn. Reeves's support attached to the wires, leaving his cape free to flop in the wind during the staged lift-offs and flights. Reeves took four or five strides toward the camera; just as he jumped, the crew pulled on the wires, raising him into the air over the camera. Once again the effect looked better on paper. Early in the production one wire broke, sending Reeves crashing to the ground like a 1957 Vanguard rocket. The incident was hushed up.

Superman and the Mole Men experimented further. The crew rigged an in-flight rescue of one Mole Man and a magnificent tracking shot of Superman soaring over the angry mob. After the dramatic flying shot, Superman delivers the first of his moralistic rebuttals to Luke Benson: "It's men like you who make it difficult for people to understand one another."

Superman and the Mole Men was released to thea-

Superman carries the wounded Mole Man back to the oil shaft. Notice the Electro-lux vacuum cleaner one Mole Man uses as his weapon. ("Superman and the Mole Men," Lippert Productions, 1951.)

ters as a feature two years before it was broadcast on television in two parts as "The Unknown People." Phyllis Coates was vacationing in Scotland when she first sensed the impact Superman would have on her life. Never figuring anyone would see it, Coates found the feature playing in Europe. For better or for worse, she had to accept the fact that for years to come people would know her as Lois Lane.

Robert Maxwell co-produced the feature with Barney A. Sarecky, then shared the producing credit on the remaining twenty-four episodes with Bernard Luber. Luber had been an attorney at Paramount Pictures before he turned producer. His experience in film balanced Maxwell's in radio; their collaboration produced a forceful, direct descendant of the Bud Collyer Superman. The Maxwell-Luber Superman had determination, strength and belligerence; qualities inherent in the forties hero. Maxwell was responsible for the editorial and creative angles, while Luber held up the business side of the production.

The remaining "Adventures of Superman" were shot through the heat of August and September at a rate of four shows every ten days. Two directors earning $600 apiece per episode alternated between shooting and pre-production conferences. Tommy Carr, a veteran of Kirk Alyn's 1948 *Superman*, joined the television crew with Lee Sholem. Both directors were talented, each with a distinct style. For Sholem it was shouting. Those who describe him speak with no malice. He wasn't a tyrant, rather a director with enthusiasm, a flair for the dramatic. According to Whitney Ellsworth, "I never heard a guy scream as loud as Sholem did when he cut a scene. He'd get it all done and yell at the top of his lungs, 'C—U—T!' " Sholem had been an experienced budget director, moving from project to project, always working, never worrying about making the Great American Film. Like most of the "Superman" directors, Sholem was weaned on a diet of Hollywood B assignments. He's remembered for a series of Tarzan films he shot, along with *Redhead from Wyoming, Tobor the Great, Emergency Hospital, Pharaoh's Curse* and *Sierra Stranger.* Since "Superman," he has directed scores of pictures for television, including two hundred "This Is the Life" episodes for the Lutheran Church.

Tommy Carr joined the company to improve the Superman work he had directed at Columbia. "We had more say with Superman on television for the simple reason that we weren't restricted to animation as we were in the serial. Our TV work looked alive! The writing was better on television, the acting was better too; it was a more intimate medium. Sure, the serial was more violent than the television series, that was their bread and butter then—the audiences loved that—but the TV show was shot better in every way."

Tommy Carr was born into a film environment. His father directed silents and his mother acted in them.

Carr himself appeared in motion pictures for twenty-five years before following the career of his father. His credits extend as far back as the Philadelphia-based Lubin Company, where he appeared as a baby with the first matinee idol team, Arthur Johnson and Florence Lawrence. "The camera was still nailed to the floor then," remembers Carr. "You didn't move the camera, the people moved up to it. If an actor was too tall for a shot or the camera angle, he'd be out of work." [3] Father and son worked together for years before the prodigal left. Meanwhile, Tommy's mother, Mary, remains a household word in families old enough to have seen *Over the Hill to the Poor House* (1920). Tommy himself has been in *Wings* (1927), *Dawn Patrol* (1930), *Hell's Angels* (1930) and a single "Three Mesquiteers" picture with Ray "Crash" Corrigan and Bob Livingston. The back-to-back shooting required of Superman directors was old hat. Carr had cut his teeth at Republic Studios, where directors were responsible for as many as six Westerns, all on the call-board the same day. Like Spencer Bennet, he was a master of the trick, once dropping dye into the mud-filled Sacramento River blue to match footage from the day before. Carr's direction included *West of the Brazos* (1950), *Captain Scarlett* (1952), *Three for Jamie Dawn* (1956), *Dino* (1957), *Tall Stranger* (1958) and *Cast a Long Shadow* (1959). Carr moved into television with "Wild Bill Hickok," and he's actually the one who named Andy Devine "Jingles." After his years on "Superman," Carr directed "Trackdown," "Wanted Dead or Alive," "Rawhide," "Richard Diamond, Private Detective," and "Stagecoach West."

One assistant director on "Superman," Bob Justman, says of Carr, "I learned a lot from Tommy; he was always intent on his work, yet that doesn't mean he was

[3] Carr's father William claimed to have predated the famous D. W. Griffith as the first director to unbolt the monstrous camera from the floor and shoot a moving vehicle from another automobile.

without his idiosyncrasies. Tommy could smoke up a storm," says Justman. "He'd start a scene with a cigarette behind his back; however, the smoke often would drift onto the set. So Joe King, the wardrobe man, and I would get an eyedropper filled with glycerin and every once in awhile drop it on his cigarette to put it out. Each time the camera rolled he'd light up a new cigarette, and we'd have to sidle past him, to douse one after another. Tommy never knew it, he just said, 'Cut—Print.'"

Yet where low-budget television was concerned, Tommy Carr was unbeatable. His philosophy is quite simple: "When you've got to produce a show, you do it the way the sponsors and the public like it. It's the only way to stay in business."

The crew assembled on that last day of July 1951 for what was to become one of the earliest marathons in television production. Of the first year's gathering, only George Reeves, Jack Larson, John Hamilton and Robert Shayne remained through 1957. All other acting, technical and managerial positions incurred a turnover at least once, not unusual for any Hollywood production over a six-year period. Oddly, all of the principal actors had earlier belonged to Warner Brothers. Reeves and Hamilton, in the early forties; Shayne a short time later; and Larson and Coates by the end of the decade.

Home that first year was the grand old RKO-Pathé lot in Culver City, California, which was rich with outdoor sets. *Variety* reported the arrival of the newly awaited tenants strictly in terms of dollars and cents. The first twenty-six episodes, including "Superman and the Mole Men," were to come in for $400,000, or roughly $15,000 each. By today's standards, the same money would hardly pay for a decent sixty-second commercial.

"Superman's" early television history is clouded with some mystery. Some sources indicate that Bob Maxwell promised a "piece of the action" to George

Reeves in lieu of a salary. Granted, the first contracts were not overwhelming, but National Comics did meet the payroll. Kellogg's bought the program on a multi-run basis from Cy Weintraub of Flamingo Films.[4] Kellogg's, in turn, pleased with the earlier success from "Wild Bill Hickok's" Sugar Pops, envisioned the same good fortune for the Man of Steel. They sent Tony the Tiger after Superman and the idea bit. The program aired on ABC, until the Leo Burnett agency handling the Kellogg's account found they could get better coverage for their needs by buying spot time on local stations, thus setting up their own controlled in-house syndication. By the time Kellogg's made the move to nationwide saturation, the FCC had opened up the industry and everybody seemed to want this most valuable showpiece. "Superman" struck gold; it hasn't let up since.

In April 1951, Robert Maxwell was hired by National to produce "Superman." Within a month after signing, he set up shop on the West Coast. The May 16, 1951, *Variety* announced his arrival, adding that a whooping fifty-two episodes were scheduled for that year. The blurb was slightly premature, if not blatantly incorrect. However, it did note the thirty-year distribution contract set up with Flamingo. A July 18 article indicated that "Superman" would be ready for viewing by January 1952. The finished product was ready, but National was not.

Maxwell's programs are undeniably more violent than those of Whitney Ellsworth. Jack Larson says it was probably Maxwell's background in radio that molded the "Superman" of 1951. "He didn't think of it as a children's show, because he hoped for an adult time slot." There are death scenes, and hair-raising fights in Maxwell's twenty-six half hours. In fact, the episodes resemble serials, where violence was sacrosanct. During the first year, Superman is an unknown force to most adversaries, his sudden appearance is

[4] National Periodicals Publications later bought out Flamingo's interest in the deal.

Superman director Thomas Carr with his mother, silent film star, Mary Carr, at the Republic backlot during shooting for the Sunset Carson Western, "Oregon Trail" (1945).

always unexpectedly dramatic. The action, adventure and mystery was everything Bob Maxwell wanted and none of what National Comics had in mind.

The "Adventures of Superman" wasn't aired until February 9, 1953. The first episode, "Superman on Earth," was broadcast in Los Angeles on KECA, while New York audiences saw it on April 1, over WABC. *Variety* reviewed the New York showing in its April 8 edition and described it with the accolades it deserved:

It was only a matter of time before "Superman," long-awaited comic book and radio favorite with the kids (and some adults, no doubt), should be put on film. It's to National Comics' credit that its television version is restrained on the scripting side and well done technically.

Kellogg has bought the pix from Flamingo Films, its distributor, and has spooned it into WABC-TV, in the station's kidfilm block. Move should pay off—station has a hefty cross-the-board slot of adventure pix for children, and "Superman" fits the bill neatly.

Initial installment told how Superman as a baby was flown to earth in a rocket by his parents on the planet Crypton [sic] just as the planet was about to disintegrate. Pix showed how the boy was found by a farmer and his wife and raised by them as Clark Kent, their son. Finally, as Kent grew to manhood, he left for the city, and with the rescue of a man hanging from a dirigible got a job with the *Daily Planet* as a reporter.

All this is familiar stuff to the kids, but there's an extra kick for them seeing it on the screen. Filming is top-notch, with no expense spared to get those special effects. George Reeves, who acts Superman, doesn't have too much of a role in the initial pix, since most of it deals with boyhood of the hero, but he registered nicely as the meek reporter and as the hero. Phyllis Coates was okay as Lois Lane, the girl reporter, while John Hamilton fits the fictitious concept of an editor. Other roles were well handled.

The Superman of television developed powers far beyond his precursors from radio, serials and comic books. George Reeves separated his molecules to walk through walls ("The Mysterious Cube," 1957), split in two ("Divide and Conquer," 1957), traveled through the telephone lines ("The Phoney Alibi," 1956), and became invisible ("The Phantom Ring," 1955). In addition, during the six years of production, Reeves's Superman called on the normal assortment of extraterrestrial abilities for microscopic and X-ray vision, superhearing, supertyping, superstrength, a mastery of foreign language and—of course—flying. There were, however, certain discrepancies—actual contradictions that were later ignored. For example, in "The Case of the Talkative Dummy" (1951) he could see Jimmy Olsen locked in a lead safe, in "Blackmail" (1955) he could not. The first year also resurrected some scripts that had entertained early radio audiences—"The Stolen Costume" (1951) and "The Secret of Superman" (1951). Such evidence reinforces Jack Larson's suggestion that Bob Maxwell and his wife Jessica were more at home with the strong, dynamic and violent radio characters. Jessica meanwhile moved from dialogue director to general-purpose consultant to allow Stephen Carr,[5] Tommy's brother, to pick up the script assignment.

Individual episodes were not shot in the order they were broadcast. Since there was a delay of two years before the first twenty-six reached local television stations, Maxwell and Luber were able to juggle the line-up to prevent obvious repetition of guests or plots. (Actual air order is shown in the Appendix.) Since the production schedule was handled by two directors, this chapter will discuss the episodes in the sequence in which they were filmed.

Superman and the Mole Men was in the can first. The next to be filmed was "The Talkative Dummy." In a nutshell, Superman rescues Jimmy Olsen from a safe before it completely falls from a block and tackle high above the ground. Clark Kent turns to Lois Lane and says, "Lois, look. It's Jim. He's in that safe!" He nearly blows his cover. Lois can see neither the safe nor its contents. In fact, she has a difficult time peering over the steering wheel of the 1951 Nash. While Lois tries to figure everything out, Clark ducks out of the car, changes into his traveling clothes and saves Jimmy, only to return to face the third degree from Lois. "How it is that you always manage to show up at the right time?" Superman quips back, "Miss Lane, that's my job."

The hallmark of the show is repetition, and the theme most often repeated is Lois Lane's ongoing suspicion of Clark Kent. In "The Talkative Dummy" Lois asks Inspector Henderson to explain Kent's disappearing act. Henderson answers, without knowing how precise his remarks are, "Maybe he runs into an alley,

[5] Stephen Carr, a bit player in the first serial, and the man with the familiar hand pointing skyward in the opening of the black and white episodes, also appears in utility roles throughout many of the 1951 pictures.

Hero, the mechanical man, sits in the laundry basket, as the bandaged inventor, Horatio Hinkle (Lucien Littlefield) sits on Clark Kent's couch. ("The Runaway Robot" 1951.)

takes off his glasses and turns into Superman!" By the 1957 episodes, these asides proliferate almost every script to the point where Lois and Jimmy have to be blind not to give the possibility more than casual thought. However, writer/producer Whitney Ellsworth says, "We couldn't have anyone come right out and make the connection. Besides, if you're willing to accept the premise of a man flying around in what looks like underwear, then it's not so hard to chew on another premise that his best friends never recognize his secret identity."

Bob Maxwell moved the action to postwar Germany for the next Tommy Carr directorial effort. The hackneyed theme of identical twins who provide alibis for one another muddled its way into "Double Trouble" (originally "The Million Dollar Mystery"). Superman

George Reeves, completely unaware that in the next second his cable would break and he would crash solidly on the studio floor ("The Ghost Wolf"—1951).

George Reeves suspended over the mattresses via his counter-balance.

crosses the Atlantic to track down a valuable cache of radium, stolen from the United States Medical Corps in Germany. "Double Trouble" was the second episode to draw a bead on former Nazis. There would be no more. Somewhere between helping the Mole Men and rescuing Jimmy Olsen, Superman mastered German, easily translating the mumblings of one von Kleben twin. After hearing what best can be translated as "Cussed Superman!" or "Cussed Stronger than average man!" (characterization deleted) Superman responds with his own retort: "I'm going to make you eat those words!" In order to get the goods on the surviving von Kleben brother, Superman enlists the aid of United States Army Colonel Redding (Selmar Jackson) and future "Mouseketeer" Jimmy Dodd.

"The Secret of Superman" finds Superman feigning amnesia to apprehend the diabolical Dr. Ort (Peter Brocco). True to form, Lois and Jimmy are taken hostage by the scientist to lure the Man of Steel into a deadly trap. However, Superman, unaffected by Ort's mind-altering drugs, watches the fanatical scientist go down in the end.

The cold war is not a dominant preoccupation of "Superman," but it does burn hot in a few plots such as "The Monkey Mystery." Superman is introduced to the Iron Curtain by Peppy, a chimpanzee clad in a mini-Superman suit. Together, they recover a formula representing the only known defense against atomic warfare. The episode is otherwise harmless.

While Carr shot his five, Lee Sholem was busy with pre-production work on the shows he would film: "The Mind Machine," "The Stolen Costume," "Mystery in Wax," "No Holds Barred," and "The Ghost Wolf." When these went into production on August 24, 1951, scenes from different weeks were shot back to back. Budget and time requirements dictated that the director stay put in certain sets, working all four scripts at once. Jack Larson describes the confusion that often resulted:

. . . **and the take-off revealed.**

refuses to identify the item stolen from a compartment in his closet. Kent simply says it has to be recovered. The exchange simply drives Candy to the point of exasperation:

Clark Kent:

Candy, I want you to find out who broke in.

Candy:

What was stolen?

Clark Kent:

Something, I can't tell you.

Candy:

What?

Clark Kent:

Just something.

Clark Kent learns that Jimmy Olsen's hunch is correct. There's something odd happening in "The Haunted Lighthouse" (1951).

The missing uniform is the only one Superman owns. Apparently, by later episodes—"Panic in the Sky," "The Face and the Voice"—he must have found a Kryptonian tailor, because he ends up with a few additional suits.

All that Candy's involvement earns him is a case of mistaken identity. Consequently, the crooks accompany Candy to their hideout, where Ace becomes disconcerted when he finds that Candy packs a revolver. Candy, unaware of the purpose of this detention, answers, "Well, you know a reporter sometimes meets some pretty hard characters." Ace leaves it at that.

When Clark catches the hoodlum's error in judgment, he begins to move as Superman. However, the stolen costume prevents him from doing the traditional off-with-the-glasses routine, and propriety demands that his business suit remain intact. This is one job for Clark Kent! Candy is seated patiently on

Ace's living room couch when Clark Kent unexpectedly crashes through the door and knocks him out.

"That's how it looks on television today," says director Lee Sholem. "If only it had gone that easily in 1951." Ace's apartment door was constructed of balsa wood, temporarily set in place by a series of two-by-fours. The door and frame were brought to the studio from the workshop, then nailed to the existing set pieces. The design allowed Reeves to split the door apart without destroying the frame. Under normal circumstances, the propmen would remove the supports before the actors played the scene. But as Lee Sholem says, "We forgot to take out the extra lumber and I called for the camera to roll. George came running up the stairs right into the frame. The balsa wood barely gave way because George bounced off the heavy wood, and fell to the floor—unconscious." The scene was reshot a few days later. Reeves was noticeably more cautious—the effects, he said *would have to be tested* before he'd try anything new.

Maxwell's episodes seemed to get more macabre as the shooting schedule progressed. "Mystery in Wax" climaxes when Perry White's picture turns up on the front page as another suicide victim prophesied by Madame Selena, a self-proclaimed medium. By the end of the tale, Superman discovers Selena has set aside a special corner of her museum devoted to those presumed to be suicide victims.

"No Holds Barred" lifted a familiar theme from a dozen B films: a crooked syndicate wrestler who pins unsuspecting "nice guy" victims with unorthodox holds. The twist to the story is a paralyzing grip that eliminates the most burly of opponents—that is, until Clark Kent moves into the picture. Kent works out a defense with Wayne Winchester (Malcolm Mealey) to prepare the young wrestler for his bout with Bad Luck Brannigan (Richard Reeves). Meanwhile, Lois begins cuddling up to Winchester, who plays every bit the man Clark Kent isn't—and no doubt the man who can deliver what Superman doesn't. As Kent sends Wayne inside the ropes, Lois goes after Clark with everything she has. She aims at his masculinity, claiming that he wants Winchester to get hurt. Lois figures Clark will find her an easier conquest that way. She's wrong, but her daggers are already sailing through the air. It is her arsenal of sharp, caustic retorts that wound Clark's Interior where hoodlum's bullets fail to penetrate.

"Superman" had its down days. Perhaps the most hushed-up was during the filming of "The Ghost Wolf." Director Lee Sholem remembers only too well. Reeves's previous ascents were shaky at best, but so far they had looked good. He had taken off via a wire-pulley assembly, but the odds finally ran out. "Just as I called cut, the pulley gave, George hit the deck." Reeves was actually more stunned by Bob Maxwell's reaction than the ten-foot fall onto his back. He complained to a newspaper reporter that his producer was callous and unfeeling. "Maxwell didn't ask, 'Are you hurt, George?' All he said was, 'My God—the star!'"

Maxwell's apparent heartlessness toward Reeves's fall gives credence to an argument already discussed. Producers don't want their leading actors to do their own stunts—even if the stars want to do them. One moment of poor timing and the entire production is out of business.

A careful viewing of "The Ghost Wolf" reveals this disaster in the making. Reeves is pulled straight up from his takeoff. He turns slightly to the right when the contraption breaks. Thol Simonson came on the set to handle the special effects, the previous man left.

The first order of business for Simonson was to prove that a fail-safe system was possible. "However, George insisted that before he would try our new counterbalance, I had to get in first, then my helper, and still one other guy to make sure it held. From there I gradually gained his confidence." Simonson threw out the leather belt and wires in favor of a new hydraulic unit. "We thoroughly tested all the flying, rolling, diving, turning and loop-de-loops that George

Jack Larson and two nubile maidens pose for the camera between scenes in "The Tomb of Zaharan" (1956).

could possibly do." Meanwhile, Tommy Carr suggested a springboard to facilitate the actual takeoffs. The new plan was rather straightforward. Reeves ran onto the springboard, vaulted over the camera, then somersaulted safely onto a wrestling mat.

The springboard itself was a novel idea; however, its debut in the production was far from subtle. Tommy Carr painfully remembers the first day it was on the set. He had been doing run-throughs of Reeves's dive out the window. When he set the springboard in place, he decided to demonstrate the fine art of a graceful takeoff himself.

Jack Larson, twenty years after Superman. (Photo by Irene Joyce Grossman.)

I said I have to try it. Well, I didn't know the thing was adjusted for Reeves's weight. He weighed about 195 pounds, and I tipped the scale at 130 soaking wet. So I hit the springboard and went out the window as planned. Outside we put a mat with a big thick pad on it, to land flat on. But, as wasn't planned, I missed the pad, and came down on the top of my head!

Upon his release from the hospital a humble and polite Tommy Carr was visibly more sympathetic to the rigors of Reeves's daily workout.

Reeves generally lacked Kirk Alyn's ballet prowess, but he was able to match his predecessor's "airs above the ground" with the addition of the springboard. Successfully executed, Reeves's takeoffs were spectacular. Yet, on occasion, his legs still drifted downward into camera view. The eyesore was eliminated when Reeves simply ran out of frame. Such a procedure saved time and money.

Tommy Carr was the first to use the springboard when the show returned to production on September 3, with "The Haunted Lighthouse." Reeves opens the episode with an eerie narration about young Olsen's visit to his Aunt Louisa's cabin on Moose Island, off the coast of Maine. Maxwell relies heavily on the more familiar radio images during George Reeves excellent onomatopoeic narration. As he speaks, Jimmy Olsen arrives wearing his horizontally striped polo shirt and white zipper jacket. Olsen notices a contradiction between what his aunt says and the rumors he hears on the mainland. "The lighthouse," says Louisa, "has been dark for years." Olsen insists he's heard reliable stories about the beacon cutting through the fog on certain nights, but his aunt dismisses the report as pure balderdash. However, an odd cry coming from the beach underscores Jimmy's curiosity. "Help, I'm drowning!" pleads the nightmarish voice. It's enough to unnerve Olsen.

At last, Olsen declares himself a reporter. He refuses to accept the story of the haunted lighthouse, and soon learns that Aunt Louisa and her son Chris are impostors. He's knocked out and left to die in a tidal cave.

Superman, realizing the lighthouse is used for smuggling, arrives in the nick of time to save Jimmy from drowning, and helps the Coast Guard apprehend the criminals. Superman then releases the real Aunt Louisa. For all the suspense it causes, the frail unnerving voice turns out to be a harmless parrot. After the Man of Steel leaves to change, the genuine Aunt Louisa asks, "Where's that handsome Superman. Well now, if I were just thirty years younger . . ." Her voice trails off as Kent enters, his hand still straightening his tie. The elderly Aunt fixes her sights on him. In a moment of recollection she begins, "My, but he's handsome too, as a matter of fact, he's . . ." Clark, anticipating the next line, turns away, touches his glasses and begins to maneuver the conversation away from its ultimate conclusion.

"The Haunted Lighthouse" holds an interesting memory for Jack Larson. The script required him to stand inside the tidal cave, while the water slowly rose to drown him.

That would have been fine if it were a one-shot deal, but they made me the resident Johnny Weissmuller, an honor I would have preferred to pass on to someone else. They used to have a lot of scenes with water. I told them I don't mind a couple of stunts, but I'm really not a wet animal. Somebody had this fixation about water. Eventually, I was trapped in all kinds of things while the water slowly rose; on the top of buildings, in water tanks ("Perry White's Scoop"), in a room flooded by a sprinkler system ("The Whistling Bird"), in the subterranean cave ("The Haunted Lighthouse"), in a suitcase ("Three on One"), in a rainstorm ("Test of a Warrior") and in a diving bell ("Superman's Wife"). It seemed that show after show I was wet. It got to the point where I had to say I'll hang from a cliff and let a car drag over me before I let them get me wet again.

" 'The Haunted Lighthouse' was a very elaborate show," continues Larson. "They had some kind of incredible special effects that Si Simonson worked up, but the bars holding me in the cave didn't work when Superman came in to lift them and rescue me. I consequently went home with a terrible cold, and when I just about got rid of it, they'd get me wet on another show. I did them all, but I tried to lay down the law. I told them, I pleaded with them, 'No more fire, no more ice and especially *NO MORE WATER!*' It didn't last."

The years have matured Jack Larson beyond the comic figure he portrays in "Adventures of Superman." Today he lives in a handsome Frank Lloyd Wright house overlooking the Pacific Ocean. He has a new, full life which Larson refuses to mix with the past. The present is Larson's challenge—the typewriter and pad are his tools. The "Superman" cast never knew of his avocation, and few beyond a new circle of friends have followed his successes. People are still looking for Jimmy

Phyllis Coates, on the wrong end of a real knockout punch from Frank Richards. A moment later she was out cold on the floor ("A Night of Terror"—1951).

Phyllis Coates in a 1948 studio publicity still.

Olsen, but he moved out long ago. In his place lives a talented, multifaceted Jack Larson who speaks to the world through creative writing, plays and music.

The man—Larson—is a concerned activist, an early resister of the Vietnam war. The patronizing, demeaning, bumbling boy reporter is gone forever. Larson hung up his bow tie over fifteen years ago. "I was a kind of kid actor; writing, or trying to write all the time. When work was scarce and studios began to shut down, I followed the advice of my manager and moved into television."

Larson's discovery was another Hollywood Cinderella story. Solly Baiano, a talent scout for Warner Brothers, had searched for an actor to fill a semi-comic supporting role for Raoul Walsh's *Fighter Squadron* (1948). Nobody from the Pasadena Playhouse fit the bill, so Baiano pressed on to other theater groups. Larson was directing a college musical he had written when the scout walked in on a dress rehearsal. Baiano stepped forward, "Now I don't want you to get excited, but there may be something in a picture at Warners for you." Larson was called the next day for a screen test, and within minutes after Walsh saw the rushes, Larson had the part.

He quickly moved into other film work: *The Redwood Forest* (1950), *Starlift* (1951), *Kid Monk Baroni* with Leonard Nimoy and *Battle Zone* (1952). He studied under Michael Chekhov; John Barrymore, Jr., and Debbie Reynolds were his classmates. Larson recalls this early period at Warner Brothers with wide-eyed enthusiasm. "I saw each day of filming as a new lesson, everyone was my teacher." It was a perspective he would carry into "Superman." But in 1951 Larson was no different than three thousand other actors who needed work. Things looked tentative at most studios; unemployment a probable future. Larson, within weeks of his "Superman" screen test, had options brewing at Twentieth Century–Fox and M-G-M. However, his manager suggested that he catch his breath in television. "Look, Jack, do them. Nobody will ever see this

'Superman'; you'll get the money, which is more than you'd make at the studio. Take it and don't worry.'' The rest is history.

"And so I did it, and television blew through the roof. Suddenly, not only did everybody see 'Superman,' but I was world famous as Jimmy Olsen. Everywhere I went people recognized me as being on television, one of the popular creatures!'' Larson's success in the new medium was phenomenal, and he was more surprised than anyone else. "I was a big Superman comics fan, and my dad once said, 'It's about time you got paid from Superman—you're just getting your money back.' I must have kept him broke buying all those comic books when I was a kid!''

The instant popularity was difficult for Larson to comprehend. The new public life made it difficult for him to maintain the privacy he so dearly relished. "It was impossible to be alone, I couldn't walk around unnoticed." In less than a year, the onetime editor of the *Montebello High School Oiler* became the world's most famous cub reporter. "I couldn't escape it. And talk about identity, Jimmy Olsen was so shallow I had to bring myself into the role. There's really not much character in 'Jeepers, Mr. Kent!' ''

"All they would give him were those 'Golly,' 'Gee Whiz,' and 'Jeepers' lines,'' adds Phyllis Coates. "Yet Jack had ability, his sight gags were good, and luckily they built more shows around him later.''

Larson reasoned that nobody could be more innocent than Jimmy Olsen. "Jimmy never realized that Clark Kent was Superman. So you start off with that premise. Sometimes it dawned on him that maybe . . . though it hit Lois Lane more often . . . but she doesn't even know who she's in love with. So the main characters are about as dumb as you'll ever get. So were the villains. Apparently, it's not hard for the American audience to accept anything, because 'Superman' remains terribly successful. The program just goes on and on!''

Nonetheless, it was the "Gollies" and "Jeepers"

Phyllis Coates and George O'Hanlon in a scene from a Warner Brothers Joe McDoakes comedy short.

that helped feed Larson during those "Superman" years, and despite the criticisms, he obviously enjoyed his work and associations. "I loved doing it, I learned a lot and worked with marvelous character actors."

Like many of the other people from the show, Larson's memories are blurred. "Superman" began twenty-five years ago, and some of the anecdotes were lost in the sheer fatigue of the shooting schedule. "The Kid," as he was called on the set, traded on his smile

Phyllis Coates and Whit Bissell ponder what they've created in "I Was a Teenage Frankenstein" (American International, 1957).

and pre-pubescent voice to bring life to Jimmy Olsen. "I tried to do the best job. I never sloughed off because I never knew who would be watching. I've met Sir Laurence Olivier and Sir John Gielgud in New York. They saw me on 'Superman' somewhere along the line and said, 'How positively charming; you were so full of life!' On another occasion, Eli Wallach hugged me, then added, 'No one else on television was ever full of more naïve energy and life.' If they think it's good—it's good!''

The Olsen character predominates in more episodes than "The Haunted Lighthouse." This first one only tested his strength, the other episodes amplified it: "The Evil Three" (1951), "The Boy Who Hated Superman" (1953), "Jimmy Olsen, Boy Editor" (1953), "Lady in Black" (1953), "Olsen's Millions" (1954), "King for a Day" (1954), "Jimmy the Kid" (1955) and "Whatever Goes Up" (1956). His character became so popular that National Comics gave serious thought to a Jimmy Olsen series after George Reeves's death.

During down time from "Superman"—usually ten months—Jack Larson was active in Philco, Goodyear, and Alcoa television shows, additionally appearing with Edgar Buchanan in "Country Editors," and "Home, Sweet Homer" with Tom Tully. In between "Superman," and jobs in the Big Apple, Larson channeled his creative efforts into his real love—writing. Today, the playwright uses fiction and verse to attack the same themes that Alvin Toffler dissects with fact and futurism. Larson's preoccupation with the dehumanization of society and a technology out of control works its way into his play *Chuck* (published by Vintage, *Collision Course*, 1968), which has been performed at the Los Angeles Mark Taper Forum, New York College, the Edinburgh Festival, off Broadway and on the Public Broadcasting System.

Larson proudly talks of a libretto he composed for Virgil Thomson, and another play *June/Moon* (published by Delta Books, *New Theatre for Now*, 1971). In his quiet way, Larson applies the same love of work that made his "Superman" days enjoyable, and although audiences have applauded Larson's works at Carnegie Hall, Lincoln Center and the Hollywood Bowl, he still prefers to leave the limelight to others.

Carr's second episode of this group is "Treasure of the Incas." As can be anticipated, Lois and Jimmy are on the heels of a headline when they stumble across a cave tended by desperadoes of the worst kind. Needless to say, Superman frees the intrepid duo after he recovers a communiqué belonging to the Peruvian government.

"The Runaway Robot," third in the series co-starred Lucien Littlefield (1859–1960). Littlefield appeared in over one hundred silent and sound pictures, specializing in playing old men while still young in real life. His films include *Tumbleweeds, The Cat and the Canary, If I Had a Million* and *Ruggles of Red Gap*. He had a walk-on in one of George Reeves's starring films at Fox, *Man at Large*, and was also seen in Noel Neill's Henry Aldrich pictures. However, for Maxwell's "Runaway Robot," Littlefield portrays Horatio Hinkle, an eccentric scientist who soldered a mechanical man that bears no resemblance to the more sophisticated Robby the Robot from *Forbidden Planet*. "Hero" is simply nuts and bolts, a garage invention held together by sheer ingenuity and love. Horatio sets the pattern for dozens of episodes to follow—the naïve innocent who falls prey to unscrupulous heavies.

Shooting for "The Runaway Robot" began August 10, 1951. Next through the mill was "The Case of the Talkative Dummy" co-starring Tristram Coffin and Pierre Watkin.[6] In much the same manner that Alfred Hitchcock fashioned *The Thirty-nine Steps,* this Superman plot relies on a vaudeville act to tie the action together. It seems a ventriloquist's dummy has two mouths, the regular onstage, another off, which tips waiting henchmen to the unpublished routes of armored cars.

[6] The "Adventures of Superman" provided work and new hope to the B actor. Tristram Coffin was one of the first carry-overs to try his hand in television. In "The Talkative Dummy," Coffin portrays Davis, the villain who seals Olsen in the safe. It was the first of many associations Coffin made with the Superman crew, later returning for "Clark Kent, Outlaw" (1954), and "Whatever Goes Up" (1956). Coffin, with his 1940s mustache, had been a regular fixture in Hollywood's low-budget Westerns; then in 1949 he put on a sleek leather jacket and visor-helmet for the Republic serial *King of the Rocket Men.* The studio mothballed the outfit for a few years, subsequently airing it out for *Flying Disc Men from Mars* (1951), *Radar Men from the Moon* (1952) and *Zombies of the Stratosphere* (1952), with a young Leonard Nimoy. Coffin later starred in a short-lived fifties series "26 Men." He also shot a quick public service National Comics production, "Stamp Day for Superman" (1953).

Coffin was joined in "The Talkative Dummy" by Pierre Watkin, familiar to Superman serial fans as Perry White. Watkin also checked in throughout the next few years for a barrage of episodes, playing both good guy, gangster, and in one episode a single-minded gentleman in a fraternity that bows in deference to the legends of King Arthur and the knights of the Round Table.

Interestingly enough the theater set used in this episode also appears in Charlie Chaplin's *Limelight* (1952). "Superman" was shooting amid the old ghosts of the RKO lot that year, and Jack Larson loved it. "The entire lot was full of magic. I marveled at watching Keaton and Chaplin at work. I was a kid, really a kid, and there was Chaplin!" It was a child's dream come true. RKO was a wonderland, a veritable time machine of great adventures and faraway places for someone with imagination. Already a film buff, Larson walked for hours through the remnants of the *Gone with the Wind* set where George Reeves had made his feature film debut twelve years earlier. The railroad station and Tara were silhouetted against the night sky, and Larson and his friends summoned Clark Gable scenes to life. He watched Howard Hawks film interiors for *The Big Sky,* and visited the fascinating backlot. For all his fascination, Larson earned a reputation as a slippery fellow. "It was wonderful to wander and imagine the times, but assistant directors wanted to lock me up within eyeshot. If somebody wanted me, I had to be there."

It seems that every so often one of the main characters ends up trapped in a cave. It happened frequently, and not just coincidentally. Maxwell, and later Ellsworth, easily realized there was no need to waste a "sophisticated" set on one script. As long as it was budgeted, perhaps amortized over the length of the season, the production might as well take advantage of it. Consequently, audiences are treated to various caves in "Rescue," "Treasure of the Incas," "The Deserted Village" and "The Haunted Lighthouse"— all the first year. When Ellsworth took over, the cave showed up in "Test of a Warrior," "Disappearing Lois," "Divide and Conquer," and "The Superman Silver Mine."

"The Deserted Village" serves up a compelling variation, when Lois puts on her investigative reporter's outfit and hops into her Nash with Kent for a trek to Clifton-by-the-Sea. The town mysteriously loses its taxpayers, apparently through a farfetched sea monster scare. Everybody but a druggist, his son, Lois' aunt and a doctor has scurried out of town by the time Lane and Kent roll in. The plot focuses on the remaining residents, who are actually squabbling over a valuable deposit of hydrozite—a rare element used in the hydrogen bomb. The group plots to take over the town, mine the property, then sell the hydrozite to the highest bidder.

Phyllis Coates's blood-curdling scream, Malcolm Mealey's decking Fred Sherman with a shovel, and Maudie Prickett's dead dog lying on the lawn emphasized the widening schism between Robert Maxwell and National Comics. As the grievances grew, it became clear that Maxwell would move on.

The last of Carr's episode, "Rescue," paralleled the initial chapter of Kirk Alyn's 1948 Superman, leaning heavily on a mine disaster story. Moments after Lois arrives on assignment, she becomes a second victim to the coal gas. Superman, of course, burrows through solid rock to bring life-sustaining air to both Lois and a trapped miner (Houseley Stevenson, Sr.).

The budget of "Rescue" allowed Tommy Carr to take Reeves and a camera crew to Iverson's Ranch in the San Fernando Valley. There Carr directed the springboard takeoff that was used repeatedly in 1951 and 1953: Kent runs behind a few New England-type boulders, whips his glasses off, loosens his tie and an instant later reemerges as Superman.[7] The Man of Steel, his arms slightly raised, surveys the terrain, then runs toward the camera, onto the springboard and into the air. The sound of wind and the Superman theme carries his flight to dozens of locations.

Superman's arrival into a scene was another matter. Reeves stood on a ladder awaiting his cue. The direc-

[7] "Rescue" is the first episode in which this particular outside takeoff is used. However, Carr also expanded the stock footage library, landing Reeves near the boulders. The scene was plugged into "Panic in the Sky" and "The Big Squeeze." The crew reshot the scene in 1954 for the color episodes.

tor signaled, and he leaped into camera view creating a realistically dramatic entrance, the deft camera work again protecting the delicate balance between the myth and reality of the superhero. "I preferred to get the camera low for the takeoffs and George's jumps off the ladder," says Carr. "The low angle exaggerated speed and distance, while it helped reinforce illusion of flight." The trick worked perfectly; the suggestion of the superfeats still holds through any viewing of the program in the seventies.

"Drums of Death," "Night of Terror," "The Birthday Letter" and "The Human Bomb" were director Lee Sholem's next episodes set for the camera. Filming began September 17 and continued until September 29. The first, 'Drums of Death," must have reminded George Reeves of his "deepest darkest Africa days" in *Jungle Jim* (1949). "Drums of Death" pounds out thirty minutes of terror for the captives Jimmy Olsen and Perry White's sister (Mabel Albertson). The pair stagger out of their wine press prison to see Superman prove that the voodoo medicine man is actually their white guide under a Kiwi shoe polish disguise.

Actually, the script was par for 1951. Whites were still portraying blacks, and what work there was for the black actor was obvious: train porter, native guide or an aspiring "credit to the race" anonymity. "Superman" was caught in the middle—a white superhero who was supposed to be champion of all. Whitney Ellsworth realized that "Superman" would have to be more. "At least my shows didn't contribute to the stereotype, but it's unfortunate we didn't go further; we could have, but we didn't, and it wasn't only 'Superman.' The thinking permeated the entire industry. It's certainly not to our credit, but at least it was a sin of omission, not one of commission. It was everyone's mistake."

Make-up for the witch doctor was an ordeal, but Jack Larson and the rest of the company knew the pain as well. "In those days they used to pile it on an inch thick," says Larson. "I used to beg the studio supervisors to let me work without it. Finally, I think somebody broke down. Until then, we just walked around with this big red stuff that caked on hard. When that happened they'd have to patch up the cracks. At the end of the day, you can imagine what we all looked like!''

The cameraman and Larson had their words over the amount of make-up actors should wear. However, it was far easier to light a scene with more pancake, and the discussion was ruled academic. The make-up went on, but Larson still complained: ''They used to think I was difficult, yet by the time I got the make-up off, showered, ate and memorized my lines for the next day, I'd say it was one-thirty or two in the morning. Less make-up would have given me more time to sleep, it was as simple as that. I wasn't a quick study as George was, so I never got much rest. Since I couldn't show up without knowing my lines, I at least pleaded for less make-up and more rest. I guess we sort of compromised.''

Lee Sholem put Phyllis Coates through unusual paces for ''A Night of Terror.'' The script never suggested that the actress get into the action as much as she did—Coates was actually knocked cold in one realistic fight scene. In ''A Night of Terror,'' the daring Miss Lane is vacationing along the Canadian border when she falls captive to a pair of mustachioed gunmen. Superman, eventually intervenes on her behalf, unfortunately, not soon enough; not before Coates goes down for longer than the mandatory ten count.

''I sure as hell was knocked out!'' says Coates, rubbing her nose and eyes. ''Frank Richards was only supposed to give me a little shot, but the guy knocked me for a loop!'' She regained consciousness to find out that Sholem wanted to finish the scene before the dazed actress' face had time to swell. ''I was willing. The thing had to go on.''

Phyllis Coates (Gypsie as she prefers) is a woman of many strengths. She brought the same determination to Lois Lane that helped her through family hardships and professional setbacks. Her Lois Lane vilifies Clark Kent and matches him step for step. Phyllis Coates was told to play the equal, not the housewife, which television relegated to Majorie Lord, June Lockhart and dozens of other women in the fifties. Phyllis Coates brought life to her character in the spirit of a 1940s heroine—a definitive individualism. "I was *never* aware of not being liberated," says Coates. "I worked hard for everyone, especially Bob Maxwell. I had to, maybe to prove women could take the load just as much as men."

"And I'll say Phyllis was one damned good actress," adds Robert Shayne. "She was open; a secure woman who knew what she was doing."

The feeling pervaded the entire crew on "Superman." Nearly everyone admired her work.

Phyllis Coates was born on a cattle ranch in Odessa, Texas. In 1943, she picked up stake for Los Angeles, to enter UCLA. Her next move plunged her headlong into the industry as a dancer for Ken Murray's *Blackouts.* She later tapped her way into Earl Carroll's troupe, and in 1946 played *Anything Goes* for a USO tour through Europe.[8] Coates is another member of the "Superman" cast who paid her dues at Warner Brothers. She was the co-star in Richard Bare's Joe McDoakes shorts starring George O'Hanlon. From 1948 until 1954 Coates appeared in almost twenty of the comedies, including two that were released while "Superman" was in production, *So You Want to Buy a Used Car,* and *So You Want to Be a Bachelor.* The one-reelers were the last long-running comedy series out of Hollywood and often saw the likes of Herb Vigran, Richard Reeves, Phil Van Zandt, Joi Lansing and John Doucette—all guest stars at one time or another on "Superman."

Phyllis Coates thinks she has survived more Indian fights than any woman this side of Belle Starr. Maybe

---

[8] Diehard fans can see her hoofing with the Dead End Kids in *Blues Busters* (Monogram, 1950).

so; the pace she describes supports her contention. "We shot back-to-back on the lot, and I had my work cut out just trying to keep the false eyelashes in place and the breast pads from falling off. Since we were so busy, we couldn't always keep up on the scripts. All I asked was whether I'm a mother, or a whore with a heart. I was always just one or the other." In either case, a horse was a new quest for this Texan. Her first encounter was during a chase scene, when in ignorance, she admitted knowing how to ride. Fifteen minutes later, she regretted having made such a confident boast. Unlike Kirk Alyn, she remained on the horse. "I ended up running through the cameras, all the lights, the reflectors—the damn thing wouldn't stop. I yelled 'Whoa horsey . . . nothing!' " From the way she enjoys telling the story, Coates would probably still be riding that horse today if the studio hadn't folded a few years later.

While the pace at Monogram was rigorous, the scripts were trivial at best. Soliloquies were traded for campfire songs with the boys, and tenderness meant getting your thirsty horse to water in time. Coates reminisces about the aesthetic qualities of a Monogram "three-shot": White-hatted hero, fair lady and stud. (The latter refers only to the horse.) It's most noteworthy that the woman of the group stood in the background behind the cowboy, and even farther behind the horse.

Phyllis Coates saw the sunset on dozens of Westerns, including *Marshal of Cedar Creek* (Monogram, 1953) with Robert Shayne and John Hamilton. But her career is not limited to the ten-day extravaganzas on the B lots. She ended the tradition introduced by Pearl White—for this, she will be most endeared to film buffs. Although her serial contributions are limited because of sophomoric scripts, Coates turns in an admirable performance opposite Clayton Moore in *Jungle Drums of Africa* (Republic, 1953) and *Panther Girl of the Kongo* (Republic, 1955). This last serial returned to the infamous Republic swamp that Clyde Beatty first sloshed through in *Darkest Africa* (1936). Coates will never forget the health precautions taken by the assistant directors. "They dragged us out and gave everyone a shot of penicillin! And believe me, that didn't help make the swamp any more popular."

Panther Girl represents Republic's last-ditch effort to keep its head above the swamp. Coates was given the exact duplicate of Frances Gifford's *Jungle Girl* (1941) outfit, a mini-skirt wraparound with bands of leather crossing the top and bottom. The similar wardrobe afforded editors the opportunity to draw from the pool of fourteen-year-old stock footage.

"When Republic Pictures ended production, I moved into spot roles on television": Three Perry Mason whodunits ("The Case of the Black-Eyed Blond," 1958; "The Case of the Cowardly Lion," 1961; and "The Case of the Ice-Cold Hands," 1964), "Desilu Playhouse" ("Trial at Devil's Canyon," 1959), "Rawhide" ("Incident of the Judas Trap," 1959, and "Little Fishes," 1961), and a "Hennessey" in 1959. She also appears in two 1959 "Untouchables" adventures—"A Fist of Five" and one called "Ain't We Got Fun" in which she plays Rene Sullivan, lover and gun moll of gangster Johnny Paycheck. The latter is the only television product in which she takes pride.

After she left "Superman," there was occasional day work on "The Millionaire," "Navy Log," "Four Star Theatre," "Richard Diamond, Private Detective," "Lux" and "Desilu Playhouse," and "Death Valley Days" when the Old Ranger was still young. In the late fifties, Coates moved into television's sixty-second wonders as a Kleenex commercial lady.

Every so often her children see their mother on reruns. " 'Hey, Mom, you're on television,' they tell me. That's the point the set goes off." However, Coates adds seriously, "I did love acting, I still love to see good actors like Tracy and Hepburn, but I don't understand people who think those of us from serials and television couldn't act. They're wrong. Years ago, I was visited backstage by some agents after a performance. One said, 'You can't be the same girl who does all those Westerns and Superman crap. You can act!' 'Of course,' I answered. 'You don't know what it takes to pitch in and do the kind of work we do.' ''

Tommy Carr is one who knows Phyllis Coates and can defend her ability accordingly, ''Phyllis read those lines with great arrogance, she had a strong sense of the bitchy character that was important for Lois Lane's credibility. She was a much better actress than the part or lines ever called for. I used her in Westerns, and I'd tell her something just once and she'd get it. She could have handled most anything.''

''George Reeves always had faith in me,'' says the actress. ''He said, 'One day I'll help you prove that you really can act.' ''

Phyllis Coates was one of ninety-five hopefuls interviewed by Robert Maxwell for the female lead in ''Superman.'' ''I'll never forget that day. My agent called and told me to wear a suit and low-heeled shoes. 'Be at RKO-Pathé at ten-thirty.' '' Forty-eight hours later she signed. ''I took it because I needed the money.''

Coates's hair color went through a change. For *Superman and the Mole Men* she was a blond; later in the series she returned to her original auburn. Jessica Maxwell, the producer's wife, cut her long locks into the kinky ''Lois Lane bundle,'' just short of an Afro. After being fit for the official ''Lois Lane hat'' and the standard issue ''Lois Lane two-piece suit'' she was nearly ready for action. ''I had one other part to the uniform, my long narrow shoes. They made George hysterical. He'd come in early in the morning just to see my big shoes.'' For some reason her footwear was the source of endless ribbing. ''George always kidded me, he'd have Tommy or Lee shoot a close-up of my feet. For some reason that really tickled George.''

The ''Adventures of Superman'' will long establish Phyllis Coates as one of the truly great screamers of our time. Besides her well-rehearsed on-screen arrogance, this Lois Lane has a most shrill yell that is certain to pin the needle on any television station's audio console. Coates says, "My vocal cords needed to be rewarded after the strain of a good scream. Every day at four o'clock George and I reached for a little nip. The production manager used to descend upon us, but we'd say, 'If you want us to finish the day's work then you've got to let us have a few minutes.' It all worked out. We never got so sloshed we couldn't finish, and I was young enough then, my eyes never got red!" Lest the Temperance League march in anger over the actors' habits, drinking was not a preoccupation of the "Superman" crew, only a way for a few to relax after a good day's work. Reeves and Coates always conducted themselves with an air of decorum, yet Coates still adds, "To this day I've never recognized one that we did without being a little tipsy."

Coates also has praise for the rest of the operation. "There was never a better crew or cast to work with— ever in town. That's why criticism of our work, and that of the entire production, really bothers me. Our acting was judged by the comic strip, and if it hadn't been for good actors and a fine production staff—'Superman' would not have made it, we brought life to the character. You have to agree with that."

Although some speak of a Hollywood caste system, the "Superman" crew often broke it. "Today it's not the same," says the first Lois Lane. "On 'Superman,' I carried stuff for grips. George even lugged equipment around. He was the star but he pitched in too.

"He was the star, there was no doubt about it in anyone's mind. I never was concerned with any kind of credit, and that used to drive agents crazy. If I got double-billed, it must have been George's idea. He would have asked Maxwell. He was that type of person. But the funny thing," continues Coates, "I was never as ambitious as I thought I was, or those things, star billing, would have mattered." Even though Coates's career might have been artistically better, her work on "Superman" will last forever. For that reason, she was sorely missed when she left the production before the show resumed shooting in 1953. "I felt badly when I had to leave," remembers Coates. "We had a rhythm, and we kidded each other an awful lot. It was very hard work, but we liked one another. We were really good buddies. If something went wrong, somebody would cover; the three of us protected each other. If somebody didn't like something, the other two would complain. And George, Jack and I—even if it meant we had to hang around late—stood by to feed each other lines off camera. Anywhere else, you would have seen a script girl handle the chore. Many times I'd tell Jack or George to leave early, but they'd say no. George, Jack and I had a tight little unit, and we worked for the best crew in television, the very best."

Phyllis Coates left for an ill-fated television pilot. By then, Whit Ellsworth had assumed the responsibility for the production and offered to double the money, but Coates was already committed to William Asher for "Here Comes Calvin" co-starring Jack Carson and Allen Jenkins.[9] Many of her friends thought that the decision was unwise, but Phyllis Coates shrugs her shoulders and says no. "My mind was closed, I needed to make more, and the new show looked good."

Lee Sholem's "The Birthday Letter" is one of those forgettable episodes which pits an invalid child against a concocted tale of intrigue. Little Cathy Williams[10] (Isa Ashdown) wants a visit from the real Superman, but her world is blitzed with terror when she inadvertently overhears an underworld tipster. John Doucette plays an overweight Superman impostor who tries to coax the message out of the crippled youngster. The plan doesn't work, and when Kent learns her life is in danger, he exclaims, "This looks like a job for Superman." Correcting himself a half second later, Clark declares, "I mean I have to find Superman." And wouldn't you know, he's able to do it.

[9] Broadcast on "General Electric Theatre," February 21, 1954.

[10] Virginia Carroll plays Cathy's mother. Carroll, of course, also portrayed Clark Kent's mother in the Sam Katzman serial *Superman.*

Whitney Ellsworth wrote the next Lee Sholem episode, "The Human Bomb," under the name Richard Fielding. He created a story in which old-time serial star Trevor Bardette plays Bet-a-Million Butler, who wagers $1,000,000 on his ability to keep Superman occupied for the duration of a museum heist. The ruse would have worked had it not been for a novel counter-offensive by Superman. He records a message on a wire recorder and slips in a stand-in, so Butler, on the *Daily Planet* ledge with Lois, will continue to think he's got Superman tied up. Meanwhile the Man of Steel leaves for the museum. Although Jimmy Olsen bungles the double cross, Superman returns with not a second to spare—saving Olsen from falling to his death.

The episode cuts every corner. The action is confined to a few sets, the barest budget and quickest shooting time. "That's why the business calls them 'telephone booth scripts.' It's a practice followed to this day," says Ellsworth. "If your budget is X dollars, and you make two episodes which cost $X + Y$ dollars, somewhere along the line you have to make one for $X - ZY$. 'The Human Bomb' was just one of those $X - ZY$ pictures."

The master sets, offices and stock footage had been amortized over the twenty-six episodes but special effects and unanticipated expenditures had sent the costs skyrocketing faster than a speeding accountant could control. The $400,000 was being eaten up too quickly; consequently, Ellsworth's "telephone boother" was seen as a short-term solution to bring the budget back into line.

Trivially, "The Human Bomb" is one of three episodes from 1951 where viewers catch a glimpse of the gallant secretary who answers Metropolis 6-0500 and puts up with Perry White's unbroken harangues. The character, Miss Bachrach, is never played twice by the same actress. However, "A Night of Terror," "Superman on Earth" and "The Human Bomb" are sufficiently distanced from one another on the rotation that the producers felt secure in their decision.

When Lee Sholem finished "The Human Bomb," Tommy Carr took over Monday, October 1, for the remaining five episodes of 1951. Three of his films slam organized crime: "Czar of the Underworld," "Crime Wave," and "Riddle of the Chinese Jade." The last episode, "Superman on Earth," retraces the mythological origins of the Man of Steel.

First of the series, however, is "The Evil Three," an episode that has been raked over the coals by Whitney Ellsworth and other critics. It appears that Maxwell had turned out another sadistic tale. The program is heavily weighted by the performances of John Hamilton and Jack Larson; Superman only joins the picture to tie up loose ends. For the balance, Perry and Jimmy register in a vacant Louisiana bayou hotel where they have to cut through the accents of Macey Taylor (Rhys Williams) and the Colonel (Jonathan Hale) to understand the danger they're facing. Unable to sour Olsen and White from spending the night, two of the evil three try to frighten them off. Money is their great secret, and the senile old lady Elsa in her wheelchair is the key.[11] The sinister Colonel, who lacks all the charm and grace his Southern position normally entitles one to, tips his own hand to the unknown man from the sky. "You might as well know now," he says, "the man and the boy is dead, and yer goin' to be dead too!" Superman answers the lunge of the Colonel's sword with a swift move of his own, easily disarming his assailant. The Colonel doesn't understand how this circus figure manages to defeat him, indeed his very presence is a departure from reality, but Superman demands attention —and those who don't know who this costumed intruder is, learn quickly. It's during these moments of revelation that Superman's true charismatic ability glistens.

[11] Ellsworth's criticism of the program comes into focus here. Elsa is pushed down the stairs and left for dead. "That," says Ellsworth, "is just the kind of thing I never allowed."

"Czar of the Underworld" tells a two-fisted tale about underworld leader Luigi Dinelli.[12] Clark Kent is sent to California as a technical advisor for the screen adaptation of his investigative reports on Dinelli. Inspector Henderson goes along for the ride. The film exposé is filmed at a make-believe National Studios where Kent and Henderson ultimately discover that Dinelli is trying to sabotage the production. Eventually, Superman captures the hoodlum and ends Dinelli's tyrannical stranglehold over the country.

Screenwriter Eugene Solow and producer Bob Maxwell got into the act. Since the "Superman" adventure follows the making of the film *Czar of the Underworld*, they name their fictional director after their own Tommy Carr. The director's real brother Stephen even played the part.

Maxwell and Luber reduced costs to a minimum for "Crime Wave." A furious montage sweeps across the screen—a ten-minute reedit job from earlier "Superman" action scenes—in which Superman declares war on Metropolis' top racketeers. Intercut with *Daily Planet* headlines are all the leftover takeoffs, arrests and fights that Carr could assemble. In addition, editor Al Joseph spliced in an assortment of police cars, motorcycle chases, sirens and explosions. The sequence ends up looking more like a Republic serial trailer than a television product.

Superman descends upon hard-nosed villains Vince Jordan, Nick Marone and Big Ed Bullock like an avenging angel. The only one left is the mysterious number-one man, whose identity, typically, remains unknown until the end. Undaunted, Superman renews his pledge to the Metropolis Citizens' Action Council to get this Moriarty/Captain Mephisto/Blofeld character who is also plotting to annihilate the Man of Steel.

Mr. Big orders one of his pretty chiquitas to develop a dossier on every aspect of Superman's life. She turns

---

[12] In the original script the episode is titled "Murder on Stage 13," and the chief hoodlum is listed as Luigi Postello.

in some candid pictures of Superman's friends, including a revealing shot of Clark Kent running into an alley and emerging as Superman. "This big sweetheart is Clark Kent," she says. Surprisingly, the revelation goes no further. The gangsters are of such limited intelligence that they fail to realize the obvious. For that reason, Tommy Carr disapproves of the script even today. "That was the one I really did not like doing, because Superman gets caught in the act and nobody picks up on it." Carr wanted a more effective story resolution. Instead, the producers kept the script as it appears, and so we see the gangsters use Kent as their go-between to lure the Man of Steel into a death trap at Dover's Cliff. Superman obviously receives the message from Kent, and arrives as scheduled. He enters a large room, and instead of finding Mr. Big, two iron doors slam shut and a series of electronic rays begins to riddle his body. An evil scientist adjusts his dials, and Superman bounces around in what we presume to be a losing battle against death. He falls to his knees, finally collapsing on the floor as the self-satisfied professor beams, "That's the end of Superman."

Mr. Big triumphantly marvels at the ease of his victory. Superman predictably jumps to his feet and proclaims, "I'm surprised any of you thought that display of fireworks would hurt me, or that I couldn't get out of here anytime I wanted to!" To all who might have forgotten his power, Superman knocks down the door as if it were cardboard. He rounds up the four conspirators and exposes the master criminal as none other than Walter Canby (John Eldredge), the respected leader of the Citizens' Action Council.

Tommy Carr, shooting a new takeoff for "Riddle of the Chinese Jade," realized additional stock footage was necessary. "Let's face it, if we had George just stick his hands in the air all the time like in the first takeoff we had, he might be floating around in the air all the time. We needed something new."

The story finds Superman investigating the robbery

Phyllis Coates. (Photo by Jeffrey Weisel.)

of a half-million-dollar jade figurine from Lu Sung's Curio Shop. Charlie Chan's number-two son, Victor Sen Yung, plays an unwilling bandit.[13]

Tommy Carr finished the first year's work with "Superman on Earth." This episode revives the universal mythology of Superman's origin. The only variation oc-

[13] It is the first appearance of Sen Yung and Reeves together since *Dead Men Tell*.

curs after the Jack Narz opening narration when Clark Kent begins to search for a job. The young man finds it difficult to get past the *Daily Planet* secretary, even harder to reach editor-in-chief Perry White. He subsequently sneaks into the stock room, out onto the ledge and into White's office. As he enters, White is collecting himself after hearing that a man (Dabs Greer) is hanging 1,000 feet above the ground at the mercy of a faulty dirigible guide wire. "If I could," asks Kent, "that is, if that man could be rescued and I get his exclusive story, sir, would you give me a job?"

"Yes, yes," barks White. "Now leave me alone!"

Kent exits, changes into Superman and miraculously catches the man who has slipped off the dirigible tether.[14] Kent returns to the *Daily Planet*, where the incredible tale is repeated for an unbelieving Perry White: "There I was, hanging . . . then I thought I must have flipped my lid from being so scared, because right then this guy in a red and blue costume comes flying through the air and catches me."

Perry White thinks the whole story is ridiculous. "There can't be any such thing as a man who flies through the air."

"Well, I know it," says the man, "but it happened. . . . My brain was whizzing around in my head and the next thing I know—this superguy landed me behind one of the hangars like on a featherbed."

Lois Lane, overhearing this surreal explanation, immediately questions the suspicious Mr. Kent. "How did you leave here later than we did, and beat us to the airport? How come you found the man behind the hangar at just the right moment to get his exclusive story when every top experienced reporter in the business was breaking his neck?"

"Or her neck," chimes in Kent.

"Or her neck to get that story," affirms Lois with a determined sneer.

Clark needs no time to ponder his answer. He shoots

[14] A dummy was used in the rescue mock-up.

back, "Maybe I'm a Superman."

Filming ended for 1951 on Saturday, October 13.

According to the closing credits, "Superman on Earth" was written by Richard Fielding, but Fielding did not exist. This was simply a house name (Jessica Maxwell's maiden name) that Robert Maxwell tagged onto work written by himself and Whitney Ellsworth.

Through production on the last episodes, Carr assumed the responsibility of clean-up work. Some of the episodes had come in short; not enough script, and not enough footage. Maxwell worked with Carr typing out a half-dozen scenes to expand the programs. Carr sighs happily, "We always had four actors who never left the set, so when we came in short, we wrote something for them. Some were short conversations between Clark and Perry White, others were telephone calls or sight gags by Jack Larson. The trick was that I always gave myself more than just my actor walking through the door. I followed him in, through the room, and took him to the desk. I never knew if I'd need it, so I shot it for protection. The same with an exit." When the show was ready for Kellogg's, it timed out to 2,376 feet and eight frames of 35mm film; that's twenty-six minutes and forty seconds of program. "If it still looked short, the editor could always fly George a little bit longer," says Carr. "And I think there's one show somewhere when he flew for a good thirty or forty seconds."

The 1951 programs originally had thirty seconds taken out of the story to accommodate a weekly preview. Although many television programs have such previews today, "Superman's" looked more like old-time serial trailers. Thereafter, Whitney Ellsworth agreed to drop the preview. Even if he hadn't, Ellsworth most assuredly would have rewritten the voice-over, for the 1951 words of the deep-throated announcer would not have applied:

Don't miss the next thrill-packed episode in the amazing "Adventures of Superman." Join with the Man of Steel as he wages war against the forces of evil—

thrilling adventure and tense excitement—pounding action and spine-tingling mystery. You'll find them all in the next startling episode of the "Adventures of Superman" so don't miss it—there's action, adventure, and mystery—in the "Adventures of Superman"!

The opening, as conceived by Bob Maxwell, showed comets crashing together in space, a quick dissolve to Superman, a superimposed image of a gun firing, then a locomotive, tall building and the crowd looking up. However, Maxwell's final version reflects Tommy Carr's suggestions. Carr thought that the gun, train and crowd should not be superimposed; rather there should be straight cuts on each, followed by a dissolve to Superman, then to Kent. The opening was edited and attached onto the twenty-six programs ready for broadcast.

The Superman portrayal in the 1951 programs is a violent hero, quick with his tongue and heavy on the force. Maxwell saw George Reeves in "The Unknown People," "Double Trouble" and a dozen other episodes as a powerful crime buster, short on patience when it comes to the underworld. Maxwell's characters are brash figures drawn from the forties. According to Jack Larson, ". . . because Bob Maxwell and his wife Jessica had done 'Superman' on radio, he created the television show with a tough kind of dialogue and heavily characterized gangsters. Whit, on the other hand, had come out of the comic book industry exactly when comic books had been under fire for violence and sadism. At National, he had been partly responsible for the disappearance of hard-edged drawings and sexuality, and the introduction of a different kind of comic hero. The emphasis was on 'comic' and 'comic villains,' and when Whit took over for Maxwell he leaned heavily in that direction."

Even though National prided themselves as being the *best* of the good publishers, Maxwell developed the tough characters with whom he was familiar. When Maxwell departed, his plots went with him. Ellsworth

John Greer (James Craven) learns that a gun won't stop the Man of Steel, as Lois (Phyllis Coates) Lane watches, in this scene from "Riddle of the Chinese Jade" (1951).

wouldn't permit his heavies to take away a crippled girl's braces ("The Birthday Letter"). And instead of Maxwell's references to postwar Germany, the Ellsworth spies report to fictional countries ("King for a Day," 1954, "Peril in Paris," 1956). Above all, there is certainly no further mention of suicide as in "Mystery in Wax"; Madame Selena and all her cronies left with the Maxwells, the show changed and most of the cast felt it was for the better.

Through all this criticism, Maxwell and Luber must be credited with a great achievement. Television was an infant medium; struggling, uncertain, totally unpredictable. Out of this, they developed the one program that is probably responsible for more families trudging back from the appliance store with a cherished television set. Can you blame anyone? We wanted to see what our childhood hero looked like—and most of us couldn't have been happier. George Reeves was tough and believable. Phyllis Coates was Lois Lane, and "Adventures of Superman" happened to be the slickest thing on the air. Bob Maxwell and Bernard Luber had done something magnificent, something they never thought would last. "Adventures of Superman" became television's longest-running success.

CHAPTER VI

1953

1953 was a year of high drama, situation comedies, endless quiz shows and the "Adventures of Superman." More children watched "Superman" that year than any other series. For some reason the "Adventures of Superman" hasn't stopped pulling them in since those first twenty-six episodes reached through the air to capture the imagination of the enraptured audience.

Bob Maxwell, who ulcerated an already acid Perry White and had invented Jimmy Olsen for radio, was out. "His casting of both Perry and Jimmy was perfect," says Maxwell-Luber successor Whitney Ellsworth. "Without wishing to take anything away from Kirk Alyn, I'd have to say that his choice of George Reeves for the Superman role was an excellent one too." However, the complexities of Maxwell's nature soured many of the associations he maintained in 1951. He was a superior business magnate, but in the words of one actor, "He was appreciated better from a distance."

When Maxwell left the "Superman" production he surely did not starve. He demonstrated his ability to produce a winner with the 1955 "Lassie," starring George Cleveland, Jan Clayton and Tommy Rettig. Before his death, Maxwell unsuccessfully tried for a TV adaptation of *Father of the Bride,* but his major contribution remains locked in those twenty-six films bearing the Superman logo.

Whitney Ellsworth assumed control in 1953. National Comics had sent him West to represent the company on their earlier Superman ventures, the late Batman serials and his own creation—*Congo Bill* (Republic, 1949). Ellsworth was no stranger to the Coast on this new trip. He had lived in California in 1937, writing for pulp magazines and dime novels. When that market evaporated, he returned East with his beautiful bride, Jane Dewey, a onetime 1930s Paramount ingenue.[1] Jack Liebowitz, who eventually commanded the National empire from atop, hired Ellsworth as his editorial director in January 1940. For four years, Ellsworth approved scripts, initiated new ideas, doing in fact "everything but mop the floor." Ellsworth remembers the days of Liebowitz and Harry Donenfeld and the esprit de corps that once existed at National Comics. It's that feeling he wanted to bring to Hollywood.

"I was with the company at the time the Superman cartoons were made. That was a long way back. Max Fleischer's studios were in Miami, and I purchased a few rail tickets South to keep tabs on the production." But the cartoons were too expensive for the theatrical market, and Ellsworth returned to New York. "Paramount studios took a considerable financial bath on the deal, and we abrogated the contract by mutual consent long before the full projected number of cartoons had been made."

The Brooklyn writer was a natural for producing Superman. He knew the product, and was the right man to mediate contract terms.

Today, Whit Ellsworth, surrounded by paintings of winter farm scenes, talks over a desk cluttered with his tools: a thesaurus, a dictionary and a collection of reference books. Ellsworth's library also reveals a myriad of interests: books on Lincoln, the Civil War, the twenties, and a score of hardbound plays. History's tug on Ellsworth even took him through an ill-fated American culture television series. "It should have taken off," says "Superman" special effects director Si Simonson. "They were Wolper-like docu-entertainment productions, but nobody picked them up."

It's the New England paintings that represent Ellsworth's true allegiance, despite his Southern California mailing address. He mixes his comics with politics,

[1] She appeared in *Wells Fargo*, *Rulers of the Seas* and *If I Were King*.

and American history with humor; just the combinations evident in his television creations.

Ellsworth visualized "Superman" as entertainment; he kept his word. After twenty-eight minutes face to face with the Man of Steel, the Ellsworth villains had regard for the law.

If he thought he was chief cook and bottle washer in New York, then he was a miracle worker in California. The producer began to move around like a visiting Romanian dance troupe on the "Ed Sullivan Show." He acted as story editor, associate and executive producer, legal advisor, company liaison and father confessor. Ellsworth observes that the industry had so changed by the time he consulted for "Batman" (1965–66) that four or more people were doing the identical work he had personally done ten years earlier. "The new people even got more money," says Ellsworth. "But that's a familiar story in any house."

He sought to tranquilize the violence on "Superman." "I honestly tried not to violate the tenets of good taste. For example, in all the shows that I made there was only one murder, and that was off screen ["The Defeat of Superman," 1953]. I just didn't want to do the show Maxwell had produced. In one of Bob's earlier shows, he showed an old lady in a wheelchair being pushed down a flight of stairs. That was not my sort of thing."

Kellogg's liked the Ellsworth approach. When he ruled that blood and guts would be taboo, his tough guys became humorous bumblers. "Most of the time, rather than Superman beating up those guys, we'd shoot them running into each other or cracking their heads on the wall. But the really fine thing about my relationship with Kellogg's is that they *never* told me how to run the show." If they had, Whit Ellsworth would have politely handed the show over to a third producer. Such was not the case. "Superman" belonged to Whit Ellsworth, and with few exceptions, he ran it the way he saw fit. "I think the kids liked the changes —you know the mug or dog heavy that Welden or

Producer Whitney Ellsworth talking with George Reeves.

Vigran played? We made them comic so we wouldn't frighten our audience. I thought we should have science fiction stories, a time machine story, some straight cops and robbers, and a few human interest scripts thrown in for good measure. And believe it or not—those human interest ones came off particularly well.''

The new producer spent a good deal of time on the set, policing the books. ''We were a low-budget operation. It was my job to keep the 'Adventures of Superman' in the black.''

In retrospect, Ellsworth thinks he would have been wise to retain Bernard Luber to help balance the books. ''Luber wanted to co-produce with me when I took over from Maxwell, but in my conceit I felt no hesitation about going it alone. That was one mistake I made.''

Even though Ellsworth was new, the crew followed his orders as if he had been there for years. ''I respected Bob Maxwell, but it was Whitney who we all really liked,'' answers Robert Shayne. ''Whitney's little touches helped us all rally around him. There were cast parties, and generally feelings of goodwill from Whit. One sweltering summer afternoon, he even ordered up a keg of ice to cool the baking studios."

Ellsworth never fully measured his impact on the comic book world until his adolescent audience grew up. The Ellsworth name is known to anyone who stayed with "Superman" through the closing credits, but he never expected that a forty-year-old writer from the "Batman" television show would remember the producer from the old days of the Ellsworth *Batman* newspaper strips. "That's when the years came crashing down on me. And now, one thing I know for sure about sixty-five—you get there a hell of a lot sooner than you expect!"

Work was made much easier by Ellsworth's decision to invite back Tommy Carr, who by 1953 was well groomed in the affairs of the "Superman" production. "Whitney learned fast," remembers Carr. "That second year the actors knew their jobs, so it was merely a question of adjusting what the actor, by experience, could do given the camera limitations. I must say, Whitney had it no better than Maxwell when it came to getting more money in the budget, but at least he listened and tried. So I had to be just as particular with film costs. Overshooting on one episode might jeopardize another. On television, it's always that way, get it— forget it. We even saved by having that standard wardrobe for our actors. 'The family' wore the same outfits all the time so that we could shoot more than one day at a time and easily intercut stock footage. It was another carry-over from the serials and program pictures we made in the thirties and forties." Every year George Reeves wore his double-breasted grays,[2] Jack Larson had the bow tie and sweater, while Noel put on her two-piece suit and hat.

---

[2] It's been reported that Reeves eventually wore his Clark Kent suit for his own funeral.

George Blair alternated directing assignments with Tommy Carr, when Ellsworth moved the production from RKO-Pathé to the less expensive California Studios on Santa Monica Boulevard. "We moved to get the best deal," says Carr. "The best deal could be easily translated into a good scene dock and perhaps a few acres of ranch property for the least amount of money."

"Another way we saved was by using Clark's office for Lois' too," explains the producer. Instead of resetting across the studio, Tommy Carr, George Blair or any of the subsequent directors only needed to shuffle a few incidentals on the set at hand, put a new name-plate in place, change a wall hanging and vary an angle, to create the illusion of another location.

"Whit always ironed things out immediately, that was the beauty of the man," says special effects super-

(left to right) George Blair, director; Hal Stine, director of photography; Whitney Ellsworth, producer; and Thomas Carr, director. August, 1973.

visor Thol (Si) Simonson. "If he had a problem, he'd share it. When he had any credit, he'd share that too. He's a guy who deserved the best but hasn't quite made it, and I could never understand why. Probably because he wasn't a conniver."

Simonson is right on target. Even Ellsworth admits that he has never been "temperamentally suited to the rat race of writing for television. They say my stuff isn't commercial enough these days. Commercial! That's a euphemism for not being sufficiently violent or dirty." Ellsworth tells his wife, "I'm, by all odds, the most talented unproduced screenwriter in the business." Thol Simonson and many others who know Ellsworth's work don't joke about it that way. They know it's true.

There was still six days of work each week in 1953. "It didn't take us long to get used to the salt mines of Siberia again," accords Jack Larson. George Reeves, who had not put on a Superman suit in the two years he free-lanced in *Bugles in the Afternoon, Rancho Notorious, The Blue Gardenia* and *From Here to Eternity*, struck an immediate rapport with Ellsworth.

"Reeves knew what he was doing," says Ellsworth. "When we were shooting, George turned in the same fine work week after week. By the second year, Tommy Carr and George Blair didn't have to direct him in the part unless a particular sequence was different. What I'd have to worry about were the guest actors, basically because the others were playing the same character."

Ellsworth worked to improve the flying stock. Acting on the producer's directive, Reeves was fitted for another torso-thigh brace. This time, however, he was suspended by a counterbalance in front of a nonreflective white curtain. The special effects department positioned a high-strength steel pipe in the center of the curtain. On one end was a universal joint; on the other, Reeves, equipped with a plastic frame. A wind machine clicked on in front of him, and when the camera rolled, the crew maneuvered the counterbalance behind the cyc to raise or lower the actor. Dolly tracks were laid for the camera, and the finished effect gave the impression of a real Superman flying—nosing up, diving and rolling to the right and left. The finished work was graceful, largely because Ellsworth and Simonson agreed upon a compressed-air cushion to eliminate any jerky moves. Reeves's body was always between the camera and the apparatus, so no matter how closely the trained eye searches today, no one can see the Rube Goldberg device. For the finishing touch, the familiar landscape of Metropolis or rural America was matted onto the flying stock. "It worked, the blessed thing worked," beams Ellsworth today.

The program was ready for production with one exception. This last bit of business concerned a former nightclub singer named Noel Neill.

"I would have continued with Phyllis Coates," indicates Ellsworth, "but during the layoff, Coates had been optioned to that other series, so I returned to Noel, who did as fine a job for us as she did for Sam Katzman's serials." The Lois Lane role was a conceptual matter. Phyllis Coates fulfilled Maxwell's idea of the reporter. She was a capable actress who played the part of a *very* "hep" female reporter. "The part as written for Noel was that of a *fairly* 'hep' female reporter, more vulnerable than Phyllis' Lois." As Ellsworth suggests, it is impossible, "if not positively erroneous to compare their performances. They were two different individuals portraying two very different characters. I think that the Noel Neill Lois was closer to the Lois of the comics, but that is not to say Phyllis Coates's characterization could not have accommodated itself to the new scripts just as competently. I liked them both." So did the audience. Phyllis Coates is hot on the motion picture stills collectors' market in New York, but Noel Neill is big box office on the college circuit.

Curiously, Miss Neill was born into a newspaper family. Her father, David Neill, was news editor of the *Minneapolis Star*. Coincidentally, Noel pecked out an earning on the typewriter reporting for *Women's Wear Daily*. In reality, she is not the clinging vine pictured in her seventy-eight "Superman" episodes. Actually, Noel Neill is a hardened veteran of dozens of serials and features from the forties. Neill first caught wind of the "Superman" television production well into the first season. She must have felt somewhat slighted, since she had established the Lois Lane role in films, yet "Superman" could wait. Noel Neill had the entire West to win at Monogram: *Abiline Train, Whistling Hills* and *Montana Incident*.[3] When Ellsworth telephoned her in the late spring of 1953, she listened attentively to his offer. Phyllis Coates was penciled in for the next batch, but it looked as if she was going to miss the deadline. Noel Neill, the original Lois Lane, was willing to return and no screen test was necessary.

Prior to Superman's television years, Noel had pioneered California video at a station on the Paramount lot. She hosted live shows in the late forties, singing at the top of her lungs to the few hundred receivers scattered throughout the city. "It was so new that people on the lot didn't even know we had our own television studio. I sang, emceed, and did acts on any of the sets where the hulking cameras could be placed."

Neill bypassed the traditional route of struggling thespians. "I tried out for high school plays, and flopped each audition! I thought for certain I'd never act." But California offered her another chance. For two years she hit high notes for Bing Crosby at the Del Mar Turf Club. After two seasons of competition from clanging dishes and couples asking for their checks over her verses, she escaped into the world of Henry Aldrich B pictures. The 5' 2" redhead ran around town in a frenzy. Between Aldrich films at Paramount (*Henry and Dizzy*) and the Katzman work at Columbia and Monogram, she did well by herself. Her best years were those at Paramount, where she appeared in Bing Crosby's *Here Come the Waves* (1944), along with the Aldrich pictures and her television work. One of her

[3] Retitled *Gun Smoke Range*.

George Reeves with his television leading ladies, Phyllis Coates and Noel Neill.

most visible roles outside the Paramount lot was in *An American in Paris* (1951) at M-G-M. "People still come up and ask me about that picture," says Noel.

She also wore through Western Levi's in thirty serial chapters of the late forties (*Adventures of Frank and Jesse James*, Republic, 1948, with Clayton Moore; and *James Brothers of Missouri*, Republic, 1949, co-starring Keith Richards). She darted in and out of *Brick Bradford* and the two Katzman Superman serials. Neill also braved Roland Winter's desperate attempt to make Charlie Chan believable in the last film of the epic series—which film critic Leonard Maltin calls "unbearable"—*Sky Dragon* (Monogram, 1949).

The Katzman "Teenagers" series for Monogram was something else. Noel, on loan-out from Paramount, was a regular in the Freddie Stewart, June Preisser, Warren Mills ensemble that gathered for *Campus*

Sleuth, High School Hero, Freddie Steps Out, Junior Prom, Vacation Days, Sarge Goes to College and *Smart Politics*. These musical-drama-comedy films were a step below Katzman's Bowery Boys pictures, yet they sported a regular following. Early fans of Noel Neill might remember this release from their hometown newspaper:

Teen-ager Noel Neill is one of Hollywood's leading sweater girls, not only because she looks well in them, but also because she has to make them. Noel was busy knitting between scenes during the filming of Monogram's Teenagers mystery film, *Campus Sleuth*.

Monogram didn't release Noel after the "Teenagers" films. She was also featured in *Gun Runner* (1949), *Forgotten Woman* (1949)[4] and *Music Man* (1948). Columbia borrowed her for its high-society *Glamour Girl* (1948), before she rolled over to Universal-International for *Are You with It?* (1948). It was back to the badlands for United Artists' *The Lawless Rider* (1954) and one RKO Leon Errol short *The Cactus Cut Up* (1949). However, of all her roles—well over one hundred—Noel Neill has never been more widely known, more widely loved, or more widely talked about than as Lois Lane.

"Superman" has its own story. "It all started when my agent said that he had a job for me in this serial. I was Lois Lane, but of course in those days there used to be so much work around we could do Westerns or almost anything else. It was the Good Old Days. I had to ask, 'What is Superman?' " remembers Noel Neill. "I had never read the comics, so I saw it just like Brick Bradford or Jesse James; something for the Saturday afternoon kids—for me, a month's work." By 1957, she was singing a different tune. "We made a few bucks, but we had the world's worst union. After playing Lois Lane off and on for nearly ten years the most I think I ever pulled in was $225 per episode.

[4] With Robert Shayne.

The only thing we walked away with after that were the fond memories of our relationships; that's why it's just kind of fun to see everyone on the reruns. But back then, we were doing two a week, thirteen a year, from 1954 to the end, and it was impossible for me to bank more than a few thousand dollars." The residuals, based on the *union* minimum, added a meager $35 on the first and second rerun, $45 on the third, fourth and fifth, and $35 for the remaining two runs. "People still think we're getting money. No way! The company hasn't had to pay us [the actors] for years. I don't think National [Comics] had any comprehension of a livable wage. Maybe they never expected to make so much, but still, when other actors were making two thousand dollars a week, Jack and I were still working for two hundred!"

Noel remembers little that kept the cast laughing.

Noel Neill (1) founders in the Henry Aldrich picture, "Henry and Dizzy" (Paramount, 1941). with Charles Smith, Sidney Coates, and Jimmy Lydon.

"Nothing was really funny working six days a week in 1953, even with the overtime. It was just hard work. We worked so fast that there was no time for prolonged humor."

Yet Noel Neill still managed to win the affection of the cast and crew. Although Robert Shayne worked closer with Reeves, he remembers, "Noel had a cutesy way that would make everyone like her. I never found Noel to be unprepared or without her breezy quality in the few scenes we had together."

"It must have been that outfit of mine Bob remember," jokes Noel. She adds, "Bob and I worked well together, but he knew me like the audience—only through that two-piece suit—you know, Lois Lane."

Today, Noel Neill takes on a constant barrage of questions from adoring college audiences. For someone who hasn't acted since the last roll of film was pulled out of the camera when "Superman" folded, Noel has certainly proved herself capable of handling any audience. In fact, she emotes charm beyond anything she created in all her films.

Wherever she speaks, she is greeted by thunderous applause and standing ovations—durable proof of her fans' affection. Some believe much of the cheer is intended for George Reeves, perhaps a thank-you for fond times in front of the television. But in the past two years more people have learned about their favorite childhood idols—Lois Lane and Superman—from the best source possible—Noel Neill. Thousands of fans see an exceptionally dynamic lady who has loved pleasing her audiences at colleges like Genesco State, Tufts, Upsala, George Washington, Emerson and Holy Cross.

Noel Neill surrounded by students of the State University of New York at Fredonia. (Photo: "Fredonia Statement," December, 1974.)

Noel shows a "Superman" episode on her tour, then address the crowd with some extemporaneous opening remarks. From there she takes the third degree from the pressing gallery:

Q. ARE YOU WRITING FOR ANY PAPERS NOW?
A. Nobody will hire me, darnit, I flunked shorthand.

Q. DID YOU EVER CALL MR. KENT CLARK?
A. If I did, we would have reshot the scene!

Q. WAS THE RELATIONSHIP COMPLETELY PLA-TONIC BETWEEN CLARK AND LOIS?
A. I'll never tell!

Q. IS THERE A REEL OF SUPERMAN BLOOPERS?
A. I hope not!

Q. WHY COULDN'T YOU GET BACK THROUGH THE TIME BARRIER IN THAT ONE EPISODE?
A. Time barrier? I went through it about thirty years ago and I've been trying to get back ever since.

Noel faces more serious questions too; inquiries on pay scales, early television techniques and the life and death of George Reeves. She speaks to an audience that has never known a time without Lois Lane on television, an audience that considers Noel a lasting friend. "I guess the whole 'Superman' thing is popular again because we represented something better than Watergate, some higher ideals for the kids. When the real world broke down, those childhood ideals were still there."

The first script conferences were held in May 1953. The six-day-week shooting grind began in early June with "Five Minutes to Doom." The schedule concluded on September 30 after the completion of "Around the World." Whitney Ellsworth decided to shoot five episodes every three weeks, replacing the whirlwind four every two weeks. It was a welcomed change.

Dabbs Greer,[5] who had appeared in "Superman on Earth," found his second paying job with the company. On his new assignment, "Five Minutes to Doom," Greer plays a convict destined for the electric chair until Superman crashes through the prison wall with a last-minute pardon from the governor.

Tommy Carr enjoyed filming "Five Minutes to Doom." While the convict, Winters (Greer), tests his "Queen for a Day" story on Clark Kent, the reporter places his hand on Winters'. The close-up of the hand-clasp is the most physical, human moment Reeves was ever asked to communicate. "Five Minutes to Doom" is the lone suggestion that Superman is not a soulless automaton. The hand-holding routine is merely a super lie-detector grip. "I know you were telling the truth," says the reporter. "I was taking his pulse all during his story and it was firm and steady," he later explains to Lois.

Lois complains, "Don't tell me you were a human lie detector!"

"Not exactly," answers Kent, as he moves to straighten his glasses.

The "Adventures of Superman," as typified in this episode, had special effects that no other producer duplicated until the "Six Million Dollar Man." "For one, there were those damn walls," say Si Simonson. "The idea was to get George through the wall fast enough so none of the dirt or dust would get on him. That was the trickiest part of the whole thing. Nothing could ever happen to Superman. When he busted through a wall, we had to get him out the other side without any dirt. That's how it looked on paper, but one day it didn't go so easily."

---

[5] Greer can also be seen as the mindless gas station attendant in *Invasion of the Body Snatchers*, and assorted bit parts in *The Vampire* (1957), *Baby Face Nelson, It! The Terror from Beyond Space* (1958) and *Shenandoah* (1965). He makes one additional appearance on "Superman" in 1957 when he tackles a dual role in "The Superman Silver Mine."

Whit Ellsworth begins the story that almost everyone was so anxious to repeat. "Our adobe brick stuff normally crumbled easily. It was used all the time in pictures. The assignment for Simonson was quite straightforward. Week after week he had to design a wall that would realistically flake apart when Reeves hit it. Timing was crucial. Reeves would have to submit himself to the seemingly harmless ordeal within hours after the wall was constructed. Unfortunately, that one day we goofed!" The trouble was simple. "We didn't get to shoot the wall scene in the evening, and it hardened overnight!"

Jack Larson picks up the story: "I was on the other side of the wall. George came slamming toward it as always, because even when they're soft he had to apply force to get through realistically. And since it wasn't all that easy to make it look good, he really went at the thing full force. This time—he didn't get through. Crash! George only got halfway, and I was still tied to a chair on the other side with this fake dynamite about to explode!"

"George got one hand and a foot through," adds Noel Neill. "It was blessed! There was dead silence, nobody yelled cut, there was just the whir of the camera. George stayed like that for a few seconds, he stepped back, pulled out his hand and foot, dusted himself off, then said, 'Good day, see you all tomorrow!' "

"George loved those goddamned walls!" adds Tommy Carr. "The wall didn't give way as it should have. The damn thing really knocked him for a stupor."

The man who built the wall, Si Simonson, says good-naturedly, "They were one-shot deals, there was no way to experiment, no way to 'feel' your way through. We made them as flimsy as possible; it was up to George to make it look difficult. He had to go into it with a lot of force, yet stop on the other side and stay in focus as though there was nothing to it. If he hit it too hard, he'd be clean through the room out the other side before he could stop. I suppose he didn't

Professor Roberts (Jonathan Hale) watches the meteor and says, "Look, it's falling now!" ("Panic in the Sky"—1953.)

have that problem this time around."

Nonetheless, Jack Larson thinks Reeves carried it off very well. "It wasn't easy being Superman, crashing or trying to crash through walls, then standing around in tights and a red cape. It wasn't the easiest thing to do at all, but George did it. He came back and took wall after wall in stride."

Carr looks at it from a more technical viewpoint: "We couldn't have a stumbling Superman. So anytime I did a shot where he would be breaking through a wall, I would use two angles, two cameras rolling for one scene. It was a lot cheaper than trying to take the wall out and put another one in. Invariably, if he'd hit the thing wrong, he'd land on the debris. Ninety-nine times out of a hundred, it was impossible to get footing on all the rocks and broken set pieces, so I always protected George with one shot holding the floor and everything else as he came through, and another angle cutting out the floor. Then, if George didn't land right on the floor, I could give Harry Gerstad the tighter angle to edit in, just missing his stumble. It was a simple matter of matching the action and cutting out the unsure footing."

George Reeves, more mindful of splinters and other worldly hazards, repeated the wall trick through the next four years of production.

A few years before Hugh Beaumont fathered the "Leave It to Beaver" family, he was busy clearing his criminal record in a "Superman" episode, "The Big Squeeze." Beaumont had previously appeared in a number of 1940 Michael Shayne films, and several other minor features. He plays Dan Grayson, all-American family man who is living down a police record, for his lone "Superman" appearance. Grayson has turned over a new leaf for his wife (Aline Towne) and son Tim (Bradley Mora), at least until Luke Maynard (John Kellogg) threatens blackmail. The script proves to be another interesting variation on the often repetitive "Superman" plots.

The 1953 episodes, with few exceptions, were originally broadcast in the order that they were filmed. So the third episode the audience saw was "The Man Who Could Read Minds," a harmless story about Swami Amada (Larry Dobkin). Lois and Jimmy are commissioned to follow up a clue regarding the identity of a phantom burglar, but before long they're in the clutches of Monk (Richard Karlan) and Lora (Veola Vonn).

Lane Bradford turned in his black cowboy hat for a pilot's helmet in "Jet Ace." It was quite a change for the veritable hangman of late B Westerns. Chris White (Bradford) is a convalescing test pilot who is set upon by nefarious foreign agents. Unfortunately, neither White's airplane nor the script takes off from there. The episode lacks any spark, and Bradford looks terribly uncomfortable without his horse. Even Tommy Carr feels that it doesn't compare favorably to his next

Clark Kent, a victim of amnesia, wonders whether the costume will provide the powers he needs to destroy the meteor in "Panic in the Sky" (1953).

episode—the exciting "Panic in the Sky."

In all the 104 episodes, Superman never stares his maker more squarely in the eyes than in "Panic in the Sky." After partially destroying a Kryptonite-laden meteor, bound on a collision course for Metropolis, Superman returns to Earth, stunned beyond description—the victim of amnesia. Superman has no idea who he is!

He changes his clothes behind a boulder, then rifles through his strange pockets and discovers he is a reporter of some merit, who lives alone in a modest Standish Arms apartment. When he reaches the unfamiliar home he is greeted by Jimmy Olsen. He allows the youngster to stay, but begs permission to undress and rest. Since he has nothing to hide, Kent disrobes, the Superman insignia flashing through the open shirt. Luckily, Olsen is behind him, and it is only by coincidence that Jimmy doesn't immediately learn the secret he has wanted to know for years.

In the next scene, Kent collapses in the shower when his superlegs weaken under the strain of Kryptonite. Jimmy helps him out, later telling Perry White, "He must weigh a ton." Despite the broken glass, there isn't a bruise or cut on Kent's magnificent hulk. White and Olsen scratch their heads; they can't get over how Kent fell through the shower stall without spilling a drop of blood. It brings Olsen to comment, "He must be the luckiest guy who ever lived." Again, they refuse to consider the obvious.

Kent is reintroduced to the trappings of his *Daily Planet* cubicle and a pretty Lois Lane. Unaware of who she is, he returns the pretty gal's stare with a wink of his own. Meanwhile, Perry White growls that Kent picked a helluva time to lose his memory: "The world may not have another day." He orders Kent to get on the horn to Superman. Clark naïvely answers, "Okay, Mr. White, how about putting an ad in the paper, or I'll check downstairs through all the files and see if I can get a lead on him!" In "Panic in the Sky," Superman faces his toughest assignment and no one, not even Superman himself, knows where he is.

Tommy Carr toys with the audience for the entire half hour. We who have the answer are incapable of helping the foundering hero. Clark has to solve this puzzle alone. He returns to his bay window apartment and bounces an uncertain idea off Olsen. For some reason, he must have needed a secret closet. Maybe it has something to do with the flashy uniforms. He wonders whether the Superman costume makes the man; whether the outfit gives the wearer certain powers. "No," says Jimmy. "It's not the suit, Superman once explained it to me."

Superman about to hit the spring board in "Panic in the Sky" (1953).

. . . soaring . . .

Superman soaring toward the deadly meteor ("Panic in the Sky").

The drama moves toward the inevitable climax without Clark putting the pieces together. He tries on the uniform, appearing incredibly vulnerable with his glasses still snug to his ears, glances into the mirror and after an eternal moment of frustration, slams his hand on the table. It splinters! There's no question anymore. Either the uniform gives him the powers, or he is, in reality, this odd fellow Perry White calls Superman. He removes the spectacles and throws himself into the evening sky. All his chances to score with Lois go out the window with him; however, there is greater purpose to his life—the Earth must be saved. Superman, or at least Clark Kent in unfamiliar garb, returns to the observatory where Professor Roberts (Jonathan Hale) is apologizing for why science cannot divert the onrushing meteor. "I'm afraid they haven't developed a guided missile yet that can go that far out into space." [7] There is no hope without Superman.

While the conversation is taking place, a recommitted Superman, fully aware of his mission, zooms toward the observatory. He accepts a shoe box nuclear device from the professor, and declares, "Well, no matter who I am, here goes." He lifts off for a fate unknown. Editor Harry Gerstad cut in some footage he had claimed from one of his earlier pictures, the 1950 PRC (Producers Releasing Corporation) science fiction *Rocketship X-M* with Hugh O'Brian and Lloyd Bridges. The $5-a-foot explosion of the meteor fills the screen, followed by a pre-NASA view of Earth. The world is saved by Superman, with an honorable mention to Harry Gerstad and Tommy Carr.

"Panic in the Sky" is more than the trite battle with an evil scientist or two-bit con man. Superman fights to save his adopted Earth. But the drama also frees Kent. If he had realized his own identity in calmer times, Superman might not have returned. However, under the circumstances, Superman knows that Clark must remain a prisoner to his own emotions. It almost takes a global calamity to prove it, but of course, it is Superman, not Clark, who saves the world from the disaster. Clark can never be the real McCoy, the Jackson Gillis script cinches it: "You see," Kent tells Lois. "I know who he is now. Just knock me out on the head sometime, you'll find out!"

Carr added brilliance to the episode with his direction. "When George hit the springboard, he'd go quite high, but by tilting the fence at the observatory toward the camera, his takeoff seemed higher to the eye." On the other side of the lens, George did a somersault in the air, finally hitting the mat on his back. "It was quite a stunt!" exclaims the director. "We also had to get some extra flying scenes on film; that didn't help keep the budget down at all." Since Superman had to carry the atomic bomb under his arm, Carr set

---

[7] It was 1953. All the V-2 stock footage in the world couldn't get them out of this predicament.

A rear screen projection, not process shot, of Superman approaching the meteor. The breast plate supporting Reeves bulges out from the back. ("Panic in the Sky"—1953.)

up for a series of special takes. The total effort remains truly memorable for viewers of any age. "Panic in the Sky" is science fiction at its 1950s best.

Whitney Ellsworth handed the second director's job to another Republic Pictures veteran, George Blair. Blair's first efforts for Ellsworth were "Shot in the Dark," "A Ghost for Scotland Yard," "The Face and the Voice," and "The Man in the Lead Mask."

"Shot in the Dark' returned graying John Eldredge to the gangster role, while a pre-"Father Knows Best" Billy Gray portrayed an amateur photographer. The episode begins when nervous Aunt Harriet barges into *Clark Kent's* office crying, "You must help me, Superman!"

Kent stands to attention. "You must be mistaken," he stutters. She most definitely is not. The reporter sees the truth as Aunt Harriet produces a candid snapshot taken by nephew Alan (Billy Gray). The photograph caught Clark Kent in the act of being Superman, his clothes half off, in what he thought was a secluded alley. "There's got to be an explanation somehow," manages Clark.

Jimmy Olsen, the third ear to the conversation, comically observes, "That must be interesting."

And again back to Earth, after the meteor is finally destroyed. Note the Daily Planet Building (Los Angeles City Hall) on the right ("Panic in the Sky"—1953).

David Chantler, Whitney Ellsworth's longtime screenwriter, submitted the script for "Shot in the Dark." By the time the show had run its course in 1957, he had written the majority of scripts, including a draft for a full-length Superman motion picture.

Superman battles with an avenging apparition in George Blair's second program, "A Ghost for Scotland

Yard." The episode opens as Clark and Jimmy stop in England before heading home from a European junket. There, their "nose for news" helps them recognize a story in the making. The strange tale concerns the ghost of Brockhurst (Leonard Mudie), who is apparently squaring some post-mortem debts. Clark Kent, by now acting as Superman, barely saves Brockhurt's first prey, Sir Arthur (Colin Campbell), from toppling his Rolls over the White Cliffs. Brockhurst quickly moves against victim number two (Patrick Aherne), but again Superman is there in the pinch.

Superman, who on at least three other occasions breaks up fake superstition rings,[8] finds a strand of the motion picture film with which Brockhurst (very much alive) had frightened Sir Arthur. However, while Superman is busying himself, Brockhurt corners Olsen and delivers his long "Karloff end-of-the-line soliloquy." The magician is quite the madman, and only Superman's climactic intervention saves Olsen from being blown apart by Brockhurst's bomb.

Reeves gives his Pasadena Playhouse training a workout when he faces a dual role in "The Face and the Voice." He is, of course, Superman and Clark Kent; however, the Jackson Gillis script also calls for him to play Boulder, a typical Bronx bruiser. As the picture begins, squeaky-voiced Percy Helton (appearing as Hamlet) prepares the final touches on Boulder; he plans to pass the heavy off as the world's best substitute since cyclamates. "I got the bilt, and da verse," says Boulder, but the one thing that bothers him is the way bullets will react to his tender hide. "Da real Superman is not a punk like me!" Hamlet reasons that another Superman, especially one involved in a series of Metropolis robberies, is bound to rattle the real Man of Steel. It might have worked completely had Jimmy Olsen not recognized one of the bad guys, a weasel-like character named Scratchy (George Chand-

<hr>

[8] "The Lucky Cat," "Great Caesar's Ghost" and "The Magic Necklace" (1954).

Hayden Rorke plays a psychiatrist years before his assignment as Dr. Bellows in "I Dream of Jeannie" (The Face and the Voice" —1953).

ler). Nonetheless, Boulder applies enough pressure early in the plan for Kent to visit friend psychiatrist at large Hayden Rorke.[9] "Nothing on earth is the matter with you," says the shrink. For that Rorke doesn't even earn a screen credit.

Kent tries to defend Superman's (Boulder's) latest escapades before Perry White. "It's not true . . . I happen to know Superman was home in bed last night." Superman doesn't walk in his sleep, he adds—"At least I don't think he does!"

Later that evening, Boulder, in a duplicate of the Superman uniform, takes the express elevator to Perry

[9] This was eleven years before Rorke opened up a full-time practice as the befuddled Dr. Bellows in 'I Dream of Jeannie.'

White's office, and delivers his ultimatum to the editor. Either White complies or the city pays: "Have you ever figured out what the consequences would be if I got mad at Metropolis?" Boulder smiles menacingly and *walks* out the door.

By now, Clark is finished with his therapy. He telephones White, who recounts what has just occurred. "I saw him here, just one half hour ago."

"That's all!" Kent has heard enough. "I've wasted too much time already." He flies to Henderson's office, where the inspector is certain that Superman is beyond help. Superman chases Henderson around the office trying to convince him of his good intentions: "Listen, Bill, we've been friends for years, I'd hate to use you for a volleyball in your own office." Henderson gives in. He'll help capture the impostor.

Boulder ends his spree in the sanctity of a prison hospital, and humbly admits to Clark Kent, "It takes more than a face and a voice; there's only one Superman."

Next ready for air was "The Man in the Lead Mask." the story of two con men who put one over on their fellow crooks, the police and the intrepid fourth estate. Everyone but Superman is tricked into thinking that Marty Mitchell, the most wanted criminal in the country, has undergone surgery to change his face and fingerprints. Superman figures it's all a ruse that the real Mitchell (Joey Ray) is carrying off with the help of a lone inside man (Frank Scannell). Mitchell is after money from the mob's best cardplaying dummies.[10] He comes as close to succeeding as any villain does on "Superman."

What television audiences do not see are the pains that went on behind the camera during the filming of "The Man in the Lead Mask." Si Simonson made a mask that was a bit snug. "I could get it on," says

---

[10] Note: Mitchell's boys knock over the Ellsworth Jewelry Company, a direct reference to the show's producer.

Simonson, "but I didn't realize George had a tinge of claustrophobia and a bigger head! He put it on for one scene and literally tore his face apart trying to get it off. It's too bad we didn't save the outtakes," adds Simonson. "As painful as it was, that one would be worth a million!"

Paul Burke was a young, thin actor when Whit Ellsworth grabbed him up from the ranks of the unemployed for "My Friend Superman," long before "Noah's Ark," "Naked City," "Twelve O'Clock High," or those Radio Shack commercials. In this episode, directed by Thomas Carr, Burke works a protection racket with ace heavy Terry Frost. They zero in on Tony (Tito Vivolo), an itinerant greasy-spoon proprietor who claims to be Superman's Kemo Sabe. Tony has no intention of paying for the "insurance." After all, what kind of protection does he need from them; allegedly he has Superman. Tony regularly serves Clark, Lois and Jimmy, so when the gangsters move in, he turns to the reporters for help. He records an incriminating conversation between the two villains on his handy-dandy wire recorder. Although the rock 'n' roll music in the background is loud, Clark Kent's supersensitive hearing easily follows their plan and Kent dashes off to capture the duo. However, before he arrives, Tony, Lois, Jimmy and a few other patrons hold the mobsters at bay with the full fury of a spectacular $200 pie fight.

"They were real pies," remember editor Harry Gerstad. "Whit insisted on giving them the best. We tried to hold onto some to eat after the shooting, but old Whit said, 'No, pitch them in there, I'll get you a sandwich later!' "

Ellsworth saw the rushes and felt obliged to add his thanks for the additional discomfort experienced by Burke and Frost:

I remember watching them throw the pies at Paul Burke. Realizing that this was a humiliating way to

earn a living, I told Bess Epstein, my accountant, to add $50 to his check, the same for his partner Terry Frost. I thought the only way I could ameliorate their embarrassment was to give them a little more money. It's a lousy way to do it, of course, I might have talked to the guys and told them I appreciated what they must have felt, but I thought the money, especially for the young actor, along with the thanks, would be more practical.

Throughout Tommy Carr's cafe scenes, there is a Wimpy-ish character who methodically munches away at hamburgers. Ellsworth remembers a related conversation on the role with Wendell Williams, vice-president of the Leo Burnett California office. In good humor, the producer insisted that his actors eat hamburgers instead of a bowl of surplus Kellogg's. "You can't believe that those guys back in Battle Creek never ate a hamburger," he told Williams jokingly. There was a compromise. "I think we ground the Corn Flakes into the hamburgers!"

Harry Gerstad remembers a similar incident on a show from 1955, "The Unlucky Number." "This time the agency happened to be on the set when I set up a Kellogg's display on the counter for a restaurant scene in 'The Unlucky Number.' When Wendell Williams came in, he said, 'Don't do that, Harry, we feel the institution is a little obvious already.' I took it down, and put up a sign that said ham and eggs."

Kellogg's got their commercials, but always outside the auspices of the Ellsworth production. Harry Gerstad thinks, "It was one of the strangest and strongest setups in television history. We delivered the series to the Leo Burnett agency on Vine Street. They made the commercials and distributed them themselves."

Nearly everyone in the regular cast had a hand in them; everyone, that is, but Noel Neill. "National Comics or Leo Burnett, I don't know which, couldn't figure out how to put me at the breakfast table with Clark Kent and Jimmy Olsen without raising a few eyebrows. I needed the extra money. However, they pleaded 'modesty' and 'good taste.' It's silly by today's standards, but that's the way they thought!"

George Reeves also popped up on the reverse side of a Sugar Frosted Flakes package promoting Superman shirts and other paraphernalia.

"Superman" researcher David Miller discovered one commercial that never made it on the air: Clark Kent interviewing himself on the nature of his favorite breakfast foods. "It was a nicely conceived thing," says Miller. "Clark Kent knocks on the door of his own house and proceeds to carry on a 'normal' interview with himself! Kellogg's must have planned a whole series of these things, but I don't remember if they ever were broadcast. I found this print, minus the synchronous sound, in a garage."

Some people believe that many of the thin plots make it difficult to follow "Superman" today, especially when the young audience has grown up on more sophisticated villains in space-age television fare. "Not so," at least according to Robert Porfirio, professor of American Studies at California State University at Fullerton. Porfirio is quick to point out that the children of nostalgia and the "UHF after-school cult" can't get enough of the Superman mystique. "Maybe we're more accustomed to crew members beaming up to a starship, but we haven't tired of this guy flying through the window." Porfirio feels the episodes that remain poignant are those that deal with the timeless topics of isolation and overtechnology. These two themes survive far beyond the transparent plots. "These are the twentieth- and twenty-first century concerns, one we began grappling with in the thirties (Things to Come), and the same issues we will have well into the future." This, of course, doesn't mean there isn't room for fun with the mad scientist plots. "Lord knows 'Superman' has those."

"The Defeat of Superman" matches the typical mad scientist, in this case Meldini (Maurice Cass), with a wrong-side-of-the-street Happy King (Peter Mamakos). This particular Dr. No plans to use what he calls the Delthinian Theory to reduce Superman to a sniveling weakling. "That which was harmless on his home environment adversely affects him here!" Meldini's television logic is flawless; Kryptonite is his weapon!

Ruffles (Sid Tomack) is loosely disguised as a bum who rigs a machine gun/motion picture camera to determine whether a Kryptonite bullet affects Superman. Meldini's hypothesis works. Now to bait a trap with Lois Lane: "This dame is practically Superman's girl friend," volunteers King.

Superman accepts the invitation to death. He joins Lois and Jimmy in King's basement, where he encounters an ominous-looking item in the shape of a gold brick. Superman reassures his friends, "Don't worry, no metal can harm me."

"But this one's called 'Kryptonite,' " adds Olsen.

"Well, I don't care what they call it." Superman pushes his body against the door—his full force has no effect on it. "Did you say Kryptonite?"

"Maybe if I bring it over here," says Jimmy.

As he slides it closer, Superman drops to the floor. Lois stops sobbing long enough to help Jimmy stuff the Kryptonite inside a lead drainpipe. Superman immediately regains his strength and announces what we have known since the early days of the comic books. "Kryptonite is the only thing in the world that can hurt me, that's why this sample is going to disappear forever." He hurtles it through the air at supersonic speed, drawing the attention of the escaping villains. The three drive off the cliff to their deaths—the only casualties Ellsworth permitted in his years as producer. Meanwhile, the mysterious green rock sinks to the bottom of Metropolis harbor until "Superman Week" (1954), when Herb Vigran plots to fish it out.

In relation to the Porfirio opinion, "Superman in Exile" is one episode that unequivocally remains as relevant today as it was in 1953. "It's that one on loneliness," says Bob Porfirio. "Superman's dual identity already insulates him from society. He can't lead a normal life, so when companionship—terribly important to his survival—is cut off, Superman is left utterly helpless." Superman glows with the poison of radioactive isotopes; his touch is far too deadly for him to return safely to Metropolis. This new cross becomes unbearable.

The predicament begins when Superman answers a call for help from Project X. The nuclear stockpile is dangerously close to exploding Metropolis right off the map, so Superman must save the day. He forces his way into the sealed room to change a defective rod (amid some of Si Simonson's most impressive special effects), exiting minutes later, victorious in his race against time, but loaded with more gamma rays than Mickey Rooney in *The Atomic Kid* (1954). He scolds the relieved scientists: "It's new, and you haven't quite figured on how to handle it." The city is saved, yet Metropolis pays a hefty price—perhaps the life of its number-one citizen.

Fiction notwithstanding, "Superman in Exile" is a warning against the imminent collision course that Jack Larson prophecizes in his one-act play *Chuck*, and what Alvin Toffler forecasts in *Future Shock*. Despite a shoddy subplot, "Superman in Exile" survives. The Man of Steel resigns himself to a makeshift Fortress of Solitude atop Blue Peak Mountain while the greatest minds of Metropolis collaborate to solve their dilemma. They decide that a severe electrical shock might discharge the radioactive matter within Superman's 6'2" frame. Metropolis Edison cannot deliver the load, therefore Superman, to the accompaniment of vibrating strings and blaring horns, flies straight into a raging electrical storm. Four lightning bolts later, a Herculean figure pulls next to the airplane hauling away jewel thief Ferdinand (Leon Askin) and his hostage Lois Lane.

Clark enters just after Superman brings the airplane down. Lois' curiosity about the reporter's and Superman's coincidental disappearance during this "radioactive period" raises the repetitious remark, "Superman and you, I still wonder."

"Wonder?" he says. "It's no wonder you wonder, you're a pretty wonderful girl." It is the series' worst closing line.

Whitney Ellsworth cannot be faulted with all of the character's shortcomings. Although he did make changes, he inherited a personality drawn relatively close to the comic book creation of 1938. It is the budget that must be considered if anyone is to criticize the program accurately. Location shooting was rare; production was often limited to available sets: usually a few offices, a hideout, cabin or living room. "Obviously," says Ellsworth, "when we went out on location we tried to shoot the elements of more than one show to save some money. In other cases, we even repeated the same heavies, allowing us to shoot stuff for show number twenty-nine and show number thirty-seven. Of course, we'd have to pay the guest actors for two shows, but it saved us the setup time we couldn't afford to waste."

Tommy Carr articulates another consideration about location work. "Oh God! The fans would start coming out of the woodwork as soon as we'd start shooting. George tried to stay by himself, but the kids came over to hound him. It was a losing battle, but I remember George was a good egg about it."

"Don't forget the budget couldn't feed too many hungry mouths at lunch," says Noel Neill. "They'd have to feed us when we were out; that never balanced well in the ledger, so as often as possible we'd do them right on our phony sets as cheaply and quickly as could be. It was all we could do." On the rare occasion when they did hit the road, it was not unusual for the "Superman" entourage to bump into as many as five companies sharing the glorious outdoors at Iverson's Ranch in the San Fernando Valley.

The home sets were permanently lit, ready for the cameras to roll. "They had to be," says Ellsworth. "The expense of moving the show to a location was prohibitive. Maybe if we were doing the show today we'd be out more, but look at a show like 'Batman' or 'Kojak,' they're the same thing—stock location intercut with studio sets. When you're producing for the nineteen-inch screen you can't move around with the finesse of a multi-million-dollar motion picture." For that reason, Ellsworth followed Maxwell's cue, using "stock clothing" as well as stock footage. "It's another one of these things for which we had no choice," remembers the producer. "I could use one shot of Lois and Jimmy coming out the front door, getting into a car and driving off maybe a half-dozen times in the course of a year. If we had it, there was no need to shoot it again." As long as the characters wore their assigned clothing, the footage could be matched in serial style. "From the viewers' standpoint," concludes Ellsworth, "it never mattered if they did notice it. It was the *same* person walking through the *same* door whether we shot it once or one hundred times!"

Individual scenes were broken down in the manner of any other filmed television program: first, a master or wide shot covering all the action; later a series of close-ups and medium shots. Robert Justman, one assistant director for 1953, says, "Ordinarily, we'd shoot our masters in one basic direction. Tommy Carr and George Blair used to lay a dolly track for the camera which bisected the axis of the set. If something broke down, or someone flubbed a line, we moved in for the close-up and picked up the dialogue. Rarely did we shoot anything in order; it isn't done that way anywhere. The difference between 'Superman' and another show I did—'Star Trek'—is that on 'Superman' we hardly ever changed the angle if George or someone else blew a piece, we just shot closer. We relied on the master shots, and pickups that were not so much changes in direction, rather changes in the size from the first shot. Although we moved fast on other shows we tried to vary something if we were forced to stop."

There's no wide assortment of close-ups, over-the-shoulder and relationship shot in "Superman." Time and money limitations never allowed Tommy Carr to be that fussy. "I had enough problems just getting the show on film without killing everybody in the process. I called 'Action!' and 'Cut!' and then we had to move on to the next scene."

Whit Ellsworth is the first to admit things were rough. "Again you have to remember production values were different then. If we were shooting today, 'Superman' would be on location, amid real urban problems. He'd be fighting drug traffic and racism. But as you know, we're not in production today and our old reruns are more popular than ever before. Figure that."

Ben Welden helped make "Superman" such a valuable product. He was called back for "The Dog Who Knew Superman," this time to play Hank, a burlesque riffraff whose dog Corky[12] puts together the scents of Clark Kent and Superman and comes up with one person. "We always had a silly premise," says Welden. "In this one, I wasn't a gangster in the real sense, I owned that dog who almost uncovered Superman."

Superman moves from one offbeat challenge to another. In "Machine That Could Plot Crimes," Uncle Oscar's oversized thinking machine, Mr. Kelso learns Superman's identity. Nowhere in the script is Mr. Kelso called a computer. It's still 1953. He is strictly a mechanical brain, an "it" with a built-in guilty conscience that spews out linear block-print messages over Uncle Oscar's laboratory floor. Kelso is a personal sort of machine, a poor man's Robby the Robot, if you will. It realizes that it is an accomplice to Ben Welden's and Billy Nelson's crimes, and consequently reprograms itself for their slipup. Kelso has also studied the question of Superman's identity, but decides to bite its proverbial analogues to keep the best-kept secret—a secret.

Mr. Kelso's inventor is not short on credits. He is

---

[12] The terrier looks amazingly like Whitey, Boston Blackie's hound which corners Ben Welden and Billy Nelson in one of the early Kent Taylor productions at ZIV.

one of Hollywood's most recognizable character actors, and thus the entire "Superman" cast and crew applauded when Sterling Holloway walked onto the set for "Machine That Could Plot Crimes." Famous for voices in such Disney films as *Dumbo* (1941), *Alice in Wonderland* (1951), *Winnie the Pooh, Jungle Book* (1967) and *The Aristocats* (1969), Sterling Holloway gave a fitting performance (his first of three) for Ellsworth. Holloway recalls an anecdote on the occasion of this first appearance:

I'm supposed to be tied up by the villains in a chair when Superman breaks through the wall and rescues me. I didn't quite know how he was going to do it. We had no rehearsal, and after the thing was over, the director complimented me, "'Gee, it was wonderful, you looked so scared and all. It was just a fine piece of acting." But what I was doing was trying to keep from laughing. It struck me so funny to see this guy bust through the trick wall—his shoulder pads slipping, the bricks bouncing all over the place. I was all bent over shaking and they thought it was a fine piece of hysterical acting!

Director Carr moved from the Jackson Gillis script to Peter Dixon's "Jungle Devil." Superman fans will most readily remember the clutch performance of Clark Kent when he wins a round of hand-to-hand combat against a berserk gorilla, then turns a hunk of coal into a magnificent diamond. The "thousands of pounds of pressure for a thousand years" idea works nicely.

George Blair cleared an entire month for an unprecedented six episodes while Carr rested, looked over his remaining scripts, and pitched in with an occasional assist. The pressure to finish was mounting, especially since the first episodes were due for delivery within weeks. A production schedule based upon maximum efficiency was worked out, thus minimizing the hours Reeves would be in uniform. "His skin used to break out when he wore the thing too long," says Jack Larson. "It was extremely hot in the clingy uniform, particularly in the throes of Los Angeles' smog."

The hectic pace ground into summer of 1953. Before anyone had a chance to breathe, six new shows went before the lens: "The Clown Who Cried," "The Boy Who Hated Superman," "Semi-Private Eye," "Perry White's Scoop," "Beware the Wrecker" and "Jimmy Olsen, Boy Editor." During this exhausting period, Roy Barcroft, the best of the serial villains, joined Herb Vigran, Richard Reeves and Elisha Cook, Jr., on the California Studios sets.

"The Clown Who Cried" is another one of the human-interest stories that Whit Ellsworth prefers. The *Daily Planet* sponsors a charity telethon with Clark Kent playing the Jerry Lewis pitchman. Rollo the Clown (William Wayne) is the big draw, but a look-alike, Crackers (Peter Brocco) impersonates his former partner to abscond with the affair's proceeds. As the action climaxes, Rollo engages Crackers in a roof-top fight-to-the-finish. However, Superman miraculously catches the "good guy." Rollo is curious; how did Superman tell the difference? "Easy," Superman answers sympathetically. "The real Rollo wouldn't have pushed anyone." Maybe; yet we have to wonder whether his X-ray vision had anything to do with it.

Roy Barcroft was king of the bad guys. For every mighty river that Superman could majestically affect, Barcroft's sneer could melt the polar ice and send the waters rushing down again. Barcroft made the devil look like Sterling Holloway's Winnie the Pooh. Roy Barcroft was bad. Plain bad, and nearly everyone in town got to kill him—at least once.

Barcroft loved his trade. He told Alan G. Barbour, in *Days of Thrills and Adventure*, that villains had work every day of the year, while the heroes would come and go. Such visibility in the forties gave few other heavies the star status of a Roy Barcroft. He had the ability to die every week. After all, what men in their lifetime itemized on their "long form" such jobs as Ruler of the Moon (*Radar Men from the Moon*—Re-

Clark Kent serves birthday cake to Frankie Harris (Tyler McDuff) and the crack Daily Planet staff in the closing minutes of "The Boy Who Hated Superman" (1953).

public, 1949), Captain Mephisto (*Manhunt of Mystery Island*—Republic, 1945), Martian Invader (*The Purple Monster Strikes*—Republic, 1945) or a Western Toughie (*Jesse James Rides Again*—Republic, 1947).

Barcroft didn't need to leap tall buildings in a single bound. His film cans, stacked one on top of another, would have taken him up one side of the Empire State Building and down the other. From *Mata Hari* in 1932, through nearly two hundred forgotten Westerns and Poverty Row quickies, Barcroft carved an indisputable spot for himself in film folklore. One week, Roy Barcroft was out rustling horses, the next running guns to Indians. He kept tabs on such Western dolls as Phyllis Coates and Noel Neill. While most of his films are only flashes in memories of long-forgotten Saturday afternoons, Roy Barcroft's corruption of one-horse towns made heroes out of Kirk Alyn, Clayton Moore and every other broad-chested, square-jawed, six-gun law enforcer type in Hollywood. Typically enough, this movie villain was an amiable and popular man off-screen.

"The Boy Who Hated Superman" was one of his few stopovers in television. In the episode, juvenile Frankie Harris (Tyler McDuff) idolizes Duke (Barcroft). When Kent's muckraking puts Duke behind bars, Frankie predictably vows to settle the account. "I told Superman not to do me any favors, the same goes for you!" he tells Kent. The delinquent, uncharacteristically dressed in a suit and tie, chums around with Olsen in an attempt to plot against Kent. Jimmy, in turn, appears to be fooled by Frankie's free spirit and fancy ways. Happily, it turns out that this is Jimmy's counterplan; a bit of detective work to befriend Frankie. However, as all carefully hatched Olsen plans go, it backfires. Olsen and Frankie are kidnapped by a hoodlum named Fixer (Leonard Penn). Duke has set up Frankie as his patsy. Frankie realizes, "He used me just like he used everyone else." Frankie is rehabilitated and Duke is sent back to jail. As safe a place as any for Roy Barcroft.

Elisha Cook, Jr., who years later defends Captain Kirk on a "Murder One" charge, teaches a few side-stepping jujitsu moves to Jimmy Olsen in "Semi-Private Eye." Lois Lane enlists the gumshoe surreptitiously to follow Clark Kent. She is again on to the absurd notion that the meek reporter and Superman might share the same jockey shorts. Lois initially plants a fifty-pound telephone book on Clark's desk that "No ordinary man could move." Clark trips her up by substituting a regular directory and tosses it back to her. The humiliation sends Lois reeling off to the inauspicious office of Homer Garrity (Cook). The subplot quickly dissolves into the basic kidnapping formula with one humorous twist: Jimmy Olsen decides to become a shamus. He tests his Humphrey Bogart lisp, and borrows a convenient set of handcuffs, a *Casablanca* raincoat and wide-brimmed hat.

Fingers (Paul Fix)[13] greets this semi-private eye and watches him bungle his way into his own handcuffs. In the following scene, George Blair utilizes the Jack Webb school of low-angle photography to give Superman more stature over a pool hall informer. The Man of Steel, in search of the permanently troubled Olsen, stands tall as he crushes the eight ball to dust, clearly demonstrating the urgency of his questions. He gets the information and flies off to Olsen's rescue. However, Homer Garrity acts on his own behalf, flipping Richard Benedict once over lightly, while Superman inhales noxious gases from a poison pellet. Olsen follows Garrity's example, tripping Fingers to bring this Keystone Kops episode to a humorous conclusion. As for Elisha Cook, chief of movie fall guys (*The Maltese Falcon*, 1941; *The Big Sleep*, 1946; and *Shane*, 1953), it is great to see him fend for himself for a change.

"Perry White's Scoop" is an excellent starring vehicle for television's patriarchal resident grouch, John Hamilton. The seasoned actor must have been one of the graduates of the William Boyd school of aging. In all his years on film, John Hamilton never looked young. He was, as director of photography Joe Biroc says, "An old-timer, an old pro, who always worked, who always knew what he was supposed to do." Harry Gerstad adds, "He was the best sitting-down actor in the business, a great improviser. He'd pull out the drawer as though he were looking for something while he thought of the next line, then he'd keep right on going. He was a lot of fun, but unfortunately, he began to fail our last year." John R. Hamilton[14] succumbed to

[13] Fix is undoubtedly better known as Sheriff Micah on "The Rifleman."

[14] Research materials on John Hamilton's career are particularly difficult to locate, for fans of Republic Westerns are familiar with *their* own John Hamilton. He is, however, John F. (Shorty), a fixture in dozens of low-budget pictures. The research job is made harder because both actors are usually listed in the same sources without the discriminating middle initial. It's a toss-up who's who on paper; on screen it's entirely another matter. "There's no mistaking our John," says Jack Larson. "He's always the senator, cop or judge."

a heart ailment October 15, 1958. The "Superman" cast gathered for his funeral; it was the last time many would see either John Hamilton or George Reeves. Reeves died eight months later.

Hamilton was born in Shippensburg, Pennsylvania, and educated at Mercersburg Academy, Pennsylvania State Teachers College and Dickinson College. He moved to New York City, where for twenty-five years his name was posted in small print on marquees promoting vaudeville and musical and dramatic productions. In those days, Hamilton played opposite Lew Fields, Sylvia Sidney, Lou Tellegen, Ann Harding, Alexander Carlisle and George M. Cohan.[15]

Hamilton acted on radio as well. His credits include "Gangbusters" and an early serial by Octavius Roy Cohen. His break in motion pictures came during his Broadway years. Warner Brothers–Vitaphone signed him for a series of S. S. Van Dine Philo Vance detective shorts—no relation to the feature films with Basil Rathbone, William Powell, Edmund Lowe, Warren Williams et al. The debut was enough for Warner Brothers to get a good look at Hamilton. In 1937, the studio sent him to California, where he remained.

The grumpy "Great Caesar's Ghost" editor that Noel Neill remembers played a stronger Perry White than Pierre Watkins had done for the serials. But she was quick to discover that Hamilton's proverbial "hair up his derriere" quality made him as unpredictable on the screen as off. "We never knew what he would say, but that was John," says Neill.

"Yes," adds Tommy Carr, "yet John could never remember two words. He was not a young man, so he had a tendency to get crotchety under the lights and muff his lines." The solution was not beyond Tommy

---

[15] Ironically, years later he portrayed the recruiting officer in *Yankee Doodle Dandy* who gives James Cagney's Cohan the impetus to write the rousing "Over There." Hamilton rounded out his New York career with Frank Bacon in Gayety Theatre's original company of *Lightnin*, and productions of *Seventh Heaven*, with Helen Menken, and the Jed Harris hit, *Broadway*.

Robert Shayne, George Reeves and John Hamilton (1954).

Carr. "We always laid out his script with other papers in front of him. He had the scene right there, but he did it so well that no one ever knew. Take him away from the desk and we were gambling. We could be there all day trying to get the words out. John was notorious for that." For anyone else it would have meant instant unemployment. Hamilton, the beloved senior member of the crew, could get away with murder.

In "Czar of the Underworld," Tommy Carr recalls Hamilton was asked to fill one of the gaps when the episode came in short. Maxwell and Carr, in order to remedy the situation, wrote a quick telephone scene between Perry White and Inspector Henderson. In the midst of the conversation, Hamilton picked up a sheet of paper as if to read a message. "And he did, word for word. His lines were typed on the paper. We gave it to John, rolled the camera and he read it! On other occasions he'd just shuffle the notes on his desk, and in one glance, bring the lines into focus. That's why we had him seated in his office so much."

The fellow on the other end of the telephone in "Czar of the Underworld" speaks of Hamilton in lasting superlatives. Robert Shayne parodies Hamilton's growl, "Great Caesar's Ghost!" before a memorable smile covers his face. "John was an easy man to work with, a likable guy, a political reactionary, but not the kind of man who would hate you because you disagreed with him."

"Bless his heart, he was in hard times and grateful for the work," says Noel Neill. "He was in his late sixties and he lived with his young son in a small hotel on Vine Street across from a market. He had a time of it getting enough money to keep him going. 'Superman' was his bread and butter and John worked for just as little as we did. He was a great actor from the dark ages, but there he was—in his old hotel-apartment. It was Hollywood's classic dead-end story; tragic because John had been in show business all his life, and in his last years he had so little."

"He was completely professional, a joy to work with," accords Harry Gerstad. "John had one of the better parts, and because of his experience, he carried it off perfectly." The old pro had been another one of the "Superman" cast groomed at Warner Brothers during the thirties and forties. In *The Maltese Falcon* (1941), District Attorney Hamilton informs Humphrey (Sam Spade) Bogart, "I'm a sworn officer of the law, twenty-four hours a day, and neither formality nor informality justifies you withholding evidence of crime from me, except of course, on constitutional grounds." He arrests Bette Davis halfway through the third reel of *In This Our Life* (1942), plays the governor's aide in *Meet John Doe* (1941), a judge in *The Big Shot*

(1942),[16] a lawyer in *They Drive By Night* (1940), an FBI chief in *Confessions of a Nazi Spy* (1939), a prison warden in *Always in My Heart* (1942) and a reporter in *Mission to Moscow* (1943). Hamilton is seen in *The Roaring Twenties* (1939), *Angels with Dirty Faces* (1938) and as the police chief who gets the goods on bad guy Ben Welden after a twenty-six-year-old George Reeves calls the precinct station house in *Tear Gas Squad* (1940).

Ben Welden met Hamilton for the first time on that Warner Brothers set, and was immediately impressed by the senior actor's virtuosity. "He was one of the studio's best cops. He played his character very well, so they used John an awful lot. He's on all those late-night films out of Warners."

"Superman" Producer Bob Maxwell defined the television role, Hamilton filled it, and actress Phyllis Coates speaks in the most glowing terms: "John was a lovely dear old gentleman. We all loved to work with him, and everybody, including George, treated him with the utmost respect. Still, he had lots of gags, but I suppose he put up with a lot of nonsense and dirty talk from us!"

Noel Neill agrees with her predecessor. "He hoped the series would continue so he'd have some work. It was funny, though, for such a dear old person, I remember him as a little lewd. Actually, it was pretty funny. He and George would come out with the wildest remarks. Not dirty . . . well, maybe . . . yes, dirty, a little far out. You know if they filmed some of the dialogue between John and George, we all would have been off the air! It broke everybody up because he had such a great sense of humor with a straight face. He was a grand old Teddy bear and gentleman rolled into one. He'd look at you and deliver those hilarious remarks out of the side of his mouth. It just broke everybody up."

[16] Hamilton played every type of judge during his career, eventually working his way up to the Chief Justice of the Supreme Court in M-G-M's *The Magnificent Yankee* (1951).

John Hamilton was more of a teacher to Jack Larson. "John and I had a rather formal and friendly relationship. He had a fine sense of grandeur and professional standing that went back to the famous Lambs Club of New York. John maintained their code of ethics from the old days in the theater. He'd never speak ill of another actor, nor call a contemporary by his first name. I called him John, but certainly when actors of his vintage got together it would be Mr. Hamilton and Miss Barrymore."

Larson wore jeans to the set, a presumption that often infuriated the elder Mr. Hamilton. "I'm sure that he was from the era when children should be seen and not heard, and no doubt I was one of them." Larson felt especially resigned after he criticized a Leopold Stokowski performance in Hamilton's presence. He quickly discovered why Hamilton was so outraged. "John told me he worked with Stokowski in a Deanna Durbin picture. He stormed up to me and blared, 'Young man, do you know anything about anything?' I kept my mouth shut for a while after that."

Jack Larson echoes what others have said of John Hamilton. "John never felt humiliated playing Perry White. He was thoroughly professional and did the best he could in any job. We all felt he succeeded." To many, his Silas Marner–Perry White is the most believable character in the production. Everyone has a grouch living two houses down the block. Others have known a soured boss or frustrated teacher, but how often does a Superman traipse across the front lawn? Or how regularly are our two best friends kidnapped? Perry White is recognizable; he is real, and it's nice to see him in scripts that get him out from behind the desk; thus the editor, condemned to his office since "The Evil Three," was happy to be out on the road in "Perry White's Scoop."

An abandoned corpse tickles White's journalistic curiosity enough for him to want in on the action. After all, a dead man in a diving suit on the top floor of the *Daily Planet* Building isn't your typical "dog bites man" story. So for the next thirty minutes, White sweats out the details in a locked steam cabinet and a burning freight car. Ashamed that he ended up needing Superman's help, he implores the Man of Steel, "Don't let Clark Kent know that I had to depend upon you to save me."

"Don't worry, he won't hear it from me," answers Superman faithfully.

Perry White figures that he can somehow outsmart the villains by wearing the diving suit. Clark doesn't allow it. He bends the helmet to fit himself, or rather Superman. White and Kent investigate the Quincy Athletic Club, where they end up locked in matching steam cabinets. Luckily, Superman is hiding in Clark Kent's cubicle, and once Perry White blanks out, Superman makes his move. In the next few minutes, White realizes the diving suit was used to fish out a secret message at the base of the club's water storage tank. Meanwhile, trigger-quick Max (Steven Pendleton) and Maria (Bibs Borman) lurch about in indiscernible accents, waiting for the reporters to crack the case. Of all the possible candidates, Jimmy Olsen gets the nod to stomp around the water tank looking for the note. In what was becoming routine, the "submariner" falls knee-deep into the water to encouraging words from his editor, "A little water never hurt an old-time reporter. You'll dry!" All Jimmy Olsen can do is stutter and slosh his way through the tank until a tiny fish squiggles its way into his pant cuff. Naturally, the fish has the coded message attached to its fins. Clark studies the note, adding, "Codes used to be a hobby of mine, it should be a cinch to unscramble." It is.

The treasure hunt finally sends them to the Metropolis Railroad Yard, where they meet Max and Maria and their carload of counterfeit paper. Clark feels it's that time to drop out of sight; his break comes when Lois rolls up in her Nash. "You better get help!" he halfheartedly pleads. Max uses the pause to deliver a right hook to Kent's rarely abused kisser. Clark falls limp under the train. Max ignites the wooden railroad car and within seconds it becomes a burning inferno surrounding Olsen and White. However, Superman, conveniently under the train, crashes through and blows out the fire.

"Perry White's Scoop" is John Hamilton's best show. Ellsworth tries to showcase his talents in "Great Caesar's Ghost" (1954), "Peril by Sea" (1955) and "Money to Burn" (1956), but none equal this earlier performance. His style is unique and altogether humorous. No one could have played the editor with the sheer tenacity of John Hamilton. However, his worsening heart condition forced the management to give serious thought to alternate plans if John passed on during shooting in 1957. Through those last thirteen episodes, Hamilton appears tired and aging, yet still full of the cigar-smoking stamina that characterizes his most famous role—Perry White.

The "Adventures of Superman" was myopic. Maybe that's a good thing. Ellsworth just stayed with the old rule of thumb, "Go with a good story." Although he didn't anticipate the political motives, Ellsworth did commission one story that suggests the violence that has now become so commonplace. In that respect, "Beware the Wrecker" is significant. The Wrecker claims responsibility for a number of Metropolis disasters involving airplanes, trains and ships. However, his motivation is not the political subversion or international recognition that many groups seek today; the Wrecker is only interested in personal gain—insurance money; certainly a more understandable goal for 1953.

Superman forces the Wrecker to show. Closely foreshadowing the 1970s' familiarity with the misuse of public trusts, the villain turns out to be a high-level official and a member of the local citizen's committee to stop terrorism.

"Jimmy Olsen, Boy Editor" returns the cast to a more hospitable environment. The cub reporter is handed Perry White's post on the eighteenth floor for the duration of Youth Day. During the ensuing twenty-four hours, White sees Olsen plant a story that draws

The suit fits Perry White, but Clark Kent bends the helmet so he can go undercover in "Perry White's Scoop" (1953).

underworld heavy Legs Lemmy (Herb Vigran) out of hiding. The bogus story is nearly a prelude to Olsen's permanent downfall until Superman intervenes.

"I'm flabbergasted to find out that I only have a record of six Superman shows," says Vigran. "I thought I had done a dozen or more." [17]

A pre-"Superman" friendship with George Reeves underscored Vigran's work on the set. "I was associated with George in a summer stock venture down in Laguna in the late forties. Unfortunately, I wasn't able to participate too much with him because I was starring in a radio show called 'The Sad Sack,' a summer replacement for Frank Sinatra's program."

Herb Vigran is a lawyer turned actor. Although he never hung up the shingle, he jokes about his willingness to "front" any law practice in Indiana. "Since I decided on the theater early, any offers from the Mid-

[17] Vigran appears in "No Holds Barred" (1951), "Jimmy Olsen, Boy Editor" (1953), "Superman Week" (1954), "Blackmail" (1955), "Mr. Zero" (1956) and "The Big Forget" (1957).

west have to be pretty good! I won the lead in the senior play in high school. It was the bug that bit, so after I graduated from Indiana University Law School and was sworn in, I hitchhiked to California to act. That was the end of my law career." He starved for eight years, living on whatever $15-a-day acting jobs were available from low-budget studios. A quick *Happy Landing* at Monogram was it until an agent finagled a stay at the El Capitan Theatre with Roger Pryor. "I knocked around those first two years in Hollywood before I ultimately decided to go to New York. Just before I left, I got three days' work for $35 a day [*Vagabond Lady*, 1935]. That was my traveling money!"

Vigran used a little Bob Cummings trick to take New York. Rather than coming back the suave Englishman, as Cummings had, Vigran used his portfolio to stretch the actual success of his career. "I had a stack of stills and every time I worked for fifteen dollars at Columbia playing a reporter with Rosalind Russell—poised with a pad and pencil—somebody would shoot a still. I would get ahold of these and take them to Warner Brothers–Vitaphone in New York. I started working like crazy!" His inventive nature helped him onto the New York stage as well. "It made quite an impression on people that, under any other circumstances, wouldn't have had anything to say to me."

Vigran's New York stay lasted three winters. And all of them "were not catered with caviar dinners." Too much of the time was spent recovering from $40-a-week flops like Walter Hampden's *Achilles Had a Heel.* "I remember one dejected, depressed and broke New Year's Eve in 1936, before I went on a farewell tour of Hampden's *Cyrano.* It was, 'Live on twenty, save twenty,' right up until I joined George Abbott's *Boy Meets Girl.*" The part came through with the encouragement of his friend Garson Kanin. "We were young kids then, and the ambition of my life was to audition for George Abbott." Kanin set it up. "If I could read for Abbott and he used me, then I thought I'd know for sure whether I was really an actor or whether I had

Arlene Towne, George Reeves and Sterling Holloway are observed through the laboratory window by Joseph Vitale and Toni Carroll in "The Whistling Bird" (1953).

better go back to Fort Wayne and practice law!'' Vigran walked off with the part of a songwriter. The play toured New England for a series of midwinter bus and truck one-nighters. ''We opened theaters that had been closed since talking pictures came in—Brattleboro, Vermont—I'll never forget Brattleboro. There was no stage door. We had to walk in the front of the house where the audience sat.''

After Vigran ambled back to New York, he finally signed with a Broadway hit, *Having Wonderful Time* with Sheldon Leonard, John Garfield, Cornel Wilde, Martin Ritt and future ''Superman'' bad guy Phil Van

Zandt. An off-Broadway company of *Golden Boy* was next, followed by the monotony of hard times. Vigran decided to swing through Hollywood once more before packing for that Fort Wayne law practice.

For a while in 1939, life looked more attractive back in old Indiana than it did in sunny Southern California. The actor was twenty-nine and hungry. "That entire year I earned $280, $50 for 'Lux Radio,' and a few bucks here and there." As chance had it, Vigran bumped into another struggling friend who had been taken off the breadlines by a new agent. "Hey, I just signed with one helluva agent," he told Vigran. "Come on with me, maybe she'll take you on too." Herb Vigran accompanied Alan Ladd to meet Sue Carol, who quickly negotiated a series of $100-a-week pictures. "I made about two grand over the next year at Monogram, Republic and all the independents no one ever heard of Those were the movies that television bought in the early days; the movies that even Brattleboro, Vermont. doesn't get to see anymore."

Throughout his career, radio has really been Vigran's bread and butter. "I never did a lot of pictures. Occasionally I'd do something decent, but the producers thought radio actors couldn't act in films. They thought we could only talk." Vigran trained with Kay Francis, Jack Benny and Fanny (Baby Snooks) Brice in the forties. "There was a clique of those of us who were radio's top working actors. Unfortunately, we couldn't get much work in pictures. Conversely, when the starlets, or stars, from films came over for a radio show, we thought they were from hunger." Vigran speaks of the stereotyping that pervades every aspect of the industry, a relatively unplanned but effective tool for class distinction.

Ever since those dark days ended, contracts have kept his stomach full. "I've had a very nice nickel in my pocket." He still records "Heartbeat Theatre" for the Salvation Army and shares a creative radio company with Johnny Gunn, cranking out what Vigran calls "somewhat humorous, but livable commercials."

Between radio jobs there were short takes in Westerns for Republic, and one-shot deals at the big lots. *White Christmas* was one.

"Fortunately, when television came in, the first people to become involved were those of us from radio. The new medium never made me a star, but I've had steady employment. My best-known work outside 'Superman' is probably as Monte the bartender in Dick Powell's 'Dante's Inferno' on 'Four Star Playhouse.' I played father confessor to Powell.

"I've played a lot of uniformed cops, storekeepers, short-order cooks and villains in everything from Jack Benny and Ed Wynn to 'Superman.' " In recent years, he's been a semi-regular on "Gunsmoke," as Judge Brooker. G-rated film fans might recognize him in *Twenty Thousand Leagues Under the Sea, Benji, The Love Bug* and *Herbie Rides Again.*

Vigran's six low-paying visits to "Superman" have meant more than could have been expected in the 1950s. "Through the years I find I have been very, very big with kids. They're seeing these reruns of 'Superman,' for which, of course, I don't get a cent. Yet the kids all know me in any locality where they still show 'Superman.' I can walk into the town and I'm a star. Kids still ask for my autograph, and I mean the kids who grew up too, those in their twenties and thirties now. When they see me they say, 'You're Georgie Glep or Si Horten or Arnold Woodman or Legs Lemmy, aren't you?' It's a great feeling!"

The villainous roles fit Vigran like a glove. Whitney Ellsworth fashioned his heavies into third-grade dropouts who speak in heavily dentalized Brooklynese. Vigran's Legs Lemmy is perfect for "Jimmy Olsen, Boy Editor." Keith Richards, Dick Rich, Anthony Hughes, Ronald Hargrove and Bob Crosson complete Vigran's Dead End mob.

George Blair retired from "Superman" until 1954. Tommy Carr took the last three weeks to wrap up the regular pictures and a U. S. Savings Bonds special entitled "Stamp Day for Superman."

One of Carr's final episodes is "The Golden Vulture." A scavenger ship returns to port after an apparently successful hunt for Spanish treasure. However, all is not as it seems. The ship's cook knows more than Captain McBain (Peter Whitney) cares to release to the newspaper. The galley-master tries a last-ditch effort to get word to the authorities, but landlubbers Olsen and Lane intercept his note. McBain, they learn, is actually keeping afloat a gigantic warehouse that transforms stolen jewelry into Spanish doubloons for eventual resale as artifacts. Lois and Jimmy become McBain's unwilling prisoners in the course of their zealous investigation. After their capture, Jimmy tries his first line of defense, "If I don't get home about this time, my mother begins to worry!" It doesn't work. McBain shoves them into the brig, where Kent joins them later.

Kent takes quite a few liberties with his secret identity in this one. He uses his finger as a gun to trick syndicate boss Sanders (Murray Alper). Kent, of course, says it is only his finger; Sanders thinks otherwise when he complains, "You've got fingers made out of steel, buddy!"

"The Golden Vulture" offers the best choreographed fight since "No Holds Barred." Kent is jumped by the ship's unsportsmanlike sea dogs. He bounds up the stairs in a flash where he takes them on four at a time. Clark tosses them about, dodging punches, and jumping over the downed sailors. For once it is Clark Kent as the crime fighter, and he looks damn good. However, this one-man stand cannot last forever. It simply doesn't do his mild-mannered image any justice. Clark is not supposed to be the burly winner, that's Superman's job. So we're not surprised when Kent decides to change into his work clothes. He tears off his glasses, pleading, "Superman! Where are you?" Before the reporter can steal away for a moment of secrecy, Lois and Jimmy blunder by, blocking his escape route. "Go on, leave me alone!" yells Clark. They don't budge. Clark is captured and forced to walk the plank. The end result is ultimately the same. Once Clark is "deep-sixed," Superman surfaces in his place and Clark Kent's lone bid for heroic status is over.

Before the end, Lois and Jimmy plead with Superman to save their whipping boy, their drowning mascot, Clark Kent. Yet Superman takes his sweet time disposing of McBain and his crew. "Superman!" cries Lois. "If you don't save him, I'll never speak to you again!"

Superman finishes his work, joking, "It's been less than a minute, he'll have to hold his breath a little bit longer."

Superman[18] dives head first into the sea. A moment later, Clark bobs up. The coincidence triggers Lois' mind again, "You appeared right after he disappeared . . . and . . ." Since Lois is one breath away from the inevitable, Clark quickly interrupts, asking for a helping hand. Lois obliges and finds herself treading water alongside Clark. She's wet and perturbed and has had enough for the day. "Never mind, Clark," says Lois, "it couldn't be, it just couldn't be."

Noticeably absent from the drenching is the previously aquatic Jack Larson. Larson discovered that a little persuasion in the right place does the job—at least for the remaining four pictures of 1953.

The shenanigans of "The Golden Vulture" are followed by even more, in the puzzler "Lady in Black." Frank Ferguson and Virginia Christine confound Olsen while the youngster stays overnight in a strange apartment. Ferguson plays Mr. Frank, the ringleader, in a complicated smuggling caper. He plans to scare Olsen with every terrifying circus trick in the book so that the young reporter's pleas to Superman will eventually

---

[18] Or Reeves' double, no one seems to remember. It must also be noted that one of Captain McBain's shiphands, a character named Scurvy, is played by a man whose voice most television viewers would recognize today. Actor Vic Perrin eventually went on to become the narrator of "Outer Limits," and the voice of "Nomad" in Star Trek's "The Changeling."

Superman flies Ann Carson (Judy Ann Nugent) "Around the World" (1953).

ring false. The Man of Steel thinks that the lad is crying wolf. "There's only one reason I can't stay here to give you another lecture," scolds Superman. "I've got to get back to the office."

Olsen catches the mistake. "Office?"

Superman ad-libs at his mediocre best. "Oh . . . oh yes, Kent has some work and he can't do it unless I'm there."

Jimmy finally convinces Clark that Mr. Frank's pranks are the cause of his frantic pleas. Superman rounds up the gang, which includes another "Superman" regular, John Doucette.

A glittering sapphire accompanies a leftover "Bela Lugosi" curse when Lois Lane gets back into the swing of things in "Star of Fate." Superman discovers that Dr. Barnack (Lawrence Ryle) is willing to utilize any malicious means to retrieve a priceless stone within an ancient Egyptian box. What he doesn't understand is why so many who come in contact with the Star instantly fall to the floor in a deathlike coma. He wants to make certain the same will not happen to his gal Friday, Lois, but alas, it's too late. In order to find a cure for his love, Superman books himself on his next regularly scheduled round trip to Egypt, where he handily picks up the Great Pyramid, reaches underneath for a leaf, then delivers it to the Metropolis hospital where it is ground into an antidote. Superman makes it all look as easy as cheesecake, but his heart is really out to Lois; he'll do anything in his power to get her back in circulation. Lifting the Great Pyramid is just a mild expression of his love—and a good special effects stunt.

Sterling Holloway returns as Uncle Oscar in "The Whistling Bird." He apparently has left Mr. Kelso in favor of a talking parakeet called Schuyler. However, there's a method to old Oscar's madness. The bird knows a key phrase to a secret formula, and thus becomes important to the drama. In due time, a nefarious couple poke their politics into the story, and steal off with the winged brain, leaving Uncle Oscar with a fake "Polly." Actually, Uncle Oscar has backed into the intrigue purely by accident. Instead of inventing a tasty stamp glue, he comes up with a highly unstable explosive: CO_2, magnesium, acetate, zinc oxide and probably a drop of butter. Glue the thieves would have ignored; the bomb formula they want. But the bird won't talk, at least until Superman captures the spies and puts them safely behind bars. Once that happens, Schuyler refuses to keep his trap shut. "Hello, Superman!" he squawks to Clark Kent. The reporter can only touch his glasses in mild embarrassment as Lois offers the final word. "I thought Schuyler was a pretty smart bird, but when he called Clark Kent Superman . . ."

One more half hour of "Superman" lit up the television tubes in 1953. "Around the World" fulfilled the hearts-and-flowers quota for the soft-touch set as Judy Nugent's blind "Queen for a Day" appeal prompts swift concern from the *Daily Planet* staff. Superman eventually reunites Ann Carson (Nugent) with her parents, then gives a nearsighted doctor a helping hand in Ann's sight-restoring operation. For the classy finale, Superman flies Ann around the world, hence the terribly clever name for the episode. Nugent plays the invalid with formidable Helen Keller character; just the model of strength for nine-year-olds to follow. Whitney Ellsworth knew how to tug at the heartstrings, his "Around the World" proves it once again.

The Superman costume would normally have been mothballed at the conclusion of the regular season. However, Uncle Sam prevailed upon the company to go one more round, a public service short subject entitled "Stamp Day for Superman." Billy Nelson volunteered for the heavy, Tris Coffin, for a schoolteacher. Larson, Hamilton, Neill and Reeves assumed their regular roles in writer David Chantler's twelve-minute pitch for security and patriotism.

Announcer:

The United States Treasury Department presents . . .
The Adventures of Superman!

The subplot covers a jewelry store robbery, while the main action concentrates on an obvious public relations message—Jimmy, we learn, manages to buy a typewriter with cash via converted bonds. "You see, the interest I got on my investment made my bonds worth a lot more than what I put in." Eventually, the main theme muddles its way past an arrest, and into Jimmy's alma mater for "Stamp Day" where Superman addresses an eighth-period assembly with a rousing oration.

The speech as it appears on film is blatant propaganda, evidenced most noticeably when Superman applauds the students' patriotism. "Every time you buy a stamp," he says, "you're buying freedom and upholding the privilege of living in this great country of ours. You're helping support our soldiers . . . you're helping to preserve our forests. You're helping to keep our Government strong. . . ."

At the end of the speech the action returns to the office, where the camera pushes past Lois, Jimmy and Clark onto a stamp book which reads "Superman." Clark pipes up apologetically, "Oh, it's for a friend of mine." Considering they believed him fifty-two times before, there's no sense forcing the issue now. Kent sits snugly as the film fades to black.

This was not Reeves's first experience as a government spokesman. During World War II, when he wasn't busy with assorted versions of *Winged Victory* or *Yellow Jacket,* Reeves was at the army's facilities on Long Island speaking into the camera on the evils that accompany a joy-filled tumble in the hay with any European waif. The films were distributed throughout army bases to the potentially infectious enlisted men.

The production ended in the early days of October, and before anyone knew it, Tommy Carr was off in a cloud of dust. "Enough of these 'Adventures of Superman,'" recalls Carr with a sigh. "I needed a change of scene, but you know I never knew when I had it good. In place of easygoing George, I had to contend with Steve McQueen in 'Wanted Dead or Alive,' then Clint Eastwood on 'Rawhide.' I kind of got a little numb. At first I thought 'Superman' was such awful trite, nobody in their right mind would write stuff like that or say the type of things our characters said. But after I worked around a little, I realized how really good some of them were. I have to admit, as crazy as it all sounds, I loved it. We *all* loved it."

Tommy Carr left only when the television show had taught him all it could; in return, he had given the

"Adventures of Superman" two years of his career. It was a good marriage, but Carr felt it was time to say goodbye. Once he had done so, the series was never the same.

The doors closed for another year.

In 1954, Twentieth Century–Fox released, for theatrical distribution, five Superman features, each a compilation of three television episodes. The packages were not re-edited for continuity, instead, merely the original "Adventures of Superman," shown in toto, and run back to back. (See APPENDIX IV for titles.)

CHAPTER VII

1954

George Reeves's renegotiated contract guaranteed fifty-two more episodes. He signed in 1954, unaware of Kellogg's and National's intentions.

Normally in the early days, a series could count on twenty-six episodes each season; not the "Adventures of Superman." The last fifty-two episodes were spread over four years—thirteen each year—which minimized pay hikes and further negotiations with Reeves. The other cast members were subjected to the rigor of company bargaining sessions. "Every $25 raise we got was an embarrassing fight," says Jack Larson, who believes the Screen Actors Guild hardly acted in their favor during pay disputes. "I think that's why Noel and I lost a lawsuit over one residual deal. People didn't realize what residuals would mean in the future, or maybe they did, perhaps that's why they were so hard to come by." Larson ended up with a residual contract that gave him as little as ten cents on the dollar.

One "day player" on "Superman" agrees with Larson's gripes. "They should have had dollar-for-dollar residuals for perpetuity. Why shouldn't they be getting residuals today, Warners and National Periodicals are making money." The answer is obvious. The residual plan was (as it is today) based upon the union minimum, and it was Whitney Ellsworth's job to save money, the company's money. Apparently, Jack Larson understands. "There were times that Whitney felt the corporation greatly abused him. So we didn't always blame Whit."

Larson has another beef. He was ambitious about acting in those days, always looking forward to Broadway and live television during the off-season. "I promised to be available for each new season, but there was a snag." His pleasure turned to displeasure when National decided he should be on thirty-day call. "New York never let me know at the end of one schedule when the next production would shoot. So I ended up fearful, never knowing whether or not at any given thirty-day period I could take on new work. That excluded my doing long-running plays, and left only slim pickings in quick television shows, unless I started something right after we finished 'Superman.' One time Whit apologized profusely. But even his hands were tied, there wasn't much he could do."

John Hamilton and Noel Neill enjoyed the same annual uncertainty. Robert Shayne, in the meantime, was given credit on all of the post-Maxwell shows but paid for only those days he worked.

Perhaps the most surprised actor to see "Superman" back in production that year was George Reeves. He spoke of quitting after the shutdown in 1953. Reeves was tired of the role. At the pivotal age of forty, and without the career fulfillment he desired, Reeves played for more money, thinking for certain that was the last time he'd see the Superman uniform. Ellsworth told reporters, "Reeves called for a salary increase I was unable to meet. My relations with Reeves are still amiable. I wish him luck."

"Consequently," wrote *Daily Variety* (September 27, 1954), "producer Whitney Ellsworth is looking elsewhere for a lead for the 'Superman' vid pix due to roll October 20, at California Studios." Yet Ellsworth and Reeves eventually came to terms. The October 27, 1954, *Variety* announced the fact:

George Reeves, who had left his long underwear behind and exited the lead as 'Superman' when he couldn't get a hefty raise, is back at it again. Reeves and producer Whitney Ellsworth have reached agreement on a new contract, with the actor receiving an uppance in coin, but not anything like his original demands.

224

Word got out that Reeves settled for a neat $2,500 per show ($5,000 each week when the show was in production) plus a lucrative residual package. However, there are those who say Reeves still wanted out. The camera captured his lack of enthusiasm when production resumed on Monday, November 15.

The Federal Communications Commission used its 1948–52 freeze to evaluate channel allocations and to decide upon the requirements of color broadcasting. In 1954, National Periodicals gambled on color, making book that their product value would eventually increase if shot with an eye toward the future. It was a sure bet. Although the FCC expressed interest as early as 1950 in CBS's revolving color disc for both camera and receiver, the Commission instead endorsed the RCA method developed in 1954. Their version relied upon an electronic scanning system; essentially, the model in home use today. By 1965, network research enthusiastically reported that ratings of color programs were up to eighty per cent higher in homes with color sets than in the traditional black-and-white television families—good news to National Periodicals, which had shot the fifty-two "Superman" episodes from 1954–1957 in color.[1]

Harry Gerstad directed the cast through the first five color shows. He went from *High Noon* to "Superman," or as he likes to says, "From the peaks to the funny papers." Gerstad knew Whit Ellsworth since his war years assignment in the Motion Picture Signal Corps. "I became a pet of National Comics, and when they made the first twenty-six 'Superman' shows, Jack

[1] The negatives were quietly sealed away, and the programs initially released in black and white. In the early 1960s, when the color boom took hold, National brought them out of storage and has enjoyed a glorious profit in them ever since. Other early color programs include "The Cisco Kid," "Sergeant Preston of the Yukon," "Science Fiction Theatre" (last season only, "The Lone Ranger" (also last season), and "Judge Roy Bean."

Liebowitz and Whit asked if I would consult with Maxwell." Gerstad had to turn them down in 1951 because of contract obligations to Stanley Kramer. However, two years later, he was able to sign as Ellsworth's editor. By that time, Gerstad had already accepted Academy Awards for editing *Champion* (1949) and *Cyrano de Bergerac* (1950). His other films include *Death of a Salesman* (1951) and *The Caine Mutiny* (1954).

In 1954, it became evident to Ellsworth that Gerstad wanted to direct. "I wanted Harry to remain as editor," says Ellsworth, "but he wanted to trade his editing table for the director's chair. He knew the stock requirements of the show, and how to put a picture together better than anyone. Harry knew when we could shoot into stock or out of stock, so he became our other director." To make the job easier, Gerstad and Ellsworth invited Kramer's Clem Beauchamp to manage the production and RKO's Sam Waxman to edit.

"At least 'Superman' got off with some fairly high-class personnel," beams Gerstad.

"1954 was no different," remarked Bob (Inspector Henderson) Shayne. "It was still a grind even though we only shot thirteen. We barely had enough time for rehearsal, and most of us learned the lines on the set each morning. We just continued to crank them out." The reduced schedule meant nothing new on a day-to-day basis. There was no financial windfall for the troops, since the schedule was axed in half. Even Ellsworth felt the pinch of rising film cost and special effects. Fewer trick shots were scheduled, and the ever sure springboard was pushed into a closet for most of the shooting; George Reeves just hoofed out of frame as fast as he could. Finally, the 1954 episodes relied too much on the swish-pan flying shots supposedly of Metropolis. While not the dullest episodes, the 1954 thirteen anticipated the depths "Superman" would hit by 1956.

Color required many changes; the first—Reeves's wardrobe. The gray and browns of old would never do.

Ellsworth ordered new sets, or at least those old ones painted with both the gray scale and color chip charts in mind. There was much to consider when pioneering a new wave and everything was apparently accounted for except some of the plots.

David Chantler and Jackson Gillis were Ellsworth's writers for the first color season. Enough *Gelt* crossed their palms to keep them coming back for more, Chantler more than anyone else. In his leadoff, "Through the Time Barrier," Chantler suggests the shape of things to come. The half hour, starring crackerjack Sterling Holloway, lacks the close-ups, the intimacy and pacing of most episodes from the first two years. Ellsworth's new policy meant more humor on the screen and a barrage of Clark Kent double entendres.

Holloway, who had been featured twice during the previous season, left Uncle Oscar behind and assumed a new name. Maybe Professor Twiddle isn't Uncle Oscar by name but he's just as flighty, this time blasting everyone on a trip to prehistoric Metropolis. Twiddle's breakthrough is pooh-poohed. Lois Lane, for one, tells him to run away and bury his toy in the back yard. Twiddle stands firm. "Time," he says, "I've conquered it with this machine." He proves his point.

Clark decides they should take the "way-back" machine to 50,000 B.C. Perry White seconds the motion. One cloud of smoke later, the entourage checks their bearings on a pre-gas-shortage Stone Age. "Mr. Kent, now I don't want to alarm you . . ." Twiddle apologizes that he's neglected to develop the reverse process to return them to the present. So Perry White, who was interested in any age before paper was discovered, is trapped in time with a criminal named Turk (Jim Hyland), along with Lois, Jimmy, Twiddle and the eternally useless Clark Kent.

The other twelve half hours add little solace to a bleak production year. Superman battles wits with a tape recorder, a black cat, a tribe of Republic Pictures Indians, Julius Caesar's ghost, a hillbilly, a mule and a Western bully. Gone—noticeably gone—are the violent stories and the action-adventure dramas that marked the first year, and much of Ellsworth's initial work in 1953. "Superman," finally, became a kiddie show.

Harry Gerstad followed his directorial debut with one of Bob Shayne's favorite shows, "The Talking Clue." "I finally knew something about myself," says Shayne. "I had a son, but whether I was a widower or what, I never knew. To this day, I can't even remember if Inspector Henderson was ever married!"

Robert Shayne had been reasonably successful in films when his agent heard about a job possibility at RKO-Pathé. "They wanted a man to play the inspector who was, generally speaking, someone in George Reeves's age bracket." Shayne was hired. "The principal thing I remember about Inspector Henderson is that he was a foil, a patsy for Superman, a nice guy, but Henderson never solved a crime. Sure, certain episodes provided me some leeway. I might arrive with the authority of the law, but I never cracked a case myself!

"To be quite honest, Henderson was kind of a dull character," admits Shayne. "I was a sounding board and Reeves played off me." Shayne remembers only two of his eighty or more segments which required any depth. One was as the local dick in "The Talking Clue," the other as the French gendarme in "Peril in Paris." Otherwise, he was typecast. Bob Shayne looked the part, and delivered the role with ease.

"I can't remember how Inspector Henderson felt about things except that Metropolis should be kept free of crime. And I don't even know if I was ever told. Like so much in the B picture era, we didn't do our scenes to develop character. 'Superman' was one-dimensional. It provided no great tax on anyone's imagination, rarely moving any of us to give a plausible simulation of a human being. I was Inspector Henderson, and that's all I knew."

Robert Shayne taking on a Franklin Roosevelt stance in Warner Brothers' "Make Your Own Bed" (1944). Jane Wyman (then Mrs. Ronald Reagan) listens.

No one had any pretensions about the minor roles. The show belonged to Reeves, and Shayne knew it. "You know, we used to have a lot of laughs on the set because it was impossible for us as actors to take this all too seriously. We tried to give a good performance, yet sometimes the ridiculousness of the dialogue or the situation would bring on cracks. I asked for more-fleshed-out scripts, but none popped up." Shayne recalls the most any one saw of a supposedly active Metropolis police force was Henderson and on occasion a few patrolmen. "That's why most of the work was a bloody bore, like so much of picture making is boring. It got so bad that I could have telephoned my part in, they were so much the same. The lines were easy to learn, and none of the scenes had any long speeches." Shayne's experience in television prompts his criticisms one step further. "There's not much left for the creative artist; those who hoped television would be their

229

John Carradine and Robert Shayne are pushed into the corner by a great dane, actually a ghost, in "Face of Marble" (Monogram, 1946).

way out were sorely wrong. You really don't learn your craft if you're picked up and put into a feature role or a television series. You're cast to type. Most of it is off the top of your head, there are no great challenges, and young actors and actresses are having a hard time for that reason." Shayne often explains in college lectures that acting should be intimate; the professional should know and understand his character in order to render it believable to himself and his audience. He concludes, "That was the missing element in 'Superman,' the major flaw of our production."

He talks of his background with far greater depth. Following high school graduation in Washington, D.C., Shayne joined his father and brother in their Rochester, Indiana, wholesale grocery business. When his father took a job with the YMCA during World War I, Shayne's mother moved the family East. He matriculated in business administration at Boston University and worked part-time as a parlor singer and an efficiency expert at the large Jordan Marsh department store.

Shayne came close to joining the ministry, but dismissed the idea. Instead, his associations with the church led to an assignment in the Unitarian Layman's League as their mid-Atlantic states field secretary. On the road, Shayne's idealism emerged. "I was raised in a liberal tradition where the search for truth and knowledge was justification enough for life." (Such idealism steered him toward political activism in the thirties—activism he was later asked to defend.)

In 1924, he left the Layman's League for a stint in Florida's blossoming real estate trade. "I remember soliciting subscriptions to the new Vanderbilt newspaper, the *Illustrated Daily Pad,* and on Christmas Eve, without a penny in my pocket, listening to the famous William Jennings Bryan. After the paper began, I moved into the city room, eventually making it as a hotshot real estate reporter." Shayne later answered an ad for secretary of the Miami Advertising Club. "The Board wanted me because I was an ex-newspaperman, and because they wanted to organize a Better Business Bureau. They thought I could be effective doing it." Shayne had good training, as his father, George Grosvna Dawe, was one of the five organizers of the U. S. Chamber of Commerce, and first editor of *Nation's Business.*

His next moves were northward; Atlanta, Georgia; then Birmingham, Alabama. On the second stop, he doubled as a specialty shop copywriter/assistant manager by day, and a member of the Birmingham Little Theatre by night. Before long he left his $50-a-week daytime work to relocate again in Atlanta, where he learned acting under the watchful eyes of Madge Kennedy, Sidney Blackmer, Walter Connolly, Natalie Schafer, and Leo G. Carroll. His teachers encouraged him to move on; Shayne sold his car and hopped a freight for New York. For a while, the closest he got to Broadway was posting press releases in an agent's scrapbook. Meanwhile, producer Johnson Briscoe persuaded him to change his name from Robert Shaen Dawe to the Americanized Robert Shayne. Of course roles would have been easier to come by if Shayne had daytime hours to audition. He did not. The Stock Market kept him busy ten hours each day. "I'd start selling stocks, bonds and securities at the top of a skyscraper, and work my way down, office to office, but those of us who worked in the market weren't very popular people on October 29, 1929." Even idealistic Robert Shayne was disillusioned on Black Friday, the day the market crashed—like millions of others he faced financial ruin.

By 1931, when he was reduced to a very survivable $50 per week, Shayne decided to make another go at the theater. This time, he won a bid on Broadway, a part in *The Rap*, a police story with actor Paul Harvey. Shayne played New York for six weeks, and later, Chicago, where his whopping $40 per week dried up when the play folded. He moved to Stockbridge, Massachusetts for a spell, where he was reintroduced to Leo G. Carroll and Walter Connolly. By fall, the bleak days of the Depression were on him again. Shayne began to question the deplorable state of affairs. "Why was there no pay for rehearsals?" he asked. "Why couldn't there be a guarantee for continued work when a play moved to another city?" The answers were there, but dangerous to press. Shayne saw too many seasoned actors, secure in life, ripe with success and age, who were reluctant to rock the boat. "Actors traditionally don't organize," says Shayne. "And organized protest didn't promise delivery from the Depression. As late as the fifties, it was unheard of for an actor to participate in politics. An actor was an actor, his life was a thing apart." Shayne saw it differently. He agitated for improvement at every stop: pay for rehearsals, protection against a producer's whimsical cut, and the security of a livable minimum salary. Robert Shayne, and a few others, inaugurated much of the reform that actors take for granted today.

In 1932, Shayne was still a struggling bit player on the outside of an angry industry. For a short time, he kept off the breadlines by twirling lovelies in a circle at an Arthur Murray dance studio. However, that ended abruptly when his feet once collapsed beneath him. "I was tired pushing old ladies around all day," remembers Shayne. "So I went into the men's lounge, put my feet on the wall, and got canned. I don't know how I survived to that point," adds Shayne. "I wanted to be an actor so badly in the beginning I could taste it. You have to have that kind of drive to put up with everything that's thrown in your face!"

Life looked rosier once he was cast in Maxwell Anderson's Both Your Houses (1933), followed in quick succession by Yellow Jack (1934), Order Please (1934) and Mother Lode (1934). Shayne also landed parts in The Cat and the Canary (1935), Ayn Rand's Night of January 16 (1936) and the mysterious Devil of Pei-Ling (1936), which the New York Times noticed:

. . . There is Robert Shayne, appearing at ease and amiable through the grim chaos of three acts. . . .

For the first time he was able to walk past the famed 5c Cracked Wheat Restaurants and the Selena Royle Actors Kitchen and eat a heartier meal. However, his real break did not occur until 1938, when he portrayed Renny in Ethel Barrymore's Whiteoaks.

The regular-season success of Whiteoaks was followed by another dry spell. Shayne had nothing of consequence except Five Alarm Waltz (1941), where he walked off with encouraging reviews at the expense of the show's lead, Elia Kazan. The next opportunity came that same year when he replaced Donald Cook in Claudia. In between performances, Shayne felt another tug. "Every actor in New York, even if he denied it, had a secret ambition to go to Hollywood. We were always promoting ourselves for tests at Warners, Fox, Universal or Paramount." RKO had him in the early thirties in a pair of films, Keep 'Em Rolling (1932) and

Wednesday's Child (1934), but the studio failed to move on his option. Nonetheless, his appearance was enough for Louella Parsons to add:

Robert Shayne, stage actor of the type of Gary Cooper and Cary Grant, has fixed his signature to the Radio contract (RKO). "The best bet in years" is the way he is described to this gullible writer. I'll take a look at him when he returns from Virginia. I personally don't know if I'll agree with Radio's reviews.

RKO's appraisal was a bit premature. He returned to New York until the last curtain of *Without Love*, starring Katharine Hepburn. On February 16, 1943, Shayne boarded a plane for L.A. ready to fulfill his long-awaited Warner Brothers contract. The ink was still wet.

Shayne's first major film for the studio was *Shine on Harvest Moon* (1944); however, Warners had conditioned him earlier in a series of two-reel grooming films; twenty-minute remakes of *Oklahoma Kid* and a few Errol Flynn features. From there the studio sent him out with their big guns: Bette Davis and Claude Rains in *Mr. Skeffington* (1944); Jack Carson, Jane Wyman and Alan Hale for *Make Your Own Bed* (1944); Barbara Stanwyck and Sydney Greenstreet in *Christmas in Connecticut* (1944); Errol Flynn in *San Antonio* (1945); and Peter Lorre in *Three Strangers* (1946). Shayne appeared in dozens of other pictures in and out of the A category until his career took a dive.

"Glenn Ford, Ronald Reagan and the newer crew of Warner contract players and young prospects filed back onto the lot after the war and I could see I was being submerged into smaller and smaller roles, so I asked to be released from my contract," says Shayne. "It was a big decision. A few years earlier I sweated out getting the option. The salary was good, but I had no choice in the films I did. If I turned down one, I ran the risk of being suspended. It happened to many of the top people in the trade. For a while I got my $750 per week, I paid off my debts, got a decent wardrobe and bought a house . . . but I left anyway." By late 1946, he was another free-lance actor. "In retrospect," remembers Shayne with an acute degree of sensitivity, "as I look back now, I've come to the conclusion that actors are rather stupid when it comes to determining what's best for themselves. I should have stayed."

His first job on his own co-starred John Carradine in the 1946 Monogram mistake *Face of Marble*. "It's undoubtedly the worst film I've ever done, it's deplorable," says Shayne. "My relationship with the lead was no better. One day I came onto the semi-darkened stage and Carradine was off somewhere on the set spouting Shakespeare. I didn't know he was there, and I made some caustic remark. After that he wasn't very friendly to me."

His free-lance days took him through Poverty Row all the way to the last Republic serial, the dull *King of the Carnival* (1955). His most recognizable films on television today include Sam Katzman's *The Swordsman* (1947), *State Penitentiary* (1950), *Law of the Barbary Coast* (1949) and *Prince of Pirates* (1953). He appeared in a myriad of other quickies including *Forgotten Woman* (1949) with Noel Neill, *I Ring Doorbells* (1946), *I Cover Big Town* (1947), *Backlash* (1947), *Welcome Stranger* (1947), a Green Hornet picture and a Monogram Bowery Boys misadventure. One other film co-starred him for a day or two with Phyllis Coates—*Marshal of Cedar Creek* (1953).

Shayne's last continuing role was in television's "Bracken's World." In recent years, he appeared in Walt Disney's *Million Dollar Duck* and the war bomb *Tora! Tora! Tora!* A few years back he appeared in the Doris Day and Henry Fonda sitcoms, and Hitchcock used him briefly in *North by Northwest*. For years he sold insurance, securities and mutual funds at night, while saving the world in the daylight hours from the horrors of *Invaders from Mars* (1953), *The Indestructible Man* (1956), *The Incredible Shrinking Man* (1958) and *How to Make a Monster* (1958). The last-named pictures were made when he was on leave from the Metropolis Police Department. And during his off-hours he defended the Old West with Tris Coffin in *39 Men*, and the South Pacific in *Navy Log*.

"Those television days wiped me out," remembers Shayne. "I guess everyone else on 'Superman' and any other show would tell you how we'd come home late after playing these one-dimensional caricatures, only to repeat it again the next day. It was work, hard and long; a terrible business when things go wrong, a rewarding career when things go right."

One of the most interesting elements of the color years was the lackadaisical attitude toward flubbed lines. "The Talking Clue" is an obvious case in point. Clark Kent, doing some shamus work on his own, reasons that Inspector Henderson's kidnapped son Ray (Richard Shakleton) might have left some indication of his whereabouts. The reporter splices a few strands of audio tape together and says, "I've threaded the two new pieces on the beginning of a new rule [reel]." There was no retake.

Ellsworth admits, "Sometimes there was just garbage in the rushes, but we were often forced to use what we had, rather than relight the set and go again." Throughout the last fifty episodes, the attitude of both cast and crew deteriorated. The added expense of color and the aforementioned salary disputes culminated in the excessive increase of flubbed lines.

Despite the dribble, David Chantler did write a cute tease for the opening. Inspector Henderson assembles a police lineup for the benefit of a robbery witness. The camera pans the rogues and stops on a character who identifies himself as Lou Chambers. We know him as Clark Kent. The reporter is standing in, purely as a favor for Bill Henderson. The inspector whimsically inquires of Kent, "How many names do you have, anyway?" "Several," replies Kent. There's a long pause, then Henderson asks, "What's this business about several names?" Usually, there is little parley between the two; business of the department forbids joking, but this encounter proves to be one of the more humorous

Robert Shayne as a general in Sam Katzman's "The Giant Claw" (Columbia, 1957). Robert Shayne, today.

exceptions.

While on the subject of strong teases, there's another in the next episode, "The Lucky Cat." Landlord Bots warns the subjective camera lens to beware of the strange doings in the house behind him. "Mark me, you'll be sorry, all of you who come here will be sorry." As he approaches, the camera pulls back to show Kent and Olsen flanking him on either side. Harry Gerstad's angle is merely a hook to get us into the story. In addition, there are a few good quips like Clark Kent's, "Maybe I'm lucky or maybe I'm Superman." But in total, this Jackson Gillis teleplay is rather dull fare. The anti-superstition club is a variation on the Sherlock Holmes "Five Orange Pips" theme.

"Superman Week" isn't anything to write home about either. Jimmy ("Golly, if I could fly like Superman instead of taking a hot subway") Olsen helps bring back the Kryptonite nightmare from "The Defeat of Superman." Si Horten (Herb Vigran) and his assistant (Paul Burke) coax the cub reporter into telling them the whereabouts of the deadly rock, lost for the past year. The villains, of course, do not know that the superhero anticipates the plan and lays a gambit of his own. The old clichés are around again——the naïve Olsen who spills the beans about Kryptonite after washing down a truth serum milk shake, and Lois Lane who momentously thinks aloud, "Now we'll find out once and for all about Clark Kent and Superman." Jimmy adds an inquisitive second to the motion. "That should be very interesting, Mr. Kent interviewing Superman." The conclusion of Peggy Chantler's script (David's sister) has Kent questioning Superman on the local television outlet. At last, Lois is certain she'll get proof that Kent is Superman, but you-know-who is still one step ahead. In place of his reporter self he substitutes a plaster bust. The fait accompli is a prerecorded narration in Clark's faster speech pattern that introduces the Man of Steel. Why nobody else remains in the studio to crew the talk show is a mystery unto itself. Still, Kent's fast thinking works; Lois tosses another of her rock-solid hunches out the window, adding, "And I really thought we had him."

"Superman Week" was fun for Jack Larson. He recalls one sight gag that took hours of practice. "I had this great telephone thing. In order to crash Si Horten's pad, I had to pass myself off as a telephone repairman, equipped with theatrical mustache, uniform grays and a toolbox. The bit called for me to get my mustache caught in the wires, that was enough to blow my cover. But the reason I remember the gag to this day is because George snapped a picture of the routine on his Minox and presented a print to me. I think that picture shows exactly the kind of business that made my Jimmy so real and so popular."

John Hamilton's stately presence in "Great Caesar's Ghost" lifts the next episode above most of the year's production. The editor is psychologically shaken by the materialization of the ghost he so frequently damns. His usual rationalism indicates to the ever present Superman that something is awry. The survivors of Morley's gang are trying to discredit White and prevent

SI Horten (Herb Vigran) and Matthew Tips (Paul Burke) prepare a truth serum milk shake for Jimmy Olsen ("Superman Week"— 1954).

him from presenting credible testimony in an important criminal case. The scheme is masterminded by Jarvis, the squeaky-voiced Universal horror-film player Olaf Hytten, and Julius Caesar himself—Trevor Bardette. However, Superman's intervention not only saves the precarious Mr. White, but also seals the criminals away forever.

The "Test of a Warrior" returned George Blair to the director's chair he would assume through 1957.

George Blair was a native from New Jersey who ventured West, eventually to sign on as a second assistant director for Republic. He worked his way through the ranks of the studio, winning the spoils of long hours and low pay. He once told Whitney Ellsworth that in those pre-union days, it was not uncommon for an assistant director to put in a one-hundred-hour week in seven days for a mere $35. "If you didn't like it," he told Ellsworth, "there were always a hundred other guys looking for the job."

Blair was in good company. Neither Tommy Carr, Lew Landers, Lee Sholem nor Phil Ford had time to be great directors and were not expected to be. "They were," according to Ellsworth, "craftsmen who had to bring in their pictures for X dollars in Y number of days." Remarkably, they were often able to do extremely credible work, and as Ellsworth concludes, "They were a natural choice when television came along with its stringent limitations as to time and money."

"Old George had some odd quirks," says Noel Neill. "I remember on the rushes of one of his episodes that year we noticed a little white dot popping up and down in the lower third of the frame. Nobody knew what it was. We looked at some more footage and there it was again. Somebody, I can't remember who, finally realized it was George Blair's tennis sneakers slipping around in the frame like a little white ball. So needless to say, we moved him over!"

Blair was known for an additional eccentricity. Whenever a scene ended, instead of folding up a page or striking a line through it in Carr's fashion, Blair ripped it out of the folder. "It was his nervousness," says Noel Neill. "He made snowballs out of them, and there'd be snow all over the set, sometimes he'd be tearing them up before we'd get through the lines at the bottom."

Whitney Ellsworth remembers one final Blair signature. "At the day's last take, most directors call, 'That's a wrap.' Not George, his sign-off was much different—'Home and mother!' "

Early television was a rugged business. Where live television survived on the quick thinking of reliable actors, shows like "Superman" were locked into a format that denied extensive characterization. Often when his actors hesitated on a line, Ellsworth had it written out of a scene. His production instincts demanded that such a scene be cut rather than reworked to the actor's

240

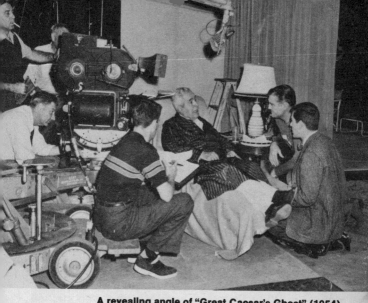

A revealing angle of "Great Caesar's Ghost" (1954).

satisfaction. Noel Neill recalls one such occasion in "Test of a Warrior" when Ralph Moody couldn't articulate his role. "He took too much time, so the order came down from above—'Chop, Chop.'" The actors tried to take it upon themselves to excise material; however, they hardly managed to raise the marking pen before Ellsworth read them the riot act. "I always made a speech about that. There wasn't to be any horsing around the set to change lines without first discussing it with me! Certainly, if somebody had a real reason, I'd hope I'd be retractable about my policy. On the other hand, it was like everything else. Somebody had to be in charge, and since I was responsible for the show, it had to be done my way. I used to say, 'This is the script that we bought, rewrote and edited, and this is the way I want it shot.'"

"Olsen's Millions" stands out as an admirable exception to the dull story lines that Ellsworth approved in 1954. It stars the aging but capable Elizabeth Patterson, George E. Stone and Richard Reeves. As the story opens, Jimmy Olsen finds he has locked a cat in a safe owned by wealthy Sarah Peabody (Patterson). Superman saves the little critter, but Peabody mistakenly thanks Olsen with an undeserved cool million. Superman learns that destroying meteors and changing the course of mighty rivers is elementary compared to the effort he must expend keeping an eye on the nouveau riche Olsen.

Tris (*King of the Rocket Men*) Coffin leads veteran "Superman" villains John Doucette, George Eldredge and Sid Tomack in the next whodunit—"Clark Kent, Outlaw." Kent leaves the *Daily Planet* offices dejected and out of work. But faithful "Superman" fans need not worry, it's only a plan to trap Coffin and his boys. Kent's undercover assignment works; the gang latches onto him and he passes their safecracking initiation with flying colors. In fact he's so good that one henchman asks, "Are you sure you've been a reporter all your life?"

Kent replies half seriously, "Do you remember Jimmy Valentine? He was supposed to have supersensitive fingers. Well, it's a gift, I guess."

Meanwhile, the initiation continues with the demands that Kent assassinate Jimmy and Lois. He takes them to Perry White's office, ties them to a chair, lights a match and bids them adieu.

While Kent is away, Stoddard (Coffin) manages to sweet-talk the truth out of Perry White. Kent returns, unaware that his cover has been exposed and he and White are forced to swallow a few knockout pills. White, who can't cope with this pharmaceutical prescription, blacks out on the spot. Clark changes his clothes, takes off his pinkie ring, dashes outside and picks up the gang's car before they make their getaway. The Man of Steel then soars off after a day's work well done.[2]

Ellsworth recalled a familiar face, Leonard Mudie, to the California Studios lot for the next adventure, "The

---

[2] The "boing" of his springboard is embarrassingly audible on the sound track.

Magic Necklace." The plot echoes the theme suggested in "The Lucky Cat": Ladders, magic beads, black cats and a rabbit's foot are no match for reason. However, logic is not Jimmy Olsen's middle name, so the lesson has to be learned all over again.

The following week, Lois and Jimmy stop off for a few days in the western corner of the studio, where they immediately lock horns with Gunner Flinch (Myron Healey), alias "The Bully of Dry Gulch." Lois, in a terror, telephones Kent, who only yawns "a so-what," until Lois adds, "Besides gunning for Jimmy, these characters have been making goo-goo eyes at me!"

"That's different. I'll be right out!" assures Kent. The receiver slams down, and by the time it stops shaking on the cradle, Superman is halfway to Dry Gulch.

"How in the world did you get out here so fast?" asks Lois.

"I flew."

Gunner quickly challenges the city slicker to a fast game of poker. "Be careful," warns Lois, who expects the cards are marked. "After all, you're not Superman." Ah, but he is, and his X-ray vision ignites the loaded deck as Lois exclaims, "That deck seemed to just explode in flames."

"Maybe it was a hot deck," jokes Clark, finally pleased with his humor.

However, later, when Clark feels the pressure, Lois sings quite a different tune: "I suppose you're going to go to your room and hide."

"Sometimes, Lois, discretion is the better part of valor." Actually, there's no discretion involved. He needs to expose Gunner as a fraud, and can best do it as Superman. The Man of Steel learns that Gunner did not really shoot down Pedro (Martin Garralaga) in a "Gunsmoke" draw. The event was merely staged to scare naïve, innocent and extremely gullible Jimmy Olsen into leaving town. However, Superman decides to turn the tables on the bully, enlisting the aid of the very much alive Pedro. Unfortunately, Jimmy is unaware of Superman's plan; he's too busy staring at his own epitaph:

**Here lies Olsen the dude,
to Gunner he was very rude.**

High noon, and the town is quiet. Pedro arrives ready for a real shoot-out with Gunner, but the toughie wants nothing of it. Pedro asks why not, adding with certainty, "Gunner, you already killed me four times this month!" Still, Gunner backs down. He picks up what's left of his battered ego, and walks to the edge of town arm in arm with his two sidekicks. Myron Healey is gone, but not forgotten. Whit Ellsworth already had him in mind for "The Jolly Roger" and "Dagger Island."

"Flight to the North" is a gem. Chuck Connors, shaved to within half an inch of his hairline, plays the good guy, while Ben Welden offers his most creative comic heavy to date. The episode's attractiveness is in dialogue and approach; probably David Chantler's best tongue-in-cheek writing. Welden recalls the episode as if it had been shot yesterday: "It was offbeat, quite fun and just different enough from the others to make it great." The formula had been the same week after week and Welden thinks that "Flight to the North" was the perfect script to break the monotony. "It always was the same. Superman somehow knocked out the heavy, or two or three of us in one blow. There was nothing strikingly original about it until we did this new one. And boy, was it different."

It's no wonder Ben Welden remembers his work so vividly; the episode is timeless. Professional hillbilly Sylvester J. Superman (Connors) rides into Metropolis atop his mule, Lilly Bell. The smelly character from Skunk Hollow has neither been to Crumbly Hotel, managed by George Chandler, nor heard of his namesake. He is just a tall, overly arid mountaineer, who can't quite understand the fuss everyone makes over him. Marge (Marjorie Owens) is the first one to place her trust in Sylvester when he answers her *Daily Planet* classified for Superman. Marge seems hard pressed to believe that this hick at the door is the real McCoy. She's even more skeptical when he asks permission to hitch Lilly Bell to the front porch.

"Oh sure," nods Marge. "But I certainly didn't expect you to look like this!"

"Oh shucks, ma'am, you should see me in my Sunday overalls." At the moment Sylvester is attired in his best manure-shoveling slacks. The woodsman, showing no sign of getting a hernia, proceeds to demonstrate his strength by moving her piano across the living room floor. However, all these demands make him equally uncertain about Marge, and when the young lady asks him to cart a luscious lemon meringue pie to an obscure air force base in Alaska, he's entirely floored. His homespun logic tells him, "There's only two ways to treat a neighbor. You either help them out or shoot them out." Marge is in luck, he settles on the former. The pie is intended for her fiancé, Steve Emmet (Richard Garland). There's one major drawback—Leftover Louie Lyman (Ben Welden) wants it for his own. Lyman bets Buckets (Ralph Sanford) $25,000 that his old high school chum Marge can bake a Betty Crocker special better than any Buckets can produce. Both are ready to salivate all the way to the bank.

Meanwhile, Clark arrives at Marge's house, never expecting Superman to be there. "Come in," she says, "I'll introduce you to Superman!"

The lines continue as if Alan Alda or Carl Reiner speak directly through David Chantler's subconscious. "You will?" chokes Clark. "I'm glad to have the opportunity to meet you!"

Back to the subplot; Leftover Louie is still desperate for the pie. He is unable to intercept it en route to Alaska, so he trails Sylvester to the relay cabin. First, the bumpkin and his mule arrive with the pie. Steve is aghast. After all, who in his right mind would trek thousands of miles with a lemon meringue pie? Even more than that, a lemon meringue pie and a mule? The serviceman either was secluded in the frozen wild since before 1938, or the cold affected his frontal lobe, because the name "Superman" doesn't even ring a bell.

A short while later, old Louie barges into the cabin, steals the pie at gunpoint, backs out the door and flies south in his airplane. Steve can't quite make hay of all this. "It doesn't matter about the pie," he says. "It's the thought that counts." There's another knock at the cabin door. "Now who could that be?" asks Sylvester.

"Oh, probably just one of those Zulu natives riding by on his elephant," answers Steve.

Superman enters.

"Welcome, sir," says Steve, now certain he has been away from civilization too long. "It's a fast relief to realize I actually have gone crazy. Now I can enjoy it!"

Superman interrupts, "Has he been here yet, the man who wanted the pie?"

"Certainly. He left just a few minutes ago. Don't fret, I've got a nice can of plum pudding for you."

Superman has no time to joke. "What kind of plane was he flying? I must have missed it."

Steve answers assuredly, "A yellow two-engine job, trimmed with lace and purple polka dots!"

Superman, ready to charge into the frigid wasteland, stops to overhear a message on Steve's wireless. Lyman's airplane has iced up and he's forced to land about six thousand miles short of Metropolis airport. Superman takes this as his cue to exit. Sylvester can't understand, but it doesn't surprise Steve one bit, nothing does anymore. Superman breaks through a wall of ice to rescue Louie; however, the crook finds little solace in the thought that his return trip will be in Superman's arms.

His peace-keeping mission finished, Superman returns to the cabin for a sampling of Marge's epic pie. The hillbilly tells Superman, "You'd better be careful, mister. You're liable to get hurt flying around like that!" Superman smiles; we know he'll live with it somehow. But Chuck Connors, a former Dodger infielder, has one hell of a story to tell at his next dinner party.

George Reeves jumps off the ladder to enter the scene in "Great Caesar's Ghost." John Hamilton, Olaf Hytten, Jim Hayword and Robert Shayne are also pictured.

"The Seven Souvenirs" kept things rolling with the kind of successful twist that writer Jackson Gillis perfected a few seasons later when he served as associate producer of "Perry Mason." Mr. Willy (Phillips Tead), a dealer in Superman memorabilia, passes off dozens of allegedly authentic daggers bent under the grip of Superman. None are legitimate, but entrepreneur Willy doesn't care. Superman deduces that another, more sinister crime is in the works. An unidentifiable figure is systematically robbing Metropolis blind of all the daggers, and Superman wants to know why. Mr. Jasper (Arthur Space) nearly weaves the perfect crime with the expert aid of henchmen Rick Vallin and Steve Calvert. The brain-heavy tricks Superman into using his X-ray vision to turn the alloy within his dagger handles to pure radium. However, Superman, according to National Periodicals folklore, doesn't like to be tricked, so Jasper goes to jail.

George Reeves demonstrates to Ralph Moody how to fly during rehearsals for "Test of a Warrior" (1954).

Clark Kent (Reeves) swallows a poisonous milkshake intended for the young prince (Jack Larson). Notice Leon (General Burkhalter) Askin waiting at the door. ("King for a Day"—1954.)

Jack Larson and Elizabeth Patterson in "Olsen's Millions" (1954).

Clark Kent (Reeves) says goodbye to Sylvester J. Superman, played by a pre-"Rifleman" Chuck Connors ("Flight to the North" —1954).

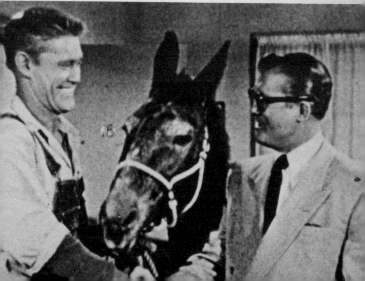

The 1954 production schedule wrapped up with "King for a Day" as Leon (Prime Minister Vallin) Askin and Phil Van Zandt lead an assassination plot against Jimmy Olsen. Both villains think Olsen is Prince Gregory of Burgonia. Their suspicions are well founded since Olsen is playing the regal role to the hilt while the legitimate monarch slips unobserved into his "Mouse That Roared" kingdom. Olsen dodges knives, knockout drugs and bullets from a firing squad while Superman, in the person of Clark Kent, keeps a close eye on him. The traitors express their surprise at the senior reporter's presence. How did he pass the court guards, they ask. "To get in one would have to fly."

"Surely you gentlemen don't think . . ." his voice trails off. Kent turns to the "twenty-four-hour prince" and admits, "I don't know about Superman, but I'm going to stick around." Olsen is one happy buckaroo.

The year was rather non-violent for Superman. Certainly, the Man of Steel had a few hair-raising encounters, but for the most part, he bested his quarry with grace and ease. There was really no reason to do otherwise. The American public was receiving its fair share of mass murders, violence and sex on "The Lineup," "Sheena, Queen of the Jungle," "I Led Three Lives" and "Ellery Queen." Ellsworth, on the other hand, had whipped "Superman" into a workable, successful production that rated high with kids and adults. Variety reported the feather in Ellsworth's cap: The "Adventures of Superman" remained top-seated in New York and most "metropolises" wherever it played. The returns were growing, and an expanding syndicated market guaranteed a bright, colorful future for decades to come.

CHAPTER VIII

1955

The transferral of the B picture market to television brought along certain inherent disadvantages. The screenwriters were swept along at a "Modern Times" assembly-line pace that left little time for thoughtful creativity. "Superman" didn't escape being so engulfed. The first two years of production stand out above the overall output essentially because Maxwell and Ellsworth juggled with a wide variety of writers. However, when Ellsworth thinned down the ranks in 1954, he failed to realize that his reliable and competent main writers, Jackson Gillis and David Chantler, were taxing their own limits by carrying the bulk of the load. Consequently, "Superman" became too ingrained, dull and lifeless. The scripts quickly lost their sparkle without a fresh supply of writers. But there was no time to debate whether the program would survive the next quarter century, the job was clear-cut; to get the show out as quickly, cheaply and efficiently as possible. To this end, Ellsworth's greatest achievement remains the program's overwhelming popularity in ratings and returns. Its revival today is pure gravy, proof that the winning charismatic elements of "Superman" were greater than the minuscule budget. Noel Neill stands as the embodiment of that phenomenon. Her Superman tour is filling auditoriums across the country. Jane Ellsworth, herself once an actress, notes that within a comparatively short time, many big stars have been completely forgotten, whereas "Noel has a secure place in the folklore of the country, and will be remembered for God knows how many years hence." There's no doubt in anyone's mind. Noel Neill and the "Adventures of Superman" have assured themselves of that niche.

In 1955, the production moved to a third home, the famed LaBrea Street studios of Sir Charles Spencer Chaplin. Each year Ellsworth negotiated what would hopefully be the most solvent deal for his thirteen episodes. And indeed it was getting harder to rent a complete setup for $750 per day. Cameras were expensive, and space was not as available as it had been.

By the time "Superman" flew into the new studio there wasn't much left of the "Little Tramp." Chaplin was in Europe, literally expelled for his political views, banished by the same country that waited so long for him to speak. Chaplin's life-style was a personal affront to many. His pleas for peace, solidarity and brotherhood in *The Great Dictator* were misinterpreted as subversive Communist ideology. *Monsieur Verdoux* and *Limelight* warned America of a dangerous Watergate mentality amid a psychotic McCarthy purge. But Chaplin, the hero for so long, the artist of incomparable dimensions, was also a vulnerable target for America's hate-slinging fringe elements. Chaplin's every word was questioned on the basis of his non-allegiance to Old Glory;[1] he had never become an American citizen. He proved an easy scapegoat. Liberal thought, combined with constant visibility, made him sure pickings. Chaplin was ironically expelled by the very weakness and hatred that had caused the Little Tramp so many difficulties. The tramp, who innocently carried a fallen red flag in *Modern Times,* was unjustifiably labeled a Commie in his real life.

Today, a supermarket stands on the corner of La-Brea and Sunset where Chaplin's finest work was filmed. The blacktop and bulldozer tribute to Chaplin's studio was America's fond way of saying goodbye to another of its great editorialists.

Jack Larson saw it coming. A cart from *City Lights*

---

[1] On June 12, 1947, Representative John E. Rankin demanded that Chaplin be deported to assure that ". . . he can be kept off the American screen and his loathsome pictures be kept from the eyes of American youth."

Mauritz Hugo and Billy Nelson pose with George Reeves and John Hamilton on the set of "Joey" (1955).

was used as a garbage receptacle, while Chaplin's elephantine *Modern Times* machinery smoldered in flames to make room for the parking lot. Larson spared a few items from the fire, but most had already vanished forever. The asphalt devoured everything in sight.

Adjacent to Chaplin's sound stage, where Ellsworth reconstructed his *Daily Planet* offices, Jack Larson discovered another lost shred of Chaplin history. "I was memorizing my lines in sort of a half trance when I walked over to a set of metal dollies the crew had put down on the sound stage. I pulled up the tracks and saw a set of footprints—Chaplin's. It was his studio dedication." A little detective work led to another revelation: "I noticed other footprints, and an imprint of a cane rubbed smooth over the years that went all the way to the bathroom. They all belonged to Chaplin. I realized it was his little walk. It must have been a big studio dedication, and Chaplin came out of the john, walked forward and signed the dedication in the wet cement. And so there was this path, at least until it was paved over."

Charlie Chaplin's studio bowed to the combined pressure of politics, years and money. What little is left belongs to Herb Alpert. Even though his buildings, with their time worn props and silent ghosts, are gone, the Chaplin films still entertain millions—and millions to come.

Season four began as they all did—in Whit Ellsworth's office. The producer delivered his fire-and-brimstone oration about scripts and the limitations of the budget. "When we're doing a television show," he would say, "particularly a low-budget show like ours, we have to watch everything all the time. There is no room for nuances. Just do what the director and cameraman want, and it'll go much easier." The "Ouija Board" decision maker, as he was called, was perhaps more impartial than New York would have appreciated. Ellsworth was at least admired as a diplomatic gentleman.

Over a friendly bowl of cereal, Ellsworth cultivated a workable relationship with his sponsor. Kellogg's bought the rights to "Superman," retaining no ownership of their own. National Periodicals simply sold the original first run and limited reruns to Kellogg's for a fixed price. They also reportedly footed part of Reeves's renegotiated salary after 1954. Ellsworth, in turn, prepared the preliminary budget; New York approved it, and Kellogg's bought in.

The procedure has changed drastically since the days of "Superman." The age of alternate and regular sponsors is long since gone. The networks, with the exception of a few quiz shows and soap operas, produce their own material. Today, each sixty-second spot costs far in excess of an original "Superman" episode.

Kellogg's budget was determined in Chicago. The Los Angeles office oversaw the production and plied Ellsworth with twelve brands of artiflcially sweetened breakfast foods. "But I had complete autonomy," declares Ellsworth with Perry White defiance. "Great Caesar's Ghost, Kellogg's had no say!"

Wally Ruggles, at Leo Burnett in Hollywood, remembers it differently. "We were there for every show, in on the meetings, and reviewing the scripts."

Ellsworth, however, calls this a courtesy. "I did not submit my scripts for Kellogg's approval, I *showed* them to the Leo Burnett people." The issue is not worthy of prolonged debate. Apparently, Ellsworth gave the agency a hand which the latter always thought extended much further. The relationship was never forced past the lines of demarcation. Ellsworth was more interested in his weekly telephone pleas to New York to refill the till. Week after week, year in and year out, Ellsworth outlined the operating costs, but Lexington Avenue never seemed to understand the nature of the sister medium. "I'd have to get on the horn every week. They'd ask how much, and I'd tell them. They'd always come back, 'So much?' "

In 1955, "Superman" was still tops. It was the year of the atomic powered *Nautilus,* so the "Adventures of Superman" launched a sub of its own ("Peril by Sea"). Churchill resigned, Argentina ousted Perón, the AFL and the CIO merged, and Superman continued to be a symbol of ever lasting democracy. "It obviously had a universal appeal for young people and adults; it still does," beams Ellsworth. "That's a thing a lot of people forget. We always had a big adult audience, we played around the world, and we were the number one show in Japan. Old George even received a citation from Emperor Hirohito!"

Ringing in everyone's ears were the familiar chords of the "Superman" theme. Far short of a resounding *Also Sprach Zarathustra,* the music from "Superman" is identifiable to millions. The main theme is owned outright by National, and the tapes are locked somewhere deep inside the vaults of Movielab in New York. Originally, Ellsworth believed the music came from Belgium, where the expense for rights and composers was considerably less than in the States. The repetitive background music from the black and white episodes had long since been dropped. In its place, Ellsworth rented a new package for $200 per episode. In addition to "Superman," the notes tinkled amid jungle screams and rocket ship engines in most of the late Republic features and serials.[2] Why no original music? Ellsworth simply says, "Our budget could not have stood the cost of composing and recording music for each segment." So the availability of a low-priced resource was the only option short of viewers sending in their own compositions typed out on a discarded Sugar Frosted Flakes box top.

Harry Gerstad directed over half of the 1955 thirteen, Phil Ford (John Ford's nephew) picked up the lighter end. First, Gerstad had to contend with a racehorse. "It wasn't an unusual request," says Ellsworth. "We had already seen an assorted menagerie made up of a mule, chimpanzee, dog and cat; a horse shouldn't be any problem." "Joey" is pitched to the six-week summer riding school co-eds who haven't yet traded in their western saddle for other invigorating social pastimes. Billy Nelson ("Machine That Could Plot Crimes") and Mauritz Hugo return as the villains who tamper with Joey, a filly owned by pretty, sweet, young and innocent Alice (Janine Perreau).

Since one show tugged at the heartstrings of little girls, Whitney Ellsworth applied the fairness doctrine to little boys. Ten-year-old Bobby Exbrook (Henry Blair)

[2] *Commander Cody, Radar Men From Mars* and *Jungle Drums of Africa.* The "Superman" theme, and background music from the first two years of production, however, have a more interesting history. Leon Klatzkin scored the theme. His other television credits include "Gunsmoke." As for the early incidental music, Bob Maxwell hired Hershel Burke Gilbert ("Four Star Theatre," "The Rifleman," "Wanted Dead or Alive"), Alexander Lazlo ("Rocky Jones Space Ranger"), and Darrell Calker. Finally, the fight music accompanying "The Golden Vulture," "Jungle Devil," and "The Clown Who Cried" in 1953, was written by Miklos Rozsa who is more widely known for his soundtracks for *El Cid, Thief of Bagdad, Spellbound, King of Kings. Madame Bovary, Jungle Book, Four Feathers, Ben Hur,* and *Lost Weekend.*

learns about truth the hard way. Dexter (John Berardino) fibs to the unsuspecting lad. We all know the sleazy character is not Superman, but poor Bobby doesn't. We also know that TV crime doesn't pay. Dexter, the penny ante hustler, falls into Dutch with his mob when Mrs. Exbrook (Elizabeth Patterson), thanks to a specially endowed reporter named Kent, correctly guesses the 2,845 jelly beans in a jar. "The Unlucky Number" is Dexter's undoing until the real Superman steps inside a closet and safely deflects a hit man's bullets intended for him.

There is a minor show of strength in "The Unlucky Number" via some trick photography. Superman twists a barbell out of shape, then back again, and melts some handy odds and ends with his X-ray vision. It's just enough training to get the Man of Steel into shape for a thorough workout next week in "The Big Freeze."

Superman next weighs anchor as a Coast Guard commando. "Peril by Sea" moves the Man of Steel onto the trail, perhaps the wake, of a submarine manned by Claude Aikens,[3] one of television's most Mephistophelian villains in the sixties and seventies. In their fourth collaboration of the year, David Chantler and Harry Gerstad have Perry White assume another of his multifarious roles—scientist extraordinaire. He had once been a lawyer, for a time a mayor, now we find White behind test tubes experimenting on his process to extract uranium from seawater.

The 35mm camera is bottoms up for another Ben Welden favorite, "Topsy Turvy," an improbable upsidedown bank robbery fable. For storytelling purposes "camera magic" has nothing to do with it. It's all the result of the crazy scientist, this time in the person of Professor Pepperwinkle (Phillips Tead). For some reason, Sterling Holloway did not fill the role he had superbly played in "Machine That Could Plot Crimes,"

[3] Aikens also shared minor billing with Reeves in *From Here to Eternity*.

"The Whistling Bird" and "Through the Time Barrier." Instead, Phillips Tead portrays the Uncle Oscar character who graduates to Professor Pepperwinkle.

Jack Larson has a dual role in the next adventure, "Jimmy the Kid." The boy wonder of American journalism is eased out by a reform school lookalike, Kid Collins (also Larson). Gridley (Damian O'Flynn) figures that Collins, doubling as Olsen, can infiltrate the *Daily Planet* offices and break an investigative reporting series that Clark Kent has developed. The dead ringer has everything going for him but the frills; Collins smokes up a storm with yard-long cigars. Collins' language is early *West Side Story*; whereas Olsen's most shocking expletive is "jeepers." While Olsen remains bound, the impostor ransacks Kent's apartment in search of the incriminating evidence.

Olsen finally frees himself and traps Collins, who has absconded with a familiar red, yellow and blue garment from Kent's apartment. "What is it doing there?" thinks Lois Lane. Clark claims he *borrowed it* for a firsthand Superman story. For the seventy-first time, his suspecting colleagues buy the double-talk—hook, line and sinker.

"Jimmy the Kid" supports Jack Larson's contention that his Don Knotts bumbling was indispensable to the program by 1955. "The Jimmy character just kept getting more popular," he says. There was talk of a Jimmy Olsen series four years later, but in the meantime, Ellsworth made certain Larson was the second busiest actor on the lot.

Noel Neill and the other women who worked for television in the fifties didn't have it so good. "The Girl Who Hired Superman" and "The Wedding of Superman," the next two episodes, stand out as much today as Thomas Jefferson would have in Richard Nixon's Cabinet. In "Superman's" day, television matured little beyond its provincial view of the female gender. The "Adventures of Superman" is no paragon of women's rights. Its portrayal of women is slightly better than its treatment of blacks. At least women had visibility in the 1950s, if only physiological. They are easy to recognize and hard to forget. There are healthy dumb blondes ("The Dog Who Knew Superman"), timid broads ("The Haunted Lighthouse"), bumbling wives ("Shot in the Dark"), elegant princesses ("King for a Day"), dangerous gun molls ("Jimmy the Kid") and rich bitches ("The Girl Who Hired Superman"). Lois Lane remains a tragic victim of the world's most publicized unrequited love. She is part of television's uncontrollable mammary fixation, a perspective that excluded the savoir faire seen in leading ladies from the forties. These women from the preceding decade were a product of a time when men were not at home. They willingly moved into the professions while men fought a war outside daily commuting distance. Thus, American women in film had a definite purpose: six parts propaganda to four parts romanticism. Hollywood rallied behind Ingrid Bergman, Katharine Hepburn,

Superman (Reeves) tells Bobby (Henry Blair), "No one can do the things Superman does, and that especially goes for flying!" ("The Unlucky Number"—1955.)

Lauren Bacall and Rosalind Russell, who thought that the war, equality, companionship and romance all preceded the marriage institution in importance.

The sex role changes of the forties didn't occur in a total vacuum. Ten years earlier, the industry invited a self-imposed regulatory commission to determine their ways. Studios learned they could present, as Arthur Knight writes in *The Liveliest Art*, six reels of ticket-selling lust and sinfulness if in the seventh reel the transgressors recognized their nefarious behavior and were everlastingly penitent. Virtue had to triumph. The 1940s films, somewhat liberated by the war, found a heroine who buttoned neither her lips nor her dress until she was sufficiently ready. She was independent and beautiful; the cinematic fantasy of all who viewed her.

But the men came home.

Demanding husbands with waiting sex glands had some vague concept about starting a post-World War II baby boom. By 1950, Hollywood echoed the feeling, and on screens everywhere women were seen turning in their working papers and heading for the bedroom; separate beds, of course. Again woman became the damsel in distress, screaming loudly for help where months earlier she had fended for herself.

It wasn't until Diana Rigg passed Scotland Yard's fitness requirements and Mary Tyler Moore left her washer-dryer combo at 148 Bonnymeadow Road that the "hope" of the forties was again fulfilled.

Myra Van Clever (Gloria Talbott) must have felt perfectly at home in "The Girl Who Hired Superman." She's a rich, spoiled, gullible broad who doesn't comprehend the meaning of "Truth, Justice and the American Way" until Superman explains the phrase. However, "American way" in the 1950s meant "male American way." She learns that as well. Jonas Rockwell (John Eldredge) dupes the young socialite into abetting his smuggling operation and drawing Superman in as an unknowing runner of counterfeit plates.

George Reeves with ace character actors Richard Reeves (center) and George E. Stone (right) in a scene from "The Big Freeze" (1955).

Myra and the *Daily Planet* regulars end up in a bomb shelter beneath her mansion. They turn to the number-one man for help. Olsen jokingly says, "You know, Mr. Kent, sometimes Miss Lane actually thinks you're Superman. So why don't you just break out of here and prove it."

He does, so to speak. During the height of an electrical storm Clark uses his body as a conductor to recharge a shortwave radio battery. The channel hails Inspector Henderson who is riding around in *the* Metropolis police car. Safely out of the jam, Myra takes a job as a copy girl at the newspaper—a lesson to all that girls can succeed if they're prone to start at the bottom.

Marriage, the most taboo issue, is butchered on two occasions. In Lois' fantasy "The Wedding of Superman," the female reporter's subconscious goes haywire. In the other, "Superman's Wife," the Man of Steel stages a fake ceremony to flush out a band of villains. "Any real wedding is impossible," says Robert Porfirio. "Marriage would have involved sex and the elimination of Superman's lone commitment to society." Porfirio believes a married Superman could not remain a champion of justice. "It's much simpler to remain the cowboy or superhero and fly off instead of dealing with an adult sexual life. Superman is always engaged in 'the adventure of life,' avoiding man-woman encounters with Lois Lane that would bring responsibility, in another sense, a loss of innocence." The comic book explanation tells fans that a gold band around Superman's ring finger would endanger other people and jeopardize his viable function as a secret operative. Porfirio concludes that a juvenile audience cannot accept a marriage or any permanent sexual relationship in episodes like "The Wedding of Superman" because "Kids don't like mush. The idea of youth is not to make a commitment; a free Superman like Huck Finn is more attractive than a married Clark Kent."

The chase remains fun for Metropolis' most eligible lady. Unfortunately for her, the only climax in "The Wedding of Superman" is the sound of the doorbell that wakes her from a snuggly, dream-filled sleep.

"The Wedding of Superman" opens with an uncharacteristic monologue: "I'm Lois Lane and this is my story. . . ." The lonely gal whines that she is the last person who should handle advice to the lovelorn, but when she barges into White's office to complain, Lois is ogled by the hungry eyes of patronizing middle-aged men. Inspector Henderson looks her up and down, Mr. Farady (Milton Frome) and Perry White check out her proportions as well. The only one who doesn't return her glance is the man she wants. "Superman, aren't you even interested in love?" she asked with a devilish grin.

Lois is desperate enough to flatter Clark. She later asks, "Does spring mean anything to you?"

He answers emphatically, "Baseball!"

"Do you think spring means anything to Superman?'' asks Lois sheepishly.

"He doesn't have time for baseball!" teases Kent.

At home in bed (alone) under a deluge of letters, Lois slips into her dreamworld—a world where she wins the affections of the man in red, yellow and blue.

"Sorry I've been so busy with the current crime wave," purrs Superman in the dream. Not only is he sorry, but he courts her with flowers and melts her with every passing gaze. Even Clark Kent flutters when he passes the lovely Lois.

Lois realizes early in the dream that Clark Kent and Superman do not share a common Roman chin by any mere coincidence. She sees Kent running into the alley, a moment later darting into the sky. Her subconscious knows very well what's going on; if only she can find reason to believe it when she's awake.

The soapiest scene is the inevitable embrace. Superman saves Lois from an explosion triggered by Farady. She romantically traces the "S" on his chest with her finger. Superman, new to the heavy stuff, squeezes one large diamond from a dozen smaller ones—a sign of his exaggerated superlove. "I'm not very good with words . . . what I wanted to say was," gulp, "will you marry me?" The dream goes on.

Henderson, who never seemed to care before, hints at how reluctant he is to see Lois out of circulation. She's touched, but the real clincher comes when Lois asks Clark to be the best man!

"Me best man?" asks Kent incredulously. "You mean stand up beside Superman at the wedding?" He utters a few sounds in disbelief, then rushes out for a breath of fresh air. Someone else will have to assume the honors.

Farady has other ideas. He figured if he can't kill her, he could marry her. Under this new contingency plan she'll never be able to testify against him in court. Lois asks "Superman darling" to fly to Switzerland and return with an edelweiss for her hair. Superman agreeingly bids adieu, "Dear, I shan't be gone long." Time now for Farady to consummate his own wedding designs. However, before he reaches first base, Superman is back and the unmolested Lois can still wear white.

Lois, after speaking ill of Clark Kent all those years, confesses she's had a torch burning for him too. "So do I," replies Superman. He lets the secret out, "Clark and I are one and the same person!"

Back at the drawing board, Farady plans another attempt to annihilate Lois. He plants a time bomb in the wedding cake that is set to explode before the blissful couple exchange their vows.

The seconds tick by. Closer, Closer. Then—"Ring!" Ring, but no boom. It's the doorbell. Lois is awakened from her sound sleep by Perry White, a perfectly innocent Farady and Clark Kent, who are all making a social call. Lois rushes up to her dream man, throws her arms about him and calls out, "Oh, Superman darling!"

Clark stands back timidly. "Lois, be careful, my glasses."

As she snaps out of her luscious dreamworld, Lois tearfully begs, "Aren't you even Superman?" The scene fades to black with Clark wondering what to say next.

Lois would have to live with her unrequited love; there was work for Superman. Big mean old Myron Healey was back in town!

"Dagger Island" and "The Jolly Roger" make it three for the Republic Western sharpshooter. (Healey's first was the "The Bully of Dry Gulch.") In "Dagger Island" Healey portrays one of three relatives vying for the estate of cousin Jonathan Scag (Raymond Hatton). The trio contest Scag's will that former lawyer Perry White is assigned to administer. However, we find that Scag is alive and well, simply testing which of his eventual survivors is worthy of his fortune. He plans a treasure hunt on an obscure island and Perry White sends Clark there as the master of ceremonies. Lois steps in as his sidekick, and Jimmy Olsen ends up in what has fast become his natural environment—the cold, wet water. While Olsen dries his bow tie, Clark discovers that Scag is not actually dead. A short while later Olsen comments, "You know what's actually amazing? We got through this thing without any help from Superman." That's what he thinks. Superman solves the caper, saves their lives and like the Lone Ranger disappears without a thank-you. All in a day's work.

"Dagger Island" is marred by one glaring error. Superman leaps through a window of one building, only to arrive in another building through the same (stock footage) window. Additional shots should have been lifted from the film library. Whitney Ellsworth explains, "Hindsight on television isn't worth a plugged nickel." He also reminds viewers if you watch any show long enough you're bound to catch an editor's or producer's mistake somewhere along the line. "Superman," at least in 1955, proves the point

The "Superman" set began taking on the air of a five-year college reunion. Most of the people called by Ellsworth's casting directors, Harold Chiles, were repeaters, with Herb Vigran the newest alumnus to return. In "Blackmail" Vigran plays Arnold Woodman, a mousy two-bit conniver who markets another in the long line of ultimate anti-Superman weapons. It backfires, as do all the other "Edsels" that are pointed in the general direction of the Man of Steel. Arnold plans to blackmail Inspector Henderson with the able assistance of Bates (George Chandler) and Eddie (Sid Tomack). Together, they try to plant $20,000 of Arnold's stolen bills on the good constable. Olsen and Lane play Sherlock again. Meanwhile, Henderson reflects about his years on the force. "It's just about the end of the road for me," he tells Kent while tossing his memorabilia into a box. The boots he wore when he pounded the beat on Delancey Street, a coffee cup and pot, and, of course, his badge are the only remnants of a heroic career.

Kent, who feels somewhat responsible, offers, "I hope you can find it in your heart to forgive." In a last-ditch effort to help his friend, Kent moves on the case himself. Soon, Henderson reaffirms his innocence, Arnold is unmasked as Mr. Big and Eddie is taken into custody. Eddie figures as much, after all he shouldn't have trusted Arnold; his boss cheats at Scrabble.

"The Deadly Rock" is one of the only episodes that ties a thread to a previous story. Jackson Gillis dusted off his two-year-old "Panic in the Sky" script, and added a new twist to it. Gary Allen (Robert Lowery),[4] a government attaché, returns from a prolonged assignment in Africa, where he had gone down in a plane crash the night Superman deflected the meteor from Metropolis. Gillis perfectly keys in the old plot. The plane crash, radiation from the meteor, and his prolonged stay in the hospital have somehow made Allen as vulnerable to Kryptonite as Kent. When Olsen notices how the G-man reacts, he immediately concludes that Allen and Superman must be one and the same. Of course, Jimmy doesn't see Kent's legs similarly weaken under the strain of the strange metal. The Kryptonite is a remnant from the meteor, compliments of a venomous professor named Van Wick (Steven Geary). The scientist wants to flush out and liquidate Superman for an inflated price, and Big Tom Rufus (Bob Foulk) is willing to pay the piper to the tune of $8 million.

Captain Midnight crime fighter Ichabod Mudd (Sid Melton) trades in his goodie two shoes to join Rufus' gang. Another stooge, the Snorkel (Ric Roman), works with the Duchess (Lynn Thomas) and the professor to trap Gary Allen, thinking the Washington agent *is* Superman. For all intent and purposes, they believe he is Superman—all but Rufus. He's skeptical enough to want more proof; he aims his .45 point blank at the al-

---

[4] Robert Lowery, the lead in Columbia's last Batman serial, also appeared in *The Mark of Zorro* (1940), *Tarzan's Desert Mystery* (1943), an assortment of campus musicals, a few choice science fiction pictures, and with Robert Shayne in an independent release *I Cover Big Town* (1947).

A gangster (Rick Vallin) thinks Jimmy Olsen is Kid Collins, in "Jimmy the Kid" (1955).

ready unconscious Allen. Miraculously, the very Kryptonite that destroys the real Superman has made Gary Allen's chest impervious to bullets. Allen lives and Rufus is convinced. The ne'er-do-well leaves with his court, and upon the real Superman's orders, Jimmy Olsen kicks the green rock into the fireplace, where the Man of Steel melts it with a nearby weed burner. (His X-ray vision is useless against his native rock.) Superman then leaps forward, barely catching a falling bottle of napalm.

The main business solved, Superman sets his sights on the gum-chewing gang. Allen and Kent exchange closing pleasantries as Harry Gerstad fades to black on the first and last meeting between the two National Periodicals greats.

Seven days later, Superman, just clear of one entanglement, is in the thick of another formidable challenge. The Spectre (Peter Brocco), courtesy of H. G. Wells, operates a very successful criminal racket.

"The Phantom Ring" co-stars the voices of Paul Burke, Lane Bradford, Ed Hinton, Henry Rowland and George Brand. For a while, we even get to see them!

Lois stays close to her Royal typewriter; this story belongs to Clark Kent. The reporter is offered a chance to throw in with the Spectre, but turns it down for the golden opportunity to fall out of an airplane. The gang sets up housekeeping in the frequently used cabin, complete with the frequently used breakaway wall. Their weapon of the week is a ring that renders each wearer invisible. Phil Ford's direction is his best to date, even David Chantler's script has that winning glow. The episode is one of the most memorable from the color years.

When Clark doesn't pick up the gang's option, he's hijacked by two invisible villains, the Spectre and Rosy (a pre-"Naked City" Paul Burke). Clark, an approved FAA pilot, is encouraged to take his plane to four thousand. There, the Spectre and Rosy rematerialize, spilling the beans to the good-as-dead Clark Kent. After their confession, they knock Kent out and send the reporter sailing earthward.

"There's a guy you can sell a parachute to real easy," quips Rosy.

Superman later explains Clark's miraculous well-being, "It's true he did get pushed out of the plane, but fortunately I was there when he fell!"

If Superman carried the force of a storm in "The Phantom Ring," he calms down to a tropical breeze when he catches latter-day pirates in his seventy-eighth trip to the storeroom, entitled "The Jolly Roger." The actors and director look vaguely similar to the congregation marooned on "Dagger Island" a few weeks earlier. It was becoming obvious to the 1955 viewer that a stock company had developed around George Reeves. Myron Healey, Dean Cromer and aging Pierre Watkin were charter members.

The episode is played strictly for laughs. Clark and his two associates "prop-jet" due west for a firsthand account of navy maneuvers off a Pacific blast site.

George Reeves is the center of attention as Gloria Talbot, John Eldredge, Maurice Marsac get ready for a Jack Larson photograph. ("The Girl Who Hired Superman"—1955.)

Once there, a band of renegade pirates captures them, pooh-poohing the story Kent tells regarding the imminent destruction of their tiny atoll. Captain Blood (Leonard Mudie) doesn't understand the politics of the cold war, and his crew look as though they'd be more comfortable in Monogram Western jeans than their Sir Francis Drake laces. Tyler (Dean Cromer) and Ripples (Ray Montgomery), two stranded hustlers from the mainland, offer no help to the correspondents. In fact, they have just the opposite idea in mind.

"Clark, for once I really wish you were Superman," says Lois in a fit of frustration. Kent laughs. He'll try detente instead. The way of negotiation goes stale, the pirates won't listen to reason; so, for the first time since "Through the Time Barrier," Kent is ready to blow his cover. As he removes his glasses, Lois delivers a backhanded compliment. "Don't tell me there's man left in you after all!"

Milton Frome (1) waits for the camera to be re-loaded during "The Wedding of Superman." Director Phil Ford rests on the floor (1955).

Humiliated, Kent says to himself, "More talk, I'll reason with the United States Navy." But, even as Superman, he learns there are very few words that stop eight-inch cannons once the government has decided to take aim. In David Chantler's best comic dialogue since "Flight to the North," the flotilla commander (Pierre Watkin) can't quote swallow Superman's far-fetched story of pirates. "What a shame," says the admiral. "I understand he was a fine fellow before."

"Yes sir," nods the first mate. "I guess the strain was too much for him." The order stands, the navy chooses to pulverize the island; pirates be damned.

Superman says no. The dauntless hero streaks into the sky intercepting the shells on their way to their mark. Superman flies left, then right, in a totally unspectacular sequence.[5] It is so dull that if Jimmy

[5] The sequence exposes another glaring error. As Superman changes direction, the footage, simply reversed on the editing table, reveals a backward 'S" on his chest alternating with the righted insignia.

The sure-fire anti-Superman gun backfires on Arnold Woodman (Herb Vigran) in "Blackmail" (1955).

doesn't add his play-by-play we'd never know what Superman is doing. The admiral halts the barrage in disbelief, and Superman tries once again to convince the navy that he is not ready to be farmed out to co-host the "Mike Douglas Show." His mission is real, the lives of his friends seriously in danger.

Back at the *Daily Planet*, the trio report their by-line story to Perry White. The editor congratulates them, then adds with a second breath, "Great story, beautiful pictures, but do you think for a moment any of our readers will accept this balderdash?"

Gruffy old Perry ejects them from his office for an extended leave. Thirteen new episodes are in the can; *Daily Planet's* ink can stop flowing for another year.

George Reeves holds the anniversary cake at the conclusion of "The Jolly Roger" and the 1955 schedule.

High above the set of "The Jolly Roger" (1955).

CHAPTER IX

1956

We were horrified to discover we had nearly completed an entire picture—and it was a good one—but we didn't have Superman in it. Just Clark Kent.

Harry Gerstad's commentary indicates the lack of vitality and creativity that greeted the production when they returned for the thirteen episodes of 1956. The temporary absence of Superman represents the corporate amnesia caused by the repetitive nature of a continuing television series.

Ellsworth moved the production from the former Chaplin Studios to the old Eagle Lion facilities, which had been renamed ZIV. Reeves also slipped on his tights for an unbilled visit to Lucy (#165).

"I Love Lucy" opens as an episode of "Superman" ends. Little Ricky (Desi Arnaz, Jr.) is on the couch enraptured by the escapades of the Man of Steel. The "Superman" music blares in the background while Ricky pleads, "Can Superman come to my birthday party Saturday?" Ricky's friend Stephen also plans a party for the same day. Although Superman is in town for a public appearance at Macy's, Lucy adds an additional stop to his itinerary—Ricky's party. However, Lucy discovers her word is one thing, the reality another.

Rather than breaking the kid's heart Lucy decides to masquerade as the Man of Steel. Looking no more like Superman than actor John Doucette does in "The Birthday Letter," Lucy hopes the red plaid shorts, tights and galoshes will do the trick. Not quite. She locks herself outside the window, clinging to the ledge during a downpour that even Jack Larson wouldn't have tolerated.

Only one person can save Lucy and the party. Ricky's father (Desi Arnaz) announces that when Superman heard it was a birthday party, he didn't want to disappoint the children. Superman magnificently crashes through the kitchen doors as Ricky proclaims in his deep Cuban voice, "It's a bird, a plane . . ." But there's a real job for Superman; Lucy is caught outside. The superhero forces open the window, and to the delight of everyone, rescues the thoroughly humiliated Lucy. Superman sharpens his eyes on Lucy's makeshift outfit, and asks Ricky Sr., "Do you mean you've been married to her for fifteen years?"

Ricky answers, "That's right!"

To the closing syncopated notes of the "Lucy" theme, Superman wryly adds, "And they call me Superman!"

Reeves was joined on the Desilu set by Si Simonson. "George wouldn't go without me," remembers the "Superman" special effects manager, "so Lucy's directors and I worked out the particulars together. But what I don't understand to this day is why George didn't get billed." No one has a good explanation; however, Ben Welden noted a marked change after George Reeves's appearance. "After that, 'Superman' was no longer a challenge to him. He was a very good actor who had possibilities beyond what he did. George liked 'Superman,' I know he enjoyed the role, and he had no delusions about that fact, but he used to remark, "Here I am wasting my life.'"

There's always been speculation over George Reeves's career had he lived past 1959. In 1976, he would have been sixty-two, a bonafide hero besieged by popular-culture disciples. He'd probably be a regular on "Hollywood Squares." Tommy Carr, a close friend, contemplates the impossible:

George would have loved to be around now to see what's happening. He often told me, " 'I wish I had fans other than screaming kids. Just once I'd like to get an

adult to come up and say, 'Hey, I love what you're doing and I appreciate the work you've done.' " But he never got that. Today George would be a great pop hero. Kirk Alyn would have to move over!

Actually Reeves and Alyn, friends in their own right, would have shared the glory. Alyn has respect for Reeves, sincerely believing George did the best possible job he could. However, Alyn agrees George Reeves needed the perspective of time to understand the good he accomplished; he never had enough.

Money was not Reeves's problem. The star's residual package was lucrative by 1956. One source attributes $200 to his growing estate each time the show aired in a primary market. Another spokesman says it was far less than advertised. An article in the *Los Angeles Times* reported Reeves's earnings in excess of $5,000 per week when the show was in production. Whatever the figure, according to Ellsworth, National bought out the estate after George Reeves's death.

The program changed little from the previous year. Kellogg's representatives dropped by regularly to confer on scripts and any other business. Ellsworth held his ground on most matters, believing as he had in the past, that as producer he could keep "Superman" a ratings giant, adding, "I don't suppose 'Superman' influenced the industry at all, we just did very well ourselves. Everyone else was too busy making Westerns to consider making spinoffs on us."

First to come out of the new block was "Peril in Paris," Robert Shayne's stab at the French Theater of the Absurd. Shayne uses the first foreign accent of his career, as he play French Inspector Lona. Kent and Olsen take one incredible look at the officer and are convinced that he is Inspector Henderson. The tease is relatively unimportant to the story; simply another Ellsworth twist that's worth a few laughs and an additional paycheck for Robert Shayne.

Lucille Ball waits for George Reeves to save her in "Lucy Meets Superman" ("I Love Lucy," 1956).

"Tin Hero" is next, and catch-as-catch-can under-cover work is on Perry White's irritable mind. He's try-ing to run a newspaper and the best his staff can come up with are birth notices and floral shows. White demands, "Crime is still going on, why don't we know about it?" Frank Smullins, a milquetoast bookkeeper, accidentally makes a dent in the Metropolis crime sta-tistics. The $45-a-week nebbish entwines a robber with yarn in the shape of a cat's cradle. Olsen snaps a picture of the event, and White immediately offers Smullins double what he's getting if he joins the *Daily Planet*. Smullins agrees, and is quickly targeted for death by three hoods: Fingers Danny, a thug called Marty and their boss, Big Jack.

"Tin Hero" follows a precedent begun with "Peril in Paris." George Reeves's credit slid back one notch to accommodate the director. George Blair's name hits the screen first in "Tin Hero," as Harry Gerstad's does in "Money to Burn." The style continues through the remaining two years.

Mauritz Hugo and Dale Van Sickel had been around for years. In 1954, they made ". . . a devilish two-some," according to Alan Barbour's description of their Republic Western *Man with the Steel Whip.* Van Sickel had been a crack stunt-man, Hugo a villain of evil proportions in low-budget stagecoach yarns of the fifties. It was a fitting tribute that Ellsworth would re-call Van Sickel and Hugo for an appearance together in "Money to Burn."

Brain-heavy Slim (Hugo) operates a good racket with his wisecracking sidekick (Van Sickel). The two follow the flames to local six-alarmers, where they set up shop as so-called Fireman's Friends. While Slim pours the coffee, his buddy darts into burning ware-houses in an asbestos suit, cleaning out the unguarded safe. The bunco jobs might have netted them an easy fortune had they not hit the *Daily Planet* facilities.

Si Simonson's inside effects look good; the realistic smoke and flames are doused by Superman's CO_2 fire extinguisher since water would have ruined the sets.

Unfortunately, the rest of the special footage is weak. Night scenes are spliced in with daytime flying, and wide shots of one fire are too often repeated for different locations.

He finds his superspeed more than ample in the next episode, "The Town That Wasn't." Superman cracks a fake police racket that has been collecting fines each time their roving policemen pull speeders into their roving court presided over by an equally roving judge (Richard Elliot). Jimmy Olsen is one unfortunate victim. Clark Kent and Inspector Henderson arrive on the scene when the youngster cries foul ball. Superman displays excellent elevation on one outdoor springboard takeoff, and Harry Gerstad's location directing is rather slick. Other than that, "The Town That Wasn't" can be easily missed.

Noel Neill tours the country with "The Tomb of Zaharan," a curious sleeper that features more good points of the healthy actress than she has previously shared with the television audience. For those diehard fans who might have forgotten, Noel is tightly squeezed into Egyptian linens and mistakenly kidnapped as the Princess Nephrodedis. Lois is told that the princess was born twenty-six years ago. Jimmy gleefully chimes to Lois' displeasure that that's her age. Of course, neither realizes until far too late, that their fate is sealed in the tomb.

Lois is given the assignment to interview Baldadian dignitaries Abdul (Ted Hecht) and Zing (Jack Reitzen) upon their arrival at Metropolis International. Little does she know the jewels she wears around her neck telegraph her destiny to the visitors. The pair invite Lane and her doting cub reporter to Baldad, where they will seal the mistaken queen in her rightful place—a two-thousand-year-old tomb. In transit, Abdul and Zing alternate every other sentence, at times every other word, pointing out the mosque of Muhammad Ali. (Ellsworth assures everyone that no attempt at foreshadowing one particular boxer's career was intended.)

The *Daily Planet* receives a telegram from the reporters that says, "All's well." Clark, noticing the message lacks the journalistic "-30-" at the close, feels another Lois Lane story has run amok. White doesn't feel particularly moved by the whole thing, but Kent assures the editor he has enough to go on. Turning down White's order to get back to his work, Kent exclaims, "Lois and Jimmy mean a lot more to me than any anniversary edition!"

In the Middle East, Clark checks in with the police for sight-seeing directions to the tomb. The authorities arrange for transportation, but "faster than a speeding bullet" Kent has means of his own.

Superman tears off the door to the shrine and carries Lois and Jimmy to safety. Back in downtown Metropolis, the two world travelers file their story and strike poses for Perry White. There is a sigh of relief, the star bunglers are safe and the anniversary edition can go to press.

Lois had her day. Time would come again for Jimmy Olsen to take the stage, but for the next episode Ellsworth chose an all-purpose script—"The Man Who Made Dreams Come True." John (Sergeant Schultz of "Hogan's Heroes") Banner goes unbilled as Bronsky, an aide to the frail King Leo (Cyril Delevanti) of Sartania. As always, there's a con man, Rutherford Jones (Keith Richards), who plots after the king's favors. He plays on King Leo's superstitious nature and arranges for the monarch's dreams to come true. First, Leo meets Superman, next his life is saved. Leo is indebted to Jones, and offers his kingdom in gratitude. Jones graciously accepts, then suggests the wise king stand in a tub of water, holding a live electrical wire to rid his body of all evil spirits. Superman intercedes in this death wish, but Leo returns for further consultation. Jones tells Leo to drive backward down the canyon road, but before his car reaches the precipice, Superman happens by again. One more try. Superman barely prevents the king from jumping out his bedroom window, again on orders from Jones. Superman feels he has played Boy Scout leader too long; he rounds up

Ben Welden thinks about doublecrossing his boss in "Disappearing Lois" (1956).

Jones, sets the king straight, then flies off for another week.

Milton Frome, a prolific comic actor, was one of the few "Superman" regulars who came to George Reeves's funeral service. There's no doubt why; Frome was a longtime friend from the days of live television. He had appeared in "The Wedding of Superman" the previous season and happily joined the cast for two back-to-back assignments in 1956: "Disappearing Lois" and "Whatever Goes Up."

Lank Garritt, Frome's second "Superman" portrayal, is better than his first. He plays a ruthless killer (within the bounds of redefined comic book taste), with Lefty (Ben Welden) his somewhat spastic hired gun.

Lois desperately wants an interview with the paroled Garritt, but she needs to evade Clark Kent in order to obtain the scoop. She switches apartments with a girl friend to confound Clark's competitive instinct. She disguises herself as a maid and walks directly into Garritt's hotel suite. Jimmy joins the charade and promises not to blow his cover. Naturally, the opposite happens. The inept pair are discovered by the equally inept villains, and the audience need only wait the required fifteen minutes to see the Man of Steel rescue the distraught duo.

"Close Shave" is no improvement. Barber Tony Gambini (Richard Benedict) encourages notorious gangster Rick Sable (Rick Vallin) to turn state's evidence and try the straight life. However, Sable's men want nothing to do with his atonement. Their reluctance to join the system makes Rick's new leaf a rather complicated item to turn over. "Close Shave" is another one of the endless moralistic messages thrust into the schedule to teach the might of right. Veteran B actor Jack Littlefield returns to help deliver the example. Harry Gerstad directs. Superman, of course, makes his timely appearance to underline the theme.

Professor Pepperwinkle (Phillips Tead) waddles out of the laboratory for his second visit to Clark Kent's office. His newest shoestring invention is a de-atmosphering chamber which telephones people to any working exchange in the world. Predictably, his machine falls into the clutches of underworld figures Brain (Frank Kreig), Old Moe (Harry Arnie) and Clippy Jones (William Challee). The trio commit their two-bit crimes, then materialize elsewhere around the world to establish their "Phoney Alibi." Superman catches on after Lois and Jimmy are phoned collect to Alaska. Superman breaks the party line, then traces the call to its source. The science fiction premise in "The Phoney

Alibi" plays well.

Raymond Hatton, one of the busiest sidekicks in the forties, earned another day's keep with "Superman." Hatton (last seen in "The Bully of Dry Gulch" and "Dagger Island"), has been around since the silent days, and is best known as the stubby sidekick in the "Three Mesquiteers" series at Republic. He rode next to John Wayne in *New Frontier* (1939), and Duncan Renaldo and Bib Livingston in both *Pioneers of the West* and *Covered Wagon Days* (1940). Hatton appeared in a few cheap Monogram Buck Jones horse operas (*Down Texas Way* and *Dawn on the Great Divide*) before making his way through the bramble in a score of one-week Westerns.

In "The Prince Albert Coat," Grandfather Jackson (Hatton) and great-grandson Bobby (Stephen Wooton) are troubled by a complicated mistake only Superman can correct. Unknown to Bobby, the old geezer keeps his life savings in the lining of a coat that the lad subsequently donates for flood relief. Lois and Jimmy join the crusade to retrieve the coat, but it is already in the hands of unsympathetic villains. Superman not only fetches the coat before the clock runs down, he also prevents a swollen dam from engulfing rural Metropolis.

"The Prince Albert Coat" deserves merit despite the dime-store attempt to reproduce Jack Arnold science fiction effects without the time and money. To Si Simonson's credit, everything else works well beyond the miniature dam, especially Superman's spring over a three-foot-high fence; his best takeoff since "Panic in the Sky."

As good as the springboard takeoff is in "The Prince Albert Coat," Superman completely avoids it in "The Stolen Elephant." He simply runs around a tree, in front of the camera, and out of frame, doing everything, in fact, but flying. If the springboard wasn't abandoned entirely, it certainly needed a mid-season overhaul.

Ellsworth took everyone to the circus again, this time

to find Suzie, "The Stolen Elephant." Perry White volunteers Superman to return the two-ton act after ringmaster Haley (Thomas Jackson) discovers that Busher (Gregg Martell) and Spike (I. Stanford Jolley) have run away with her.

Kent soon realizes that trying to find an elephant is not a simple matter.[1] The action changes to rural, rural Metropolis and the farm of humble Mrs. Wilson (Eve McVeigh) and son Johnny (Gregory Moffet). Johnny celebrates his birthday, but poverty prevents them from doing it in a big way. The simple fatherless family deliver their love message to each another in monosyllabic words to the accompaniment of soft violin strings playing counterpoint. Mother and son have moved to the farm, away from the memories of downtown. Unfortunately, Busher and Spike choose their barn for hiding the ransomed elephant. Johnny, who's moping around without a proper birthday present, sees Suzie. "Just what I've always wanted!" he shouts. The poor kid thinks the elephant belongs to him, a present from old Mom.

The ringmaster posts the $10,000 demanded for Suzie, but Superman has other plans. Meanwhile, the gangster waltzes Johnny out of his euphoria by flashing an elephant registration number declaring his rightful ownership. Actually, it is Busher's telephone number, but what does little Johnny know of such things. He stubbornly stammers off complaining, "I never want to have another pet as long as I live!"

Johnny's mother, a member of the soap opera school of dramatic acting, admits she lied when she told Johnny he could keep Suzie. "Sometimes we hurt people because we love them a lot." However, Johnny is not out of the picture yet. The *Daily Planet* carries the story of Suzie, and when the heartbroken boy sees the

---

[1] Superman's counterpart in the comics had already learned to use his X-ray vision to scour the city for villains. However, what counted on television was twenty-eight minutes' worth of script. For the sake of live action, Superman took his time.

report, he cranks up the durable country telephone and rings the famous Clark Kent. The story comes to a close with the Man of Steel now on the case. Busher and Spike are sent behind bars, and Superman declares, "When they get out, Suzie will be a full-grown elephant." It's the welcomed end of another tired adventure.

Billy Curtis, the Oscar Mayer wiener kid, seems forever relegated to extra-human roles. In 1951, he crawled six miles up a pipeline to see the moonlight in *Superman and the Mole Men* (broadcast as "The Unknown People"). Five years later he rockets to earth as the green Martian Mr. Zero Zero Zero Minus One (shortened to Mr. Zero for expediency). "Mr. Zero" happens to be a Mr. Peepers character; lonely, naïve and vulnerable in his new world, a fellow who can't quite grasp earthly ways, especially as taught by shyster Georgie Glep Herburt Vigran.

Lurking within this Peggy Chantler[2] script is peril of the worst dimension. Indeed, Superman's body is impervious to bullets and perhaps two thousand charging troops in full battle array, but one poor story can stop him in his tracks. "Mr. Zero" does just that. It is the low point of the 104 episodes.

Mr. Zero has a touch all his own. He can freeze people in place with a point of a finger. Actually, the setup is a variation of David Chantler's "Topsy Turvey" from 1955. Mr. Zero becomes the unknowing dupe of Glep and Slouchy McGoo (George Barrows). The Department of Defense asks Perry White to track a rocket ship they've spotted on their radar. But the UFO pilot with Vidal Sassoon olive hair and Rocky Jones Space Patrol outfit finds his way to the *Daily Planet* building himself.

Ironically, Whit Ellsworth's only female writer dashed off the most chauvinistic lines ever uttered by any "Superman" character. When Glep tells Zero why bank tellers take Lois Lane's money, he explains, "Being a

---

[2] She also wrote much of television's "Family Affair."

285

lady, not knowing any better, she let them have it!"

In order to help the fair Miss Lane, Zero points his finger at the bankers while Glep collects poor Lois' money. The Martian proudly confides his good deed to Lois, who quickly admits, "This sounds more like a job for Superman."

"Superman?" answers Zero. "We've heard about him on Mars."

While they all wonder where Superman is hiding himself, Clark says, "This is no time for idle feminine curiosity."

Mars Central Control, tuned in to the proceedings, decides to recall Mr. Zero on good behavior. Perry White reaches for a token of Earth's appreciation, and the four-foot-high explorer goes home with a few Havana cigars. No doubt he would have preferred Tang.

Jimmy Olsen takes a spin as a Gilbert chemistry set scientist in the concluding chapter for 1956, "Whatever Goes Up." Professor Pepperwinkle's dabbling has visibly brushed off on the maturing Olsen, as he ends up with a concoction that is as far from the formula as anything Pepperwinkle contrived. Jimmy's chocolate cake mix boils over into an anti-gravity amalgamation. Frank Adams, alias Gannis (Milton Frome), strolls by Jimmy's basement laboratory. The floating liquid triggers his mind; there might be a market for this brew.

Major Osborn (Tris Coffin) wants Uncle Sam to have the formula. Gannis, posing as government agent Adams, wants it for himself. However, Olsen can't remember what goes into the thing. Major Osborn, in typical cold war double-talk, takes the soapbox for a laudable oration on why Jimmy must return to his Bunsen burner:

Now, son, you just can't quit. We need you. Don't you realize how important your work is? Of course we can't force you to, but I just want you to know that your country will be eternally grateful. Think of what you'll accomplish. Why, we could build spaceships to the stars using your anti-grav fluid.

George Reeves and his director Phil Ford (1956).

Osborn is about to release copies of his magnificent speech through the Government Printing Office when Perry White hits a nerve closer to Jimmy Olsen's heart.

"Anyone, even you, would be able to fly like Superman!"

Olsen's jaw drops to the floor. "Yeah! I would be able to fly like Superman, wouldn't I!" He marches back to his Mr. Wizard lab and continues his experiments.

Gannis eventually steals the remaining anti-grav but doesn't know how unstable the mixture becomes when diluted with water. Superman has already swallowed one batch, and he's intent on not repeating the heart-burning experience again. That's why Superman lets it blow up in the gangster's face.

Milton Frome remembers standing knee-deep in soot. "The thing was a real explosive! That special effects man set up one mighty charge." But Frome needn't have feared; he was in good hands; Si Simonson was a pro. Simonson had been at RKO for over sixteen years before he moved into television. "There aren't many of us left." Since "Superman," he's furthered his reputation as one of the best mechanical effects men in the industry. *Papillon*, *Lost Horizon*, *Oklahoma Crude*, *Blazing Saddles*, *The Longest Yard* and *The Klansman* stand as his outstanding examples of recent years.

"Superman" was one of Simonson's best assignments. His five-year association with Ellsworth and Reeves was unlike any other he has had.

An outfit like Whit's didn't have the time and it didn't have the money. That's why Whit was so great. He got the most out of what he had to work with—which is where a lot of people lost out. They demand what's in the script, and when they don't get it, they're at a loss to get anything. But Whit would understand, and consequently, get more out of us than anybody I knew. Whit was one of the pioneers in the industry, it was a tribute to him that our work went so well.

The effects on "Superman" were unique. Up until

Special effects supervisor Si Simonson prepares the deadly gas audiences see in "The Tomb of Zaharan" (1956).

George Reeves's most frequently exploited task—charging through a brick wall—this time in "The Prince Albert Coat" (1956). (Photographic effects by Bob Rubin.)

A breather, and a dusting off ("Whatever Goes Up"—1955).

Simonson and his crew experimented, little time had been devoted to the special requirements of flying, crumbling walls et al. Previously, motion picture effects were devised laboriously. Month after month of testing might only produce one small effect. "Superman" could never afford to take such liberties. Simonson says, "We'd never admit we couldn't do something, we just put it on a time and money basis. We could do most anything some way, but we couldn't do it quickly and we couldn't do it inexpensively unless it was a regular 'Superman' gag. All our things had to be done yesterday. We had the smoothest-working operation," explains Simonson. "I did eight years for ZIV, and they did more TV shows for a while than anybody, but no matter how hard they tried, nobody, but nobody could get an operation as smooth as 'Superman.'

"In order to make our effects different, more spectacular, better than something we did before or the other guy has done, we had to add a little more each time." Simonson garnished his explosions with more smoke, higher water—more pizazz. "Sometimes to the point where we added a little bit too much. But I guess we were lucky. George was excellent to work with and very little went wrong."

Simonson saw the fundamental disciplines in film production working together for the first time. "There are always people on the set who represent the money, a group of artistically inclined individuals, and those cognizant of the practicality of the production. Traditionally, each temperament views the production from its own limited focus. For some reason that wasn't the case with 'Superman.' That's why Whit had such a good operation. He had a gang that was interested in making it good and cheap. We did a good job because we wanted to. 'Superman' crews were paid better than other television and motion picture crews in town but more than that we enjoyed being together. We had better working conditions, and a surefire job for five or six years."

On other productions in town, most special effects were performed on screen by stunt men and doubles, but Simonson reports that George Reeves wanted in on all the scenes. Producer Ellsworth watched from behind the camera, trying to explain to Reeves, "It doesn't make sense, George. Why take a chance to prove you're a he-man." There'd always be an argument and Ellsworth would lose a pound of sweat in pure worry. "There was a manhood thing involved with George," says Whitney Ellsworth. "He didn't want a man to double for him in one stinking little scene, but I'd always come back with, 'That isn't it, George, you can twist your ankle and be out for three days leaving us sitting around doing nothing.' '' As in Maxwell's ''A Night of Terror,'' Reeves stepped aside for the stunt man in the big fights. He wasn't happy, but it was the law.

Simonson's special effects were an integral part of every show. The fights, crumbling walls and smoky explosions were standard fare, and Jack Larson knew when Reeves played a fight that probably meant he'd have to stay in the scene, too. ''When that happened, I was in line for a punch if I didn't duck in time. But the thing I never got used to were those guns going off. George used to step in front of Noel or me, and I knew perfectly well George was no Superman. I was always aware that by some accident the gun might have been 'live.' Maybe that's why I was always happy somebody was jumping in front of me.''

It seems that every Jack Larson recollection of ''Superman'' includes a scene of him being tied back to back with Noel Neill with an explosive nearby, and George Reeves leaping off a ladder to the rescue. Even though Thomas Carr says they made the dangerous look simple, Larson still maintains, ''I suppose looking back we were reckless; jumping off things, gunpowder [often compressed air and dirt] going off, walls caving in, the water rising. Things could go wrong, they often did, but Si Simonson was a good man, and we were lucky.''

Si Simonson sums up his years on ''Superman.'' As tough as the work was, as long as the hours were, as hot as the studios got, ''People would have rather helped Whitney Ellsworth for nothing, than work for somebody else for top dough.''

The show went on.

CHAPTER X

1957

Script conferences began on September 18 for what was to become the final season of "Superman." Thomas Carr, the durable director, assumed the reins for the first installment under the aegis of the ABC network. Carr was a last-minute substitution. Ellsworth had intended to hire his regular director, George Blair. However, Carr believes that Blair didn't want the responsibility for the special requirements of "The Last Knight." "The script had George jumping out the window in a suit of armor and Whit couldn't get anyone on the staff to shoot it. So Whit called me back to do it as a special favor." [1]

" 'The Last Knight' is the only color show Carr directed on the series," explains "Superman" expert David Miller. "Carr, whose leadership made those black-and-white shows what they are, could have improved the color episodes had he remained. For example, the close-up of Reeves crashing through the wall in 'The Last Knight' was the best he looked in three years. That was Carr's work."

The director himself adds, "The others would shoot with their safe wide angles, while I could vary the composition without wasting time or money. I wasn't interested in a safe shot, I wanted an interesting show."

Carr originally left "Superman" at the conclusion of the 1953 schedule. The veteran had tired of the work. "I wasn't happy with the serial effects. I wanted real flying, not just animation. After we moved to TV and I had done thirty or more of the first fifty-two, I realized I had accomplished all I wanted to do. It was time to leave. Ellsworth asked me on for more, even George

---

[1] No one else is certain whether the account is quite true, yet even Whitney Ellsworth admits it makes a good story.

Reeves asked me to stay. But it was too late, my mind was made up." Carr left.

No one was more surprised than George Reeves when Tommy Carr returned to the director's chair for "The Last Knight." The first problem to confront the veteran was Clark Kent's inimitable glasses. The forty-three-year-old actor switched from the empty tortoise-shell glasses to his own prescription, despite the consternation of Carr and cameraman Joseph Biroc. The two shot and reshot around the annoying light flare off the lenses, only to see the reflection retained in the final release print.

The episode begins with Lois and Jimmy reviewing a museum exhibit in downtown Metropolis. Their presence soon leads them into an adventure they would have preferred to read in another newspaper. The 1957 David Chantler script only waits three pages before providing for the unavoidable kidnapping of Lois and Jimmy. The two are ushered out by a trio of over-the-hill swashbucklers, Sir Gawaine (Paul Power), Sir Lancelot (Pierre Watkin) and Sir Henry (Jason Johnson). Lois, undaunted as ever, riddles, "What girl wouldn't want to date three knights in a row!" Sir Arthur (Marshall Bradford), the senior member of the Society for the Preservation of Knighthood and Dragons, cuts the humor short, saying, "I'm afraid you missed the point, fair lady."

"Somehow I always do."

The two reporters play along with the fraternal knights, who whisk them far from Clark Kent's concerned telephone calls. Sir Henry is sent to Kent's apartment to search for an incriminating cuff link dropped by Olsen. Kent stumbles upon the country squire. He quickly surmises, through inexplicable intuition, that the society members are merely the gulls of Sir Arthur. Furthermore, Sir Henry supplies Kent with enough information so that the latter is able to deduce that the knights are pawns in an illegal attempt to collect on a survivor-take-all insurance policy. The reformed knight removes his battle regalia and departs.

Kent dons the full outfit over his Superman uniform (recalling Reeves's days as Sam Katzman's Sir Galahad). He instantly masters Sir Henry's voice and, at Tommy Carr's command, takes off through the open window. En route, Superman lifts the visor to the helmet, checks his bearings and heads over the hills toward Batmore Woods.

In due time, Superman/Sir Henry is unmasked as an impostor, and shackled in the basement stockade with fellow captives Lois Lane and Jimmy Olsen. The two know nothing of the medieval character's identity.

Shortly thereafter, Superman pulls his bonds from the wall, tosses off his helmet and removes his disguise. In a few short moments, standing in place of a nameless knight is the mighty Superman.[2] The Man of Steel inhales the fumes of a poison gas pellet, leaps up the stairs, dodges bullets and swords, then neatly wraps a shining saber around the evil Sir Arthur. Another dastardly crime is averted.

Whit Ellsworth felt it was time to junk the old Nash coupes and Chevy convertibles in favor of the spanking-new 1957 Plymouths with their oversized tail fins. To introduce them to the audience, Superman easily flips one on its side in the opening minutes of episode ninety-three, "The Magic Secret."

Next to the expired auto, Superman picks up an army issue walkie-talkie and serves notice on the airwaves to Metropolis' newest crime boss, D. W. Griswald (Freeman Lusk). However, the villain sneers back, "Get this, Superman, somehow, some way I'll get you." For the next thirty minutes he tries to do just that.

Griswald enlists the aid of Professor Von Brunner

[2] Carr chose to stay on reaction shots of Lois and Jimmy during the transformation, reasoning that clothes falling to the ground and assorted hosannas from the onlookers would better serve the scene than to see Superman struggling with a zipper or pant leg that refused to budge past the boots. For the same reason, no one ever showed the complete metamorphosis of Kent to Superman. It would take too much time, and the entire business would appear anti-climactic.

(George Selk), who designs a plan to destroy Superman with a "piece of the rock"; his own—Kryptonite. Von Brunner claims that since "Superman came here when his planet exploded into a supernova," the particles of Krypton could be drawn to Earth as well, forming a deadly beam that can cut down the Man of Steel in his tracks.

The Kryptonite ray works. Griswald uses Olsen and Lane as bait, luring Superman into a well. He pushes a button in his lab that sends the walls of the shaft closing in on the trio. Luckily Superman recalls the levitation act Perry White performed earlier. He slips Lois into a quick trance, flips her body between the closing walls, and orders Olsen to climb out and divert the Kryptonite ray gun. Jimmy, safely on the surface, aims the ray at Griswald's lab, causing a monumental explosion.

One week later, in "Divide and Conquer," Lois, Perry and Clark (Jimmy has the day off) hop aboard an airplane bound for another "Mission Impossible" republic. The goodwill trip is booked to confirm the publication of a Spanish edition of the newspaper. However, what follows is not on the original group itinerary.

The three happen to be in the right country at the wrong time. Clark's sensitive hearing catches the ticking of a time bomb during an interview with President Bateo (Donald Lawton). He makes an excuse to leave, returning as Superman to deaden the explosion. However, Vice-President Oberon (Robert Tafur), party to the assassination attempt, recalls an obscure law and orders Superman's arrest.

Oberon has his superior on the horns of a dilemma. If Bateo doesn't authorize the arrest, he would likely be impeached; the Vice-President would then assume the reins of government. If the President does authorize the lockup, then his life would remain in peril.

The hairsplitting situation offers no solace for Superman or his worldly alias, Clark Kent. The prison door slams shut; the American hero, for once, is apparently lost in an insoluble quandary.

Superman, who promises to honor the law, wriggles away on a magnificent technicality. He splits in two. Professor La Serne (Everett Glass), a tenured myopic university researcher, flies south of the border with a theory. Superman listens attentively to his teacher's lecture. "If I can expand my atomic structure by driving the molecules further apart, then separate them," answers Superman, "then . . ."

The professor gets so excited explaining the process, he interrupts Superman and muddles his own lines.[3] Nonetheless, La Serne still manages to throw in one disparaging note, "There might be two of you instead of one." Ordinarily, Superman's molecules are packed more closely together than those of Homo sapiens, "giving you superstrength, making it impossible for you to be injured or hurt." That's the good news. The bad news is different. "It may be impossible to fuse yourself into one single Superman," says La Serne. "If this should happen, both of you shall perish." The professor describes how the two separate supermen will be half as strong as the original, they can be wounded (as one is), hurt by enemies and weakened by flight.

Superman, upon hearing the warning, quips, "It's unfortunate I wasn't born twins." Indeed.

Superman finds it quite valuable being in two places at one time. His secret identity is kept intact and the law is observed. Simultaneously, President Bateo is conducting Perry and Lois on a tour through the national mines while the deceitful Oberon plants a dynamite charge above their unsuspecting heads.

Perry White admits, "We'd be in a bad way if our air supply was cut off." A half second later, the mine is solidly on top of them.[4]

[3] Director Phil Ford chose not to reshoot.

[4] Phyllis Coates handled a parallel situation with more savoir faire in "Rescue" (1951). When a dramatic cave-in sends deadly coal gas into the mine, Lois (Coates) and an old prospector have something really serious to contemplate in their last minute. The miner is ready to pack it in, but this Lois is willing to get her hands dirty and fight to the last. "Do nothing?" she says. "Not me!"

Superman One and Superman Two decide it's time to reunite. "It's a cinch we're no good the way we are." Individually, they're barely able to fly faster than a speeding bulldozer; they're vulnerable. Providentially, La Serne's prophecies of doom dissolve when the two merge again into one indomitable Superman.

Superman burrows through rock, then crashes through the mine wall, delivering fresh air to the trapped *Daily Planet* party.

Later that day, Lois and Perry pay a respectable house call on Clark. The boss casually mentions, "At one time, Miss Lane had the ridiculous idea you were Superman."

"I do see what you mean," answers Kent. "It's difficult even for Superman to be two places at once, isn't it?"

Ellsworth and Simonson dug deep into the hat for a potpourri of new special effects for 1957. Financial interest in "Superman" had picked up. National signed with ABC, the scripts looked better and the situations a bit less childish. Unfortunately, Reeves often appeared tired, overweight and bored with what he was doing. His low-keyed performance was acceptable on "Divide and Conquer" but remaining episodes wore heavily on the actor. The signs were obvious to Ben Welden, who moved back to the set one more time:

It was only in the last of the last year that George showed signs of being weary. Before that he seemed okay. George enjoyed life quite a lot, but he got very down. Not that he didn't think he could do well, he was a good actor, and still a young man. He knew what he was doing, and he could have carried on very well. But it was no longer a challenge, George simply became too emotionally involved outside of it.

Si Simonson agrees. Reeves made a public appearance at an Inglewood theater, but fell apart when the audience pressed too hard. "At first all the little kids gave him such a rare treat. He loved kids, but when a little joker from the front row yelled, 'Oh, ya bum, let's see ya fly!' it so unnerved George that he left the stage. He didn't show up for the opening of a new television station, and he didn't come to work for a day. Just that little thing."

"George didn't have an easy time of it," confides Robert Shayne. "I was able to go in, do the role and go home at night as Bob Shayne. George had more difficulty. He was Superman in too many people's minds, he couldn't walk away from it at 5 P.M."

"The Mysterious Cube" affords Ben Welden the opportunity to assume his normal position as the mug heavy. Jody Malone (Welden) helps Paul Barton (Bruce Wendell) count down the years to freedom from a sealed police/Superman-proof compartment. There, Barton awaits the end of his seven-year vigil, outlasting the statute of limitations. Inspector Henderson and the representative members of the fourth estate know Barton's whereabouts, but no one, including Superman, can do a thing to prosecute the rogue. Superman is at a loss. Jody Malone, Paul Barton and brother Steve (Keith Richards) have the criminal justice system beat until Superman heeds a lecture from Professor La Serne.

"It's been a long time, too long, my friend, too long," the scientist tells Superman upon his arrival. Apparently, both forgot their conversation of the previous week, for the professor from "Divide and Conquer" is back again and the problem with his tongue hasn't cleared up yet. The scientist flubs a laudatory comment to Superman on the occasion of his newest achievement: walking through walls. "By George, you did it!" Of course, the professor adds his note of warning: "Once inside the wall you might not be able to reconstruct yourself, you might remain forever in that mysterious metal." It's worth the chance and Superman decides to penetrate "The Mysterious Cube."

Meanwhile, Jody and Steve develop a contingency plan. The two use Lois and Jimmy as collateral against a last-minute assault by Inspector Henderson. Superman vanishes into the wall, where he overhears that his friends' lives will end if he continues. However, Superman also knows that Barton sets his dial by the minute hand of the Naval Observatory clock, and plans to exit *precisely* at the end of his seven-year stretch. Consequently, when he asks for official permission to slow the time down, he gets it. "Superman wants something done," says Eisenhower, Kennedy, Johnson, Nixon, Ford, ad infinitum, "we'll do it!" On orders from the commander in chief, the clock drags on for the next ten minutes. Barton enters the world a seemingly free man until Inspector Henderson, with time to spare, clicks the handcuffs around him with the full authority of the law.

Superman springs Lois and Jimmy, but it's Clark who files the story first. Lois is adamant, but Kent stands on his constitutional rights. "Even a reporter can't reveal all his sources."

George Reeves had gone the distance since the dramatic days of "The Haunted Lighthouse," "Rescue," "The Unknown People," "Double Trouble" and "The Golden Vulture." Quite frankly, the stories didn't survive the years with him. In 1957, the scripts were less violent and pitched to a young, more innocent audience. Already the Mattel "Fanner-Fiftys" were beginning to be pulled off the market; the toys were just too dangerous. A corresponding tranquillity recommended itself to the "Superman" management. Violent scripts went into the circular file, the garbage bin, to be replaced by more lighthearted human interest stories. Consequently, the later yarns of spies and mysterious ladies never matched the macabre stories of Maxwell's era. The change was made to weather the criticism of the fifties, pacifying the vocal antagonists who spoke of Superman and vigilante justice in the same breath. No one was surprised when Ellsworth ordered that serial-style violence must stay in the theaters. Where accents were once unquestionably German, and references to World War II Nazis obvious, Superman dealt in his last episodes with bumbling villains, two-bit con men and frazzled reporters. "The Atomic Captive" reflects this posture.

Clark, Lois and Jimmy move onto a Nevada test site in their own bomb—the late-model Plymouth. However, Lois and Jimmy, bored with the countdown's seven procedural delays, take to the desert to interview Dr. Latislav (Raskin Ben-Ari). The kindly scientist is in self-imposed isolation after undue exposure to radioactive materials. He tries to explain this to Lois and Jimmy, but nothing short of brute force can penetrate their consciousness. Unknown to any of them, agent X-29, agent X-249, Igor and Nicoli plot to kidnap the nuclear physicist.

As Latislav runs off with Lane and Olsen, he explains how he arranged a rescue pact with Superman. When the doctor is in trouble, he need only press his lips together and aim for a high C (much like Jimmy Olsen's signal watch in the comic books), for the Man of Steel has tuned his ears to Latislav's whistle. Unfortunately, the physicist is too dry to sound the air.

This last attempt at a semi-serious espionage drama fails miserably, but it's not because Superman is invincible. The simple fact of the matter is that the script is bad. "Superman," like "The Avengers," chooses its own reality, then operates within it. The natural laws of science and behavior are of little consequence. The entertainment comes in the experience, not the truth. However, the happenings are so contrived in "The Atomic Captive" (and many of the last days of "Superman") that the individual scenes are painfully slow and ludicrous.

"The Superman Silver Mine" gave Dabbs Greer a dual role, one good (Pebbles), the other bad (Dan Dobey). It was fitting that Greer should make one of the last episodes, since he had been on hand for "Superman on Earth" and "Five Minutes to Doom" the first two seasons. Goodbyes were in order for all the old-timers; Greer was no exception.

Mr. Pebbles, a philanthropic Texan, promises a rich silver mine to the Children's Camp Fund in honor of Metropolis' number-one citizen. However, Dobey, his double, kidnaps him and assumes Pebbles' identity and bank passbook. However, regular withdrawals don't satisfy him; Dobey lusts for the riches of the hidden silver mine. He bumps into Lois Lane and Jimmy Olsen, locks up his second and third prisoners and waits for Superman to sort out the facts. The Man of Steel uses his X-ray vision to discover that there's a metal plate inside the impostor's skull. Superman, by now running out of creative rescues, magnetizes an iron bar and easily apprehends the escaping criminal.[5]

"The Big Forget," one of David Chantler's four scripts for 1957, dares show what we have all waited to see—the day Superman admits to the world that Clark Kent is his taxpaying name. Lois and Jimmy guarantee that they can produce a front-page exposé on racketeer Muggsy Maple (Herbert Vigran) without an assist from Superman. The dubious editor in chief promises them a ten-dollar-a-week raise if they can fulfill their outrageous pledge. Professor Pepperwinkle (Phillips Tead) makes it possible with his newest diversion, a fifteen-minute anti-memory vapor. When it's time for everyone's timely rescue, Clark tears off his glasses, opens his jacket and slips off the rest of his disguise—in full view. Perry, Lois and Jimmy are stunned beyond belief. Yet it's one item that will never reach the front page. Superman has filled the room with Pepperwinkle's anti-memory spray, wiping clean all recollections of the preceding fifteen minutes. At the fade, Clark, quite satisfied, asserts, "There are a great many things it would be better for people not to remember."

In one of the earliest episodes produced back in

[5] The scene shows how obedient writer Peggy Chantler could be to the show's low-budget conscience. She simply suggested that George Blair reverse the footage to return Greer, backward, up the hill.

1951, Superman tangles with Lucien Littlefield's runaway robot Hero. In one of the last, Ellsworth returns to the theme with Professor Pepperwinkle's Mr. McTavish —better known as "The Gentle Monster." However, Pepperwinkle unknowingly powers the tin man with an innocent-looking rock, green in color, harmless to the touch of all, but one.

The episode suffers the hazards of the year: misread lines, day flying footage substituted for night scenes, and an aimless script. However, "The Gentle Monster" is unusual in one respect. Ellsworth hired old-timer Howard Bretherton to direct this single episode. Bretherton had called the shots eleven years earlier in Kirk Alyn's lone Monogram Charlie Chan feature, *The Trap*. By then he had already carved out a solid niche for himself in Hollywood folklore extending as far back as 1914. *The Redeeming Sin* (1929), *Ladies They Talk About* (1933), *Chasing Trouble* (1939), *The Girl Who Dared* (1944), *Prince of Thieves* (1948) and *Whip Law* (1950) are only a few of the hundreds of films that have survived his 1969 passing.

John Eldredge, the most visible of all "Superman" villains, accepted one last offer for work. Eldredge, in his final role, plays enemy operative Mr. X. Opposite him is the opulent Joi Lansing as Police Sergeant Helen J. O'Hara. Lansing, who had appeared off and on with Phyllis Coates in the Joe McDoakes shorts at Warner Brothers, fulfills every Lois Lane fantasy when she becomes "Superman's Wife.'

It happens quickly. Superman arrives at police headquarters, where Inspector Henderson introduces him to the very healthy, fair-haired agent. Superman, without prior warning, extends both hands to the young lovely and makes her an offer she can't refuse: "Sergeant O'Hara, will you marry me?"

"Why, I'd be delighted," she says as her eyes flutter in amorous anticipation.

Poor Lois Lane is left high and dry. Although Superman gives her the scoop (some consolation after carrying a nineteen-year torch), the century's most scorned woman shoots an eyeful of daggers at the bride. But Mrs. Superman is unmoved, for she has work to do.

Mr. X plans to clean out the armored car market. He calls Perry, Jimmy and Lois and tells them to cut across town to Pier 96, where a bathysphere promises a front-page story. Meanwhile, Superman is sent on the trail after appropriate lead time. So far so good. When Superman enters the already occupied deep-sea apparatus, X shuts the door by remote control, then sinks the diving bell [6] 250 feet to the ocean floor. The Man of Steel learns his wife is also in danger in another section of greater Metropolis. Seemingly, there is nothing he can do, and Mr. X knows it!

However, Superman can raise the bell to the surface by pulling the guide cable down. Certainly some water might leak in, but Jimmy can coach everyone on the graceful art of looking serene while watching tons of water rise above you. (And so it goes except for the colds Noel Neill and George Reeves carry to the set in the next episode.) When they finally break water level Superman kicks open the door, ushers his friends out, then lets the cable swing free. The bathysphere sinks to the bottom again, and Superman heroically soars off to save his pretty mistress.

The wedding was expectedly phony; a mere fabrication to pull Mr. X and his henchmen Blinkie, Duke and Whitey out into the open. When Lois gets wind of Superman's eligibility it takes her no time to serve notice on Sergeant O'Hara. The policewoman accepts the challenge: "I think I'll just wait around for Superman to ask me again for real."

Longtime serial villain Rick Vallin stars as Pallini, "The Human Fly," in Landers' second episode, "Three in One." Pallini is supported by strong man/giant Atlas (Buddy Baer) and magician Harmon the Great (Sid Tomack). The three merge to become one superperson,

[6] Reeves had found himself acting inside a diving bell once before—sixteen years earlier in the Charlie Chan mystery *Dead Men Tell*.

capable of throwing a calm Metropolis into havoc, and Henderson and Kent into a frenzy.

Perry White drafts his associates for the story when circus boss Tex Dawson (Craig Duncan) announces he's forced to close his unsuccessful operation. Cash is missing from the tills; the circus has to fold. White, a popcorn connoisseur, guarantees to put the show back on the road and end the rash of unexplained robberies that trouble Metropolis. The burden falls on his staff. Inspector Henderson, in the meantime, begins to lean on Superman. The modus operandi short of incriminating fingerprints, suggests that only one person could have committed the burglaries: Superman! Kent assures the constable that the idea is ludicrous. However, Inspector Henderson is now ready to take Superman into custody. He only relents when the Man of Steel politely asks, "Would you mind if I escaped?"

"Well," says Henderson, "I can't give you my official permission, but I can turn my back."

Superman captures the trio, the money is returned, Dawson's circus is saved and Clark (going on vacation for a week) Kent volunteers Superman as the center ring attraction under the big top.

There was no vacation for George Reeves. He was about to embark on a new career. Reeves became the eighth "Superman" director. In David Miller's mind, Reeves had the stylistic flair of Tommy Carr and the expert eyes of Joseph Biroc[7] when the camera rolled for his three television directorial efforts.

George Reeves joined the Directors Guild in April 1957. The experienced production crew was well systematized, so Reeves's debut did not present the usual problems of a novice. Everyone knew his job, Reeves only needed to say "go" when he got Ellsworth's nod to take over. Consequently, Jack Larson thinks all that was left was directing traffic. " 'Superman' couldn't get into serious screen metaphors. You can't compare Eisenstein to Tommy Carr or George. But directing traffic doesn't just prevent people from bumping into one another. It's how a scene is staged, whether we're told, 'faster, slower, pick up the lines, show a little more terror, or you're terrific.' George did all that well, exceptionally well."

Larson adds that fifty per cent of the director's success depends upon good casting. "Here again, George was fortunate. He had people like Mauritz Hugo, Phillips Tead, Richard Elliot, George Eldredge, Jack Littlefield and other seasoned actors at his disposal." Reeves concentrated more on his guests' characterizations, leaving everyone else to their established roles. "We had ours," continues Larson, "so George moved on to his guests. From time to time he would say, 'I want a little bit more here, or a little less there.' But essentially Jimmy Olsen had life. I was on my own. Our shows were very well made considering how hard it became for any director, including George, to figure out how to make scene after scene look interesting."

George Reeves's first bid at directing came with "The Brainy Burro," an entertaining tale co-starring actor-singer-director-friend Natividad Vacio. Vacio, already rich with experience from *The Hitchhiker* (1953) and *Green Fire* (1954), plays a Mexican policeman. After his sole "Superman" appearance, he appeared in *Escape from Red Rock* (1958) and, most significantly,

---

[7] The cinematographer was no latecomer to the medium. Biroc's camera credits extend from Mervyn LeRoy's *Home Before Dark* and *The FBI Story* to a twenty-year association with Robert Aldrich. *It's a Wonderful Life, Magic Town, Red Planet Mars, Hush . . . Hush, Sweet Charlotte,* and *The Russians Are Coming, The Russians Are Coming* all were exposed through the Biroc camera. Television audiences might recall his Director of Photography credit in 1974's "Wonder Woman"; however, he's understandably more proud of his riotous *Blazing Saddles* and *The Longest Yard.* Biroc stepped in for Harold Wellman during the 1956 "Superman" episodes and remained alongside Ellsworth through the last year. " 'Superman' just happened to be another job," says Biroc. "But it was kind of a close-knit company. Everyone had been friendly enough. What made it that way was the group; they had been working together for so long. Most of the people knew each other." (Biroc also picked up an Academy Award for his photography in *The Towering Inferno*.)

The Magnificent Seven (1960).

"The Brainy Burro" begins in a stereotypically sleepy Mexican village. Lois and Jimmy are enjoying their stay in the country while feeding travelogue material to the *Daily Planet*. Perry White, after reading a dispatch from Lois concerning a burro with ESP, sends Clark Kent racing south to verify this seemingly ridiculous report. Kent, upon his arrival, discovers it's true. Two visiting crooks, Tiger (Mauritz Hugo) and Albert (Ken Mayer), agree. Soon, Lois, Jimmy and Carmelita's owner Pepe (Mark Cavell) manage to get arrested by Inspector Tomaio (Vacio). Carmelita is held as an accessory.

Pepe orders Carmelita to break them out of jail, but they're free no more than five minutes when Tiger nabs them again. Superman enters the drama, playing twenty-one questions with the clairvoyant animal. Carmelita obliges by tapping her front hoof seven times. Somehow, Superman knows this means he should jump off the southwest-bound springboard to save dear Lois. Later, the burro promises not to tap out the reporter's moonlight occupation on the condition that Kent keeps Carmelita's mind-reading act to himself. Superman's identity is safe, and Carmelita becomes the newest member of the growing list of animals and machines that share his secret.

Episode #103 represents the closest link "Superman" ever makes to the serials of days gone by. "The Perils of Superman" reinforces the time-honored tradition.

Whitney Ellsworth had carried the Superman heritage through the comic book, cartoon and serial days. In lasting tribute he would once again tie them together. His script was a gem, borrowing from all the cliff-hanger clichés that both Noel Neill and George Reeves experienced in Sam Katzman chapter plays at Columbia: a mysterious intruder in a lead mask—the heroine tied to the train tracks—a failing brake system on a crashing car—the buzz saw at a lumber mill—

and the hero suspended over a vat of boiling acid. All was as it should be, just ten or twenty years beyond its time.

A masked assailant (Michael Fox), hoping to settle a score with Superman, marks Jimmy, Perry, Lois and Clark for death. He sets an elaborate trap. Clark initially dismisses the threat, but when he begins to follow the helmeted man, he bumps into more similarly masked figures along Metropolis' main street. Inspector Henderson gives credit to the villains' novel ploy. "Anyone who can figure out how to keep Superman off his track is plenty smart."

Clark adds, "And plenty dangerous."

The gangsters further challenge Superman when they trap Lois, Jimmy and Perry. A few double jumps later, Kent is captured, and suspended above a tub of deadly liquid. He's told, "When I get through with you even Superman wouldn't recognize you!"

Meanwhile, Henderson has misgivings about stock in his friend's future. "If anybody ever needed Superman, Kent needs him."

The pride of directing a good solid script brings out the best in Reeves. His own performance is without precedent in recent episodes. He strikes a brave James West pose above the boiling acid, exhibits the calm patience of a Sherlock Holmes and pries a complete "television confession" from the intended killers before they lower him to what they assume will be his unjust reward. However, they leave too soon to witness a soaking-wet Superman emerge from the pot. He steps over the set, crashes through another Si Simonson wall and takes off to complete a super hat trick.

Sam Waxman translated Reeves's editing cues into this serial pattern lost to audiences for years. When we figure Perry White is as good as sliced in half by a saw mill blade, Superman is there. When Lois is tied to the tracks while a locomotive with a full head of steam charges toward her, Superman is there again. And when Jimmy Olsen's car plummets off a dangerous cliff, Superman saves the day one last time. It's good wholesome fun, Pearl White style, and "Superman" at his mighty best.

Back at the office, Clark speaks the friendly words *everyone* is willing to hear, "Well, all I can say is, if it weren't for Superman I wouldn't be here!" But the episode doesn't end yet. Director Reeves takes us to the Metropolis jail where two new disappointed inmates set up housekeeping. The realization that Clark Kent survived certain death carries a special meaning to them.

"You know, there's one thing I don't understand, boss," says one to another. "We saw Kent go into that tub of acid, but we didn't see . . ."

"Shut up, you fool!" answers the second villain (Steve Mitchell). "Don't ever say anything about that again. Don't even think it!" They now know what we've known all along; but nobody will believe it. "I don't even believe it myself," adds the boss.

For the first time, those who discovered Superman's identity live to see the dawning day. The two in "The Perils of Superman" were lucky, however; with only one episode left, there was no time to take their story to the people. After all, who would accept the word of known conspirators locked behind bars?

"The conclusion was foregone. We all knew Superman would triumph," says Jack Larson, reminiscing over his six seasons with George Reeves. But time has passed. "On a holiday in France a few years ago, I walked into a 'Superman' retrospective. Figure that, a 'Superman' retrospective. The episodes were dubbed French with Arabic subtitles, and they showed seven or eight times each night. It was a surprise to see that 'Superman' was already part of a historical culture." Larson continues, "As the years have gone by, I'm so glad that I did 'Superman.' I'm prouder in some odd way having done them than I would have 'Dr. Kildare' or something which seems boring to me. And when you look at them now, 'Superman' is not boring. They were well made. They had a lot of humor, and obviously a rich fantasy life. And I notice that the things I loved to watch—Laurel and Hardy, Our Gang comedies, the Keystone Kops—it's the things that 'Superman' is lumped into by people. Somehow now, 'Superman' is part of those things that were classic to me.''

It's not surprising that a Jimmy Olsen series was considered in New York. After Reeves's death, National seriously thought of weaving new Jimmy material around old stock footage from the color episodes. However, the idea of keeping George Reeves alive in such a manner struck Larson ''. . . as a sick case of necrophilia.'' He would have nothing to do with the proposition. The plan was filed away forever, and Whit Ellsworth and Jack Larson were just as pleased.

The ''Adventures of Superman'' was nearly out of film. With 103 on the shelves, Whitney Ellsworth owed only one more to everyone's contracts. National Periodicals felt 104 episodes would be sufficient, hoping the reruns would reap a handsome profit. Initially, they felt no need to pour new cash into an already mined gold reserve, so the crew prepared for their good-byes. Yet Noel Neill declares that within eighteen months, overtures were flowing back and forth for a new season of twenty-six. Scripts were ordered and the costumes were sent out to the cleaners. George Reeves was back on the ZIV lot raring to go, passing the hours playing cards. ''He was in good spirits,'' according to Neill and Larson. ''We saw no signs of discontent on him at all.'' Yet, for some reason, he would lie dead two days later.

By 1960, Whitney Ellsworth had two new Superman spinoffs cooking. One was a ''Superpup'' pilot will Billy Curtis (''Mr. Zero'') in a canine caped costume and the street clothes of Bark Bent. Every other four-foot-high guild member that was available tested for Pamela Poodle, Perry Bite, Sergeant Beagle and Professor Sheepdip. Obviously, the show never made it. More important than "Superpup" was the 1962 "Adventures of Superboy" starring a young George Reeves lookalike, John Rockwell. Thirteen scripts were written, but even "Superboy" never took off. According to David Miller, the pilot film provided evidence for its own demise. The program begins with a montage in outer space "Superman" viewers would have recognized, but director George Blair then cuts to Rockwell standing in limbo—his hands folded on his chest, his body slouched and his uniform in need of a two-dollar pressing. The music sounds like early Mantovani ground through a miracle Veg-O-Matic. The only redeeming quality is Rockwell's remarkable copy of Reeves's bored expression whenever some two-bit thug tries the old bullet-to-the-chest routine. The plot, juvenile in every respect, pits longtime "Superman" adversary Richard Reeves (Bad Luck Brannigan in "No Holds Barred") against Superboy/Clark Kent and Lana Lang (Bunny Henning). They listen to their Smallville High School speech teacher announce an assignment on the subject of "My Father." Each student is told to report, but Jimmy Drake has little to say. "My father is a doorman at a theater, that's all." The other students giggle as Jimmy slinks into his hardwood seat. His dad Fred Drake (Ross Elliott) feels differently about his occupation. Recalling Emil Jannings' doorman dignity in *The Last Laugh*, Fred delivers this rousing motherhood, flag and apple pie discourse:

Jimmy, not everyone can be an airplane pilot, or great surgeon, or a builder of dams in faraway places. Background circumstances, responsibilities—these are factors which place some of us in ordinary jobs for all of our lives. So we hope for better things for our sons. And Jim, between us, we're going to get you through college and into your chosen profession. Now when that's accomplished, I'll consider myself as successful as anyone you know.

Jimmy's depression over his father's insignificance gradually melts away; it's Whit Ellsworth's insulin injection that puts him back on his feet.

The Smallville theater schedules a premiere run of *Rajah's Ransom*. The debut, complete with film trucks and spotlights, brings the movie moguls in with a valuable necklace purporting to be the stolen heirloom in the motion picture. Shifty Barnes (Richard Reeves), however, plans to act out the plot for real, making the necklace his own.

While Shifty keeps the lone Smallville policeman, Chief Parker (Robert Williams), at bay, Barnes's accomplices lift *Rajah's Ransom* from the display case. Meanwhile, Lana Lang and the disguised superhero are minding their p's and q's at Clark's home when the lights in the parlor begin to blink. It's a signal that Chief Parker is on the line with news of the robbery. Rockwell makes the typical George Reeves excuses and ushers Lana home, so that she can bake a tin of cookies for the church picnic.

In what was obviously intended for the stock footage files, Clark opens a bookshelf in the living room, slips into a secret room and picks up a Batman-style telephone. Parker fills him in on the current predicament, Clark hustles through a trapdoor heading into a cave, takes off his glasses, tucks in his boots and runs past a camouflaged entrance. He takes the springboard in stride and soars over the camera.

"His takeoffs were just as good as things Reeves had done with his springboard," says historian Miller. "But the flying was horrendous. Ellsworth used four basic stock shots: a flight path across the country, one against Smallville, a forty-five-degree angle up, and the same down. It was basically a bad imitation of Superman flying; no dramatic music or theme, just dull, boring violin strings. The only consolation is a decent landing."

Fred Drake submits a rough sketch of Shifty Barnes that proves to be the robber's undoing. A proud Jimmy Drake again addresses his class; this time singing a different tune. His father is "A brave man . . . a smart man . . . and a kind man, why one time . . ." At the fade-out, the camera zooms in to a close-up of Clark winking to Lana. It's the end of the pilot, and the end of Johnny Rockwell's career as Superboy.

"Superman" had seen a decade of change, six of the years with George Reeves. The actor's appearance, once the dynamic personification of the Hollywood leading man had begun to show the sure signs of age. The black, wavy hair had changed into a thinning, white replica of the early years. Life had changed too, and the series rolled with the fifties. First-season episodes were rich with those timeless Culver City sets, high-key lights and long dark shadows. However, as "Superman" moved on with the years television became more powerful. For that reason, Ellsworth maintained his undying belief: that America's parents should be able to relax in the comfort of their kitchen while the kids sit harmlessly in front of the tube watching *his* show—the "Adventures of Superman." He maintained this credo for the last episode, "All That Glitters."

The slightly senile Pepperwinkle returns with a machine that produces gold. Clark reminds his disbelieving colleagues that while Pepperwinkle has invented some strange things in the past, "They've all worked." Perry White, using his traditional superlatives, asks Pepperwinkle to unplug his machine ". . . for the good of the United States . . . the good of the world."

It's too late. Heavies Nick Mitchell (Len Hendry) and Elbows Logan (Jack Littlefield) greedily order the alchemist to tune up his machine. However, the bumbling mollycoddle is not completely powerless. He's rigged his lab with automatic crook-remover sandbags; unfortunately they find their mark on Olsen before anyone else. The reporter slumps to the floor, dazed, and awakes to Pepperwinkle's newest amusement, positive and negative Kryptonite. The professor explains that positive "K" yields Superman his strength, while negative Kryptonite drains all the power from his body. Since the professor has isolated the non-harmful element and successfully treated a supermouse with one small dose, Olsen and Lane volunteer as the first human subjects. They take a tiny pill and behold: two new superpeople! Their first thought is "Clark Kent will never be able to scoop us." The incongruous pair, Lois in heels and Jimmy wearing his bargain-basement bow tie, fly off toward the Metropolis skyline.

Noel Neill remembers the thrill of the mock flying. "Si Simonson fashioned molding to both our bodies and George suspended us above the set. It was great. Absolutely fantastic! For once it looked as if our fantasies were acted out."

Jimmy and Lois cut through the sky with the speed and grace of the real Superman. Their initial stop is the Fifth National Bank, where the president (Richard Elliot) humorously observes, "I thought only Superman did that." Next, they round up the scoundrels that threaten Pepperwinkle. Olsen, who chauvinistically jumps in front of Lois to deflect the criminals' bullets, exclaims, "That'll teach them to fool around with Super Olsen!"

The two complete their excursion with a quick trip back to Pepperwinkle's lab. Olsen walks through the same doorway, and is knocked out by the same sandbags. When he regains consciousness, he disappointedly realizes that the last ten minutes between Kellogg's commercials have been a dream; what's more, they're all as helpless as ever—the gangsters arrive.

Mitchell and Elbows ready the gold-making machine. First the ingredients: apple cider, peanuts, assorted spare parts and platinum. "Platinum!" shouts Mitchell. "Oh yes." Pepperwinkle neglected to explain that his process requires $10,000 of platinum to produce one pound of gold worth $500. The villains show their teeth, they can't be more displeased. Mitchell orders his henchmen to tie Lois, Jimmy and Pepperwinkle to the confounded machine and prepare the dynamite.

For George Reeves's last dramatic Superman feat he tears—hands first—through the laboratory wall, beating the clock to the explosives. He picks up the sticks and shields the blast from his friends. Si Simonson's machine topples to the floor in a heap of rubble; all is well. *Finally* all is well.

The crowning lines to thirty chapters of serial dialogue and 104 episodes of television script—for years, the extent of live-action "Superman"—have more significance than anyone realized at the time. Jimmy Olsen, the constant nuisance to Clark Kent, the fawning hero worshiper to Superman, bubbles, "Golly, Mr. Kent, you'll *never* know how wonderful it is to be like Superman."

Reeves sets his eyes on the camera and begins with words that rang true on June 16, 1959.

"No, Jimmy," he says, "I guess I never will."

George Reeves pauses forever and winks.

Johnny Rockwell poses as Superboy in Whitney Ellsworth's ill-fated pilot film.

Addendum

The Adventures of Superman was co-produced in 1951 by Bernard Luber and Robert Maxwell, as reported. However, Luber, who remains a successful West Coast producer, wishes to clarify some of the finer points.

According to Mr. Luber, Maxwell was given 40% interest in the program. The $18,500 budget was so low that only a per centage deal could carry off the program. Luber, in turn, received 10% of Maxwell's share as well as $500 for each program.

The casting of George Reeves, says Luber, was solely his responsibility. "I had known George when he worked at Paramount. The studios had essentially forgotten about him after the war, but he was just right for us." Luber continues, "One evening I was dining in the "Cock'n Bull Restaurant" when I saw George looking around rather forlorn." His co-producer agreed upon the selection and Luber rounded out the crew with people he had worked with at Republic and Paramount including the very capable Barney Sarecky, Tommy Carr and Harold Chiles. And the background music, says Luber, was obtained for $150 per show.

Mid way through the filming that year, the company hit a snag. "We had made our deal with George Reeves, but he wanted more money. His lawyer threatened that he'd walk off. I placed the whole thing before the Screen Actors Guild which ultimately supported me." Luber indicates that some of the stickier issues were compromised by offering George a substantial chunk of the personal appearances. "The problem was that if George had even asked for double we couldn't have given it to him; we didn't have it." The budget was so low that salaries and special effects left no room for contingencies. "The demands were only outrageous in context with 1951. As it was George Reeves was offered 3% of the profits from the theatrical release of *Superman and the Mole Men*. Today, actors are given quite naturally, the things that George couldn't get then.

At the conclusion of production in 1951, Luber left the show for a series of European projects, declining to rejoin the *Superman* set in 1953. "Jack Liebowitz wanted me to come back alone, just the opposite of what Whit Ellsworth says, but I told him that Whitney could handle the program. He did a splendid job."

In conclusion, Luber remembers that he took an adult viewpoint on *The Adventures of Superman*. "In 1951, the show wasn't strictly for youngsters. We offered the dream of everyman—to fly, to be super. It's a theme that *The Six Million Dollar Man* uses today. And I'm happy I was associated with such a memorable and exciting part of early television.

* * * * * *

The biggest unsolved mystery that plagued the course of writing *Superman: Serial to Cereal* was who reached into the depths of his vocal cords to announce: "Faster than a speeding bullet, more powerful than a locomotive . . . ." The question has finally been answered. The deep-throated announcer was Willard Bill Kennedy, a veteran character actor who also vyed for the lead in The *Adventures of Superman.*

Since the mid 1950's Kennedy has hosted a movie program on WKBT-TV in Detroit, Michigan where viewers can still delight daily knowing that they are watching one of the world's most famous announcers.

Kennedy remembers the night that his voice-over was recorded on the sound stages of General Services. "We started at midnight and finished around 3:30 in the morning. Charlie Chaplin was waiting to use the facilities to preview his music from *Limelight.* After we wrapped up, Chaplin walked forward to say, 'Young man, you have the most powerful voice I've ever heard. It was absolutely amazing what you did!' "

There was another announcer on the program, however. And credit must also be given to Charlie Lyon, for years the familiar off-camera voice on television's *Truth or Consequences.* In 1951 Lyon stepped up to the microphone and said, "Kellogg's, the greatest name in cereals, presents *The Adventures of Superman.* Presumably, he was picked by Kellogg's ad firm, The Leo Burnett Agency. After Charlie Lyon's spiel, Bill Kennedy went into the major opening, with Lyon later adding, "We'll return to *The Adventures of Superman* in just a moment," and the monologue, "Don't miss the next . . ." heard over the previews issued with the first year episodes. Lyon concluded with "Superman is based on the original character appearing in *Superman* magazine." Bill Kennedy announced the full closing.

—Gary Grossman
1977

APPENDIX

Superman Cartoons

Produced by
Paramount Pictures and Fleischer Studios

1941—SUPERMAN (also referred to as THE MAD SCIENTIST)
1941—THE MECHANICAL MONSTERS
1942—BILLION DOLLAR LIMITED
1942—DESTRUCTION, INC.
1942—ELECTRONIC EARTHQUAKE
1942—SHOWDOWN
1942—TERROR ON THE MIDWAY

1942—ARCTIC GIANT
1942—THE BULLETEERS
1942—THE ELEVENTH HOUR
1942—THE JAPOTEURS
1942—THE MAGNETIC TELESCOPE
1943—VOLCANO
1943—JUNGLE DRUMS
1943—SECRET AGENT
1943—THE MUMMY STRIKES
1943—UNDERGROUND WORLD

The Superman Serials

1948—SUPERMAN
1950—ATOM MAN VS. SUPERMAN

Superman and the Mole Men
(1951)

Original Broadcast Sequence
"Adventures of Superman"

1951—filmed at RKO-Pathé Studios, Culver City

#1 "Superman on Earth"
#2 "The Haunted Lighthouse"
#3 "The Case of the Talkative Dummy"
#4 "The Mystery of the Broken Statues"
#5 "The Monkey Mystery"
#6 "A Night of Terror"
#7 "The Birthday Letter"
#8 "The Mind Machine"
#9 "Rescue"
#10 "The Secret of Superman"
#11 "No Holds Barred"
#12 "The Deserted Village"
#13 "The Stolen Costume"
#14 "Mystery in Wax"
#15 "Treasure of the Incas"
#16 "Double Trouble"
#17 "The Runaway Robot"
#18 "Drums of Death"
#19 "The Evil Three"
#20 "Riddle of the Chinese Jade"
#21 "The Human Bomb"
#22 "Czar of the Underworld"
#23 "The Ghost Wolf"
#24 "Crime Wave"
#25 and #26 "The Unknown People" (broadcast in two episodes, originally *Superman and the Mole Men*)

1953—filmed at California Studios

- #27 "Five Minutes to Doom"
- #28 "The Big Squeeze"
- #29 "The Man Who Could Read Minds"
- #30 "Jet Ace"
- #31 "Shot in the Dark"
- #32 "The Defeat of Superman"
- #33 "Superman in Exile"
- #34 "A Ghost for Scotland Yard"
- #35 "The Dog Who Knew Superman"
- #36 "The Face and the Voice"
- #37 "The Man in the Lead Mask"
- #38 "Panic in the Sky"
- #39 "Machine That Could Plot Crimes"
- #40 "Jungle Devil"
- #41 "My Friend Superman"
- #42 "The Clown Who Cried"
- #43 "The Boy Who Hated Superman"
- #44 "Semi-Private Eye"
- #45 "Perry White's Scoop"
- #46 "Beware the Wrecker"
- #47 "The Golden Vulture"
- #48 "Jimmy Olsen, Boy Editor"
- #49 "Lady in Black"
- #50 "Star of Fate"
- #51 "The Whistling Bird"
- #52 "Around the World"

Public Service Program: United States Savings Bonds "Stamp Day for Superman"

1954—filmed at California Studios

- #53 "Through the Time Barrier"
- #54 "The Talking Clue"
- #55 "The Lucky Cat"
- #56 "Superman Week"
- #57 "Great Caesar's Ghost"
- #58 "Test of a Warrior"
- #59 "Olsen's Millions"
- #60 "Clark Kent, Outlaw"
- #61 "The Magic Necklace"
- #62 "The Bully of Dry Gulch"
- #63 "Flight to the North"
- #64 "The Seven Souvenirs"
- #65 "King for a Day"

1955—filmed at Chaplin Studios

- #66 "Joey"
- #67 "The Unlucky Number"
- #68 "The Big Freeze"
- #69 "Peril by Sea"
- #70 "Topsy Turvey"
- #71 "Jimmy the Kid"
- #72 "The Girl Who Hired Superman"
- #73 "The Wedding of Superman"
- #74 "Dagger Island"
- #75 "Blackmail"
- #76 "The Deadly Rock"
- #77 "The Phantom Ring"
- #78 "The Jolly Roger"

1956—filmed at ZIV Studios

- #79 "Peril in Paris"
- #80 "Tin Hero"
- #81 "Money to Burn"
- #82 "The Town That Wasn't"
- #83 "The Tomb of Zaharan"
- #84 "The Man Who Made Dreams Come True"
- #85 "Disappearing Lois"
- #86 "Close Shave"
- #87 "The Phoney Alibi"
- #88 "The Prince Albert Coat"
- #89 "The Stolen Elephant"
- #90 "Mr. Zero"
- #91 "Whatever Goes Up"

1957—filmed at ZIV Studios

#92 "The Last Knight"
#93 "The Magic Secret"
#94 "Divide and Conquer"
#95 "The Mysterious Cube"
#96 "The Atomic Captive"
#97 "The Superman Silver Mine"
#98 "The Big Forget"
#99 "The Gentle Monster"
#100 "Superman's Wife"
#101 "Three in One"
#102 "The Brainy Burro"
#103 "The Perils of Superman"
#104 "All That Glitters"

Superman Features

Released by 20th Century-Fox
1954

SUPERMAN'S PERIL
1. "The Golden Vulture"
2. "The Semi-Private Eye"
3. "The Defeat of Superman"

SUPERMAN FLIES AGAIN
1. "Jet Ace"
2. "The Dog Who Knew Superman"
3. "The Clown Who Cried"

SUPERMAN IN EXILE
1. "Superman in Exile"
2. "The Face and the Voice"
3. "The Whistling Bird"

SUPERMAN AND SCOTLAND YARD
1. "A Ghost for Scotland Yard"
2. "Lady in Black"
3. "Panic in the Sky"

SUPERMAN AND THE JUNGLE DEVIL
1. "Machine That Could Plot Crimes"
2. "Jungle Devil"
3. "Shot in the Dark"

"Superpup"
1958

pilot film for "Superpup"

"The Adventures of Superboy"
April 1961

"Rajah's Ransom"

A Warner Brothers Film Gallery
Release

SUPERMAN

Marketed for non-theatrical use only, September 9, 1973. Four color episodes from the "Adventures of Superman"— considered the best examples of the series. 104 minutes.

Edited together in total:
1. "The Mysterious Cube"
2. "Superman's Wife"
3. "Tin Hero"
4. "The Town That Wasn't"